Regency Rail Cruises

 City of York

UPM

aledonian Paper

0025

YEOMAN ENTERPRISE

ELECTRO-MOTIVE

British Rail Main Line Diesel Locomotives

Previous page: Six Class 20 locomotives were taken over by Kilmarnock-based Hunslet-Barclay in autumn 1989 for contract hire and classified Class 20/9, numbered 20901-906. In reality the locomotives saw little work except for the powering of the annual weed-control trains in the early and mid-1990s. In 1998 the locomotives were sold to private rail operator Direct Rail Services. A 'top and tail' Class 20/9 formation, with locomotives Nos. 20904 and 20901, is seen at Berkley, near Frome, on 9th April 1992.

Colin J. Marsden

Above: RES-liveried Class 47 No. 47791 departs from Liskeard on 9th April 1995 with a northbound 'Statesman' charter from Penzance to Manchester. The train is formed of the privately-owned ex-"Manchester Pullman" stock.

Colin J. Marsden

First published 1988
Second revised edition 2000

ISBN 0 86093 544 2

© C. J. Marsden & G. B. Fenn 2000

Published by Oxford Publishing Co.

an imprint of Ian Allan Publishing Ltd, Terminal House, Shepperton, Surrey TW17 8AS.
Printed by Ian Allan Printing Ltd, Riverdene Business Park, Hersham, Surrey KT12 4RG.

Code: 0003/A2

British Rail Main Line Diesel Locomotives

Colin J. Marsden
&
Graham B. Fenn

Oxford Publishing Co

Introduction

Following the demise of steam traction in the 1960s, a huge number of railway enthusiasts turned their backs on the railway scene and took up other hobby and interest subjects. However, many have returned to the rail scene in recent years, to join new followers of the interesting subject of modern diesel and electric traction.

With many new followers of the locomotive scene and the constant quest for more and more technical information on traction units, in addition to drawings which are of specific use to the ever-growing field of railway modellers, it was decided to write a book in the 1980s which covered these broadly neglected areas. At the time no title had ever been put together with a complete set of detailed line drawings of locomotives showing side, roof and front elevations together with major sub-class variants and modifications. Thus the pen of joint author Graham Fenn set about the task of producing well over 200 new drawings of the main line diesel classes. Information (or at least accurate information) was sometimes hard to come by, and in all cases original designers, drawings and those retained by the rail industry were studied before any of the enclosed drawings were produced.

The drawings reproduced in this book are to the most popular modelling scale of 4mm to the foot, equating to the 'OO' gauge. Each class of locomotive has been given its own section, headed with a comprehensive technical description, and wherever possible a full split of sub-classes has been given. A basic write-up of the class follows, with each section finished with a full set of line drawings. As a minimum, each class shows one side, end and roof detail, and this is considerably expanded for the larger classes, and where sub-class modifications exist.

In a very few places, technical information for a specific subject has been omitted; this has arisen where neither the official records from the builder nor those held by the erstwhile British Rail exist or agree. Throughout this book, the assistance of the locomotive construction businesses, British Rail and the new private rail sector has been gratefully received — without their help the production of this book would not have been possible.

Since the production of the original imprint of this title, while some new locomotive classes have emerged — principally the Classes 57, 66 and 67 — the number of locomotive types has reduced. However, the overall scene has largely provided a more interesting subject, with a vast new array of liveries, private owners and, in some areas, sub-classes. It is expected that, over the next few years, following the full introduction of Class 66s for both the English, Welsh & Scottish Railway (EWS) and Freightliner, Class 67s for EWS and the launch of new multiple-unit-based trains for many operators, the number of older locomotive classes will be further reduced — this is likely to see the virtual elimination of the Class 31 and 37 fleets and a huge reduction in the Class 47 fleet size. However, it is good to note that, following Freightliner's initiative to rebuild a fleet of 12 Class 47s with General Motors power units as Class 57s, this 1960s design — the backbone of British modern traction — will be seen for many years to come.

This title also covers the prototype and production IC125 power cars of Classes 41 and 43; while many people regard these more as multiple-units, they are officially classified as locomotives, and have arguably made the largest single contribution ever to rail traction in the UK, being without doubt the most successful diesel locomotive ever to have operated in the world. The book does not include details of the passenger vehicles.

The illustrations for this book have been selected to try to show as many variations and liveries as possible in the limited number of pages available for each class. This revised edition now includes for the first time full sections on Classes 57, 59, 60, 66 and 67, with a set of new specially-commissioned line drawings.

Special thanks are due from the authors to a huge number of people from within the rail industry who have made official and private papers available for inspection. All the major traction-builders in the UK have been very helpful in supplying information, some of which has not previously been released in the public domain. With the construction of many new locomotives overseas, General Motors in the USA and Canada, and Alstom in Spain have also been especially helpful. The authors would also like to record a special thankyou to the photographers who have supplied material for this book.

Colin J. Marsden
Graham B. Fenn

January 2000

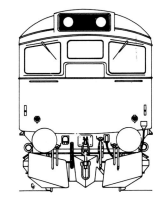 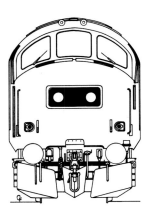

Throughout this title, the drawings have not shown the three piece miniature snowploughs as fitted to a number of classes, as this would have detracted from the detail shown. These two drawings show on the left a Class 27, and on the right a Class 37, with standard three-piece snowploughs.

Contents

Notes

(1) Rebuilt as prototype 25kV electric locomotive.
(2) Randomly numbered within fleet.
(3) 43000-43001 also carried numbers 41001-41002.

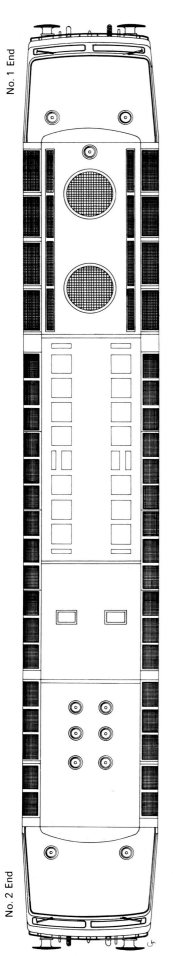

No. 1 End

No. 2 End

DWG 2

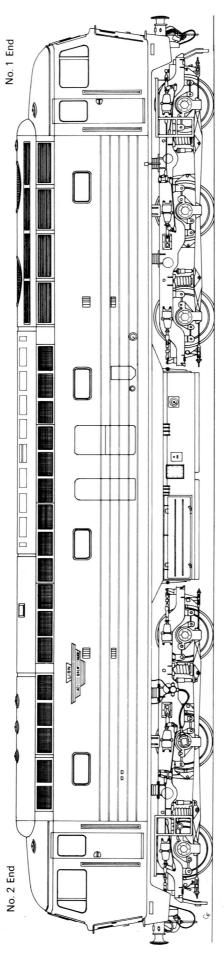

No. 1 End

No. 2 End

DWG 3

DWG 4

DWG 2
Roof detail of No. D0260 *Lion*.

DWG 3
Side elevation of AEI/BRCW/Sulzer 'prototype' No. D0260
Lion, the No. 1 end is on the right.

DWG 4
Front end detail of No. D0260 *Lion*.

D0260 Lion

Class	—	Steam Heat Boiler Type	Spanner Mk 3
Number	D0260	Electric Train Heat Generator	AEI AG106
Built by	BRCW-Sulzer-AEI,	Multiple Coupling Restriction	Not fitted
	by BRCW	Brake Force	tonnes
Introduced (On loan)	1962	Engine Type	Sulzer 12LDA28C
Wheel Arrangement	Co-Co	Engine Horsepower	2,750hp
Weight (operational)	114 tonnes	Power at Rail	2,080hp
Height	12ft 9^1/$_{16}$in	Tractive Effort	50,000lb
Width	8ft 10in	Cylinder Bore	11.02in
Length	63ft 6in	Cylinder Stroke	14.17in
Min Curve negotiable	4 chains	Main Generator Type	AEI TG5303
Maximum Speed	100mph	Aux Generator Type	AEI AG105
Wheelbase	50ft 9in	Number of Traction Motors	6
Bogie Wheelbase	14ft 6in	Traction Motor Type	AEI TM253
Bogie Pivot Centres	36ft 3in	Gear Ratio	17:70
Wheel Diameter	3ft 9in	Fuel Tank Capacity	850gal
Brake Type	Vacuum	Cooling Water Capacity	gal
Sanding Equipment	Pneumatic	Lub Oil Capacity	gal
Route Availability	6	Boiler Water Capacity	1,260gal
Heating Type	Dual		

Built by a consortium of three leading rail traction companies – Birmingham RC&W, Sulzer Brothers and Associated Electrical Industries, the *Lion* project was a privately sponsored 'prototype'. It was assembled at the BRCW works as a showpiece in the hope that the newly formed BRB would favour the design in projected second generation Type 4 orders.

Lion, painted in a staggering white livery with gold lining emerged from the BRCW Smethwick works in Spring 1962, visiting Marylebone for a BRB inspection on 28th May. After its acceptance onto BR tracks the locomotive was allocated to Wolverhampton Stafford Road shed, from where it was used on West Midland – Paddington line services. After minor teething problems during the early summer of 1962 the locomotive was returned to its builders for modification, but the machine resumed main line testing on the WR in July with trains often including the Swindon dynamometer car.

One of the most significant test programmes was on 14th August 1962 when the locomotive complete with 16 Mk 1 coaches and the dynamometer car traversed the South Devon banks to Plymouth. By the end of September a number of technical problems had been experienced with the locomotive and in addition a number of BR recommended modifications led to *Lion* being returned to BRCW for several months. It did not reappear on the main line until April 1963 when further tests were effected on the WR. From September 1963 the locomotive was transferred to the ER being housed at Finsbury Park depot.

Once on the Eastern Region the locomotive operated local services out of King's Cross in addition to main line duties such as the "Master Cutler" and "Yorkshire Pullman" trains. In late 1963 a number of major power unit problems were identified which necessitated the locomotive's transfer to BR Doncaster Works. After a short period there the machine was transferred to the BRCW works. Regrettably the BRCW Company was by now having grave financial problems, and with BR's decision to opt for a Brush built second generation Type 4 this led to the scrapping of *Lion* at the end of 1963, after only 18 months in service. In addition to its name the locomotive carried the number D0260, which was derived from its builder's No. 260.

Long before *Lion* was constructed this drawing of the projected design emerged from BRCW, showing as early as 1961 a yellow warning panel on the front end.

Author's Collection

Resplendent in its white livery, and specially prepared for the official handing over to the BTC, No. D0260 *Lion* is shown from its No. 2 end on 27th May 1962. Whilst arguably unsuitable for general service painted in white, the locomotive looked quite stunning even to the casual observer.

Author's Collection

After its acceptance onto BR tracks for evaluation running *Lion* was allocated to Wolverhampton Stafford Road shed, from where Wolverhampton–Paddington diagrams were operated. This view shows the locomotive still in pristine condition at Wolverhampton prior to departure for London, the white painted buffers being indicative that the locomotive had not been coupled the other way since painting!

Author's Collection

After a short return visit to its builders *Lion* was back on WR Birmingham services in July 1962, and is seen storming through Iver on the up fast line on 4th July, heading a Wolverhampton–Paddington express.

BR

During July 1962 to gauge performance on various train consists, *Lion* was deployed on selected vans and secondary passenger duties. On 2nd July the locomotive is seen near Twyford heading the 1.30pm Paddington–Plymouth vans formed of a mixture of GWR and LMS vehicles.

BR

B. End

A. End

DWG 5

B. End

A. End

FALCON

DWG 6

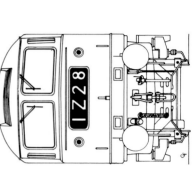

1Z28

DWG 7

DWG 5
Roof detail of No. D0280 *Falcon*.

DWG 6
Side elevation of Brush 'prototype' No. D0280 *Falcon*.

DWG 7
Front end detail of No. D0280 *Falcon* in original condition with vacuum only braking.

D0280 Falcon

Class	53	Engine Type	2 x Maybach
Number	D1200		MD655
Former Number	D0280	Engine Horsepower (total)	2,700hp
Built by	Brush Ltd	Power at Rail	2,165hp
Introduced (On loan)	1961	Tractive Effort	60,000lb
(To BR Stock)	1970	Cylinder Bore	7^1/$_4$in
Wheel Arrangement	Co-Co	Cylinder Stroke	7^7/$_8$in
Weight (operational)	115 tonnes	Main Generator Type	2 x Brush TG110-56
Height	12ft 9^7/$_8$in		Mk 2
Width	8ft 9in	Aux Generator Type	2 x Brush TAG
Length	68ft 10in	Number of Traction Motors	6
Min Curve negotiable	4 chains	Traction Motor Type	Brush TM73-68 Mk 2
Maximum Speed	100mph		
Wheelbase	56ft 4^1/$_2$in	Gear Ratio	
Bogie Wheelbase	14ft 11in	Fuel Tank Capacity	1,400gal
Bogie Pivot Centres	42ft	Cooling Water Capacity	gal
Wheel Diameter	3ft 7in	Lub Oil Capacity	gal
Brake Type	Note: 1	Boiler Water Capacity	800gal (Note: 2)
Sanding Equipment	Pneumatic		
Route Availability	6	
Heating Type	Steam – Spanner Mk 3 (Note: 2)	
Multiple Coupling Restriction	Not fitted	
Brake Force	59 tonnes	

1. When introduced the locomotive was fitted with vacuum brake equipment. After being sold to BR this was replaced by air brake equipment.

2. When built steam heat equipment was fitted, which was removed in 1972.

Project 'Falcon' or Brush contract No. 280 was authorised in April 1959, for the design and construction of a lightweight Type 4 2,800hp locomotive, with the feasibility for a production run of second generation Type 4 locomotives. As no suitable power unit of the required output was then available it was decided that *Falcon* would incorporate two smaller units each rated at 1,440hp. The units adopted were UK built Maybach engines constructed by an associate company of Brush, Bristol–Siddeley. Coupled to each power unit were Brush 915kW main generators, providing power to six Brush traction motors.

Construction of *Falcon* commenced in December 1960 and was completed in September 1961 when the gleaming lime green and chestnut brown locomotive, carrying the No. D0280 and bearing a 'Falcon' transfer nameplate emerged from the Brush works at Loughborough. After release the locomotive was the subject of a detailed BR inspection before entering traffic on the Eastern and London Midland Regions. On a number of occasions during the first few months the locomotive was returned to Brush for various alterations. At the end of 1961 the locomotive was allocated to the Western Region from where it operated a number of controlled road tests to evaluate power unit performance. In March 1962 *Falcon* was again returned to Brush for equipment observation and while present was fitted with cast alloy 'Falcon' nameplates.

D0280 returned to BR tracks in April 1963 and was then shedded at Sheffield Darnall, from where it operated services such as the "Sheffield Pullman" and a selection of heavy freight diagrams. The Sheffield testing continued until November 1963 when the locomotive was returned to Brush, its original testing having been completed. More than 12 months later the locomotive was returned to BR in January 1965 for active service, but by now was painted in Brunswick green livery with small yellow warning panels. From January 1965 the locomotive came under a special contract between BR and Brush, whereby the machine would be operated and maintained by BR, but any major electrical repairs would be referred to Brush.

Once on BR the locomotive was allocated to Bristol Bath Road and used alongside the 'Western' diesel-hydraulic locomotives on Paddington–Bristol line services. This operating arrangement continued until 1970 when BR approached Brush to purchase the locomotive at its scrap value. This was eventually agreed, but with the proviso that once its operating life was over it had to be sold for scrap. This arrangement was accepted and in January 1971 the locomotive entered Swindon works for a major overhaul, emerging in February painted in standard BR blue with full yellow ends and carrying the Number D1200. Under BR ownership the locomotive was classified as Class 53.

The locomotive was again allocated to Bristol, being subsequently transferred to Newport Ebbw Junction, where it was used on Llanwern iron-ore duties. Due to its non-standard equipment No. D1200 was withdrawn from 5th October 1975 and sold to Cashmores of Newport who broke the locomotive up in March 1976.

On 13th October 1961, Brush 'Prototype' No. D0280 *Falcon* was delivered to Finsbury Park depot on the Eastern Region to commence trials. The locomotive is seen posed outside the shed. Note the transfer name and emblem on the bodyside. Livery at this time was lime green and chestnut brown.

Author's Collection

After a lengthy period out of service at Brush, Loughborough No. D0280 was returned to BR in January 1965 painted in Brunswick green livery with a lighter sole bar band, together with small yellow warning ends. Showing its cast aluminium 'Falcon' crest and nameplate the locomotive is seen outside the Brush works at Loughborough.

Author's Collection

After its 1965 return to BR *Falcon* was allocated to the Western Region, where it was deployed on Paddington–Bristol/West of England line services. On 10th October 1968 the locomotive is seen hurrying through the countryside near Tilehurst with the 12.45 Paddington–Bristol service.

John Cooper-Smith

Following the January 1971 Swindon overhaul and transfer of ownership to BR, *Falcon* was renumbered into the BR series as D1200, being first used on passenger and latterly on freight operations. Photographed a year before final withdrawal No. D1200 is seen at Orb steelworks, Newport with a mixed rake of unfitted steel carrying wagons.

Graham Scott-Lowe

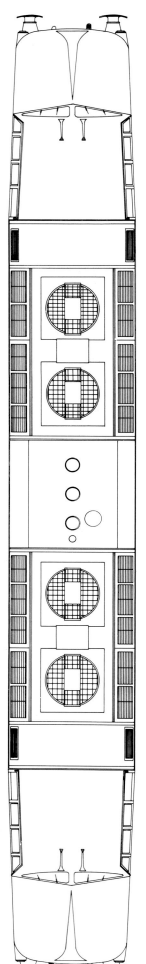

DWG 8

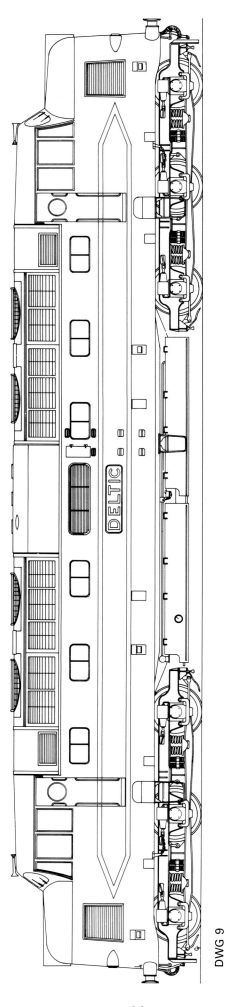

DWG 9

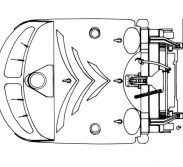

DWG 10

DWG 8
Roof detail of *Deltic* 'prototype'.

DWG 9
Side elevation of EE 'prototype' *Deltic*.

DWG 10
Front end detail of *Deltic*.

(Drawings show the locomotive in original condition.)

14

Deltic

Allocated Number	DP1 (Note: 1)	Engine Horsepower (total)	3,300hp
Identification	DELTIC	Power at Rail	2,650hp
Built by	EE – Dick Kerr	Tractive Effort	60,000lb
Introduced	1955	Cylinder Bore	7in
Wheel Arrangement	Co-Co	Cylinder Stroke	3.45in
Weight (operational)	106 tonnes	Main Generator Type	2 x EE 831A
Height	12ft 10$\frac{1}{2}$in	Aux Generator Type	2 x EE 912A
Width	8ft 9$\frac{1}{2}$in	Number of Traction Motors	6
Length	66ft	Traction Motor Type	EE 526-1A
Min Curve negotiable	6 chains	Gear Ratio	59:21 (Note 2)
Maximum Speed	90mph (Note: 4)	Fuel Tank Capacity	800gal
Wheelbase	58ft 4in	Cooling Water Capacity	gal
Bogie Wheelbase	14ft 4in	Lub Oil Capacity	gal
Bogie Pivot Centres	44ft	Boiler Water Capacity	600gal
Wheel Diameter	3ft 7in	Boiler Fuel Supply	From main supply
Brake Type	Vacuum		
Sanding Equipment	Pneumatic		
Route Availability	Not issued	1. The number DP1 was never carried.	
Heating Type	Steam – Clarkson (Note: 3)	2. Gear ratio originally 61:19.	
Multiple Coupling Restriction	Not fitted	3. Stone Vapor steam generator later installed.	
Brake Force	tonnes		
Engine Type	2 x Napier D18-25 'Deltic'	4. Maximum speed later increased to 105mph.	

The most adventurous of the early prototypes was *Deltic*, designed and built by English Electric (Dick Kerr) and loaned to BR for operational testing. At the time of the design the EE company had considerable hopes in the export field, hence the fitting of a large bonnet headlight, but alas this was not to be. The prime mover incorporated was two D. Napier & Son 'Deltic' D18-25 opposed piston units, each developing 1,650hp.

The bodyshell incorporating the two 'Deltic' engines was constructed by EE at the Dick Kerr Works in Preston during early 1955, being ready for testing in October. During construction some deliberation had been made over a number or name for the locomotive; these ranged from DP1 (Diesel Prototype 1) to *Enterprise*. However, when the machine emerged it carried the name given to the power units, *Deltic*. After initial acceptance tests *Deltic* was allocated to Liverpool Edge Hill depot, from where it commenced work on 13th December 1955 on London services. After only a short time, power unit problems befell the locomotive, which was returned to English Electric for attention.

During mid 1956 the locomotive was temporarily reallocated to Carlisle Durran shed from where trials with BR test vehicles were conducted over the arduous Settle route. By Autumn the machine was returned to Liverpool, again working on London services such as the "Merseyside Express" or the "Shamrock". From early 1959 *Deltic* was transferred to Hornsey depot on the ER, from where the ER (GN) trials were undertaken, although not totally successfully. On one occasion the locomotive hit the platform edge at

Manors, and on another it lost its cab footsteps at Darlington. By March 1959 high speed performance tests were carried out on the ECML, which involved operations at up to 105mph with a BR dynamometer car. Until June 1959 *Deltic* had always operated south of the border, but late in the month five days of testing were carried out in the Edinburgh area and over the Waverley route.

By July 1959 most testing was complete and *Deltic* was diagrammed for general ECML operation alongside the East Coast racehorses — the A4 Pacifics. In March 1961 a serious engine failure befell *Deltic* and it was removed to English Electric's Vulcan Foundry and stored pending a decision on its future. A proposal was made in September 1961 to modify *Deltic* for operation in Canada in an attempt to attract overseas sales but the idea was not pursued. Under BR operating the locomotive had covered over 450,000 miles.

Deltic remained at Vulcan Foundry until 1963, when a decision was made to restore the bodywork and present the machine, non-operational, to the Science Museum in London, where it arrived on 28th April 1963 on the back of a road low loader. The locomotive remained in the Science Museum until a re-design required it to be found another home. In October 1993 *Deltic* was lifted from its bogies, removed from the Science Museum hall and taken by road to the National Railway Museum, York, where it is now on display.

For its entire life working on BR tracks, the locomotive was painted in a distinctive powder blue livery with aluminium mouldings with yellow 'whisker' markings applied to the ends.

In all but complete condition *Deltic* is seen inside the English Electric Dick Kerr works at Preston in March 1955, while undergoing a rigorous static test period. It will be noted that at this time no number or name was applied as the final decision on this controversial subject was still to be taken.

GEC Traction

Approaching Preston from the Blackpool line *Deltic* heads a lengthy rake of ex LMS stock while undergoing active testing during 1956. Note that the headlight, which was never used on BR, appears to be blanked off.

GEC Traction

From 1959 until its withdrawal *Deltic* was operated on the Eastern Region, usually at the head of Anglo-Scottish express services operating on A4 steam diagrams. With a haze of exhaust above the roof *Deltic* passes Sandy during 1960 with an up express.

John C. Baker

On the day of its arrival at the NRM, York, *Deltic* is seen on the turntable in the Great Hall, where it is now on display along with other great railway locomotives. The transfer from London by road required it to make one final journey by rail, from the Adtranz site adjacent to the NRM to the museum complex, as the road vehicle could not gain access to the museum.

Colin J. Marsden

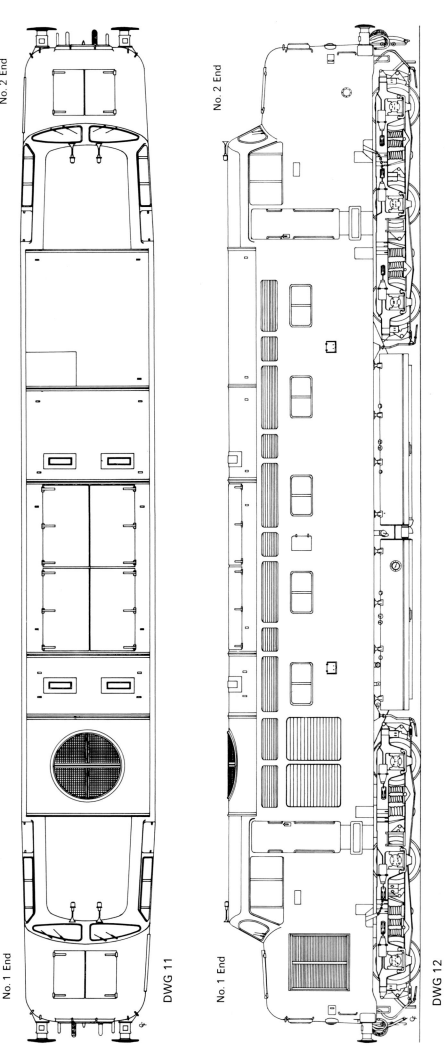

No. 2 End

No. 1 End

DWG 11

No. 2 End

No. 1 End

DWG 12

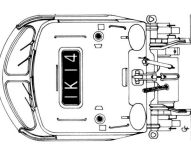

DWG 13

DWG 11
Roof detail of English Electric 'prototype' No. DP2.

DWG 12
Side elevation of English Electric second generation 'prototype' No. DP2, with No. 1 end on the left.

DWG 13
Front end elevation of No. DP2, clearly showing the near identical appearance to the production 'Deltic' type.

DP2

Number	DP2	Multiple Coupling Restriction	Not fitted
Built by	EE Vulcan Foundry	Brake Force	tonnes
Introduced	1962	Engine Type	EE 16CSVT
Wheel Arrangement	Co-Co	Engine Horsepower	2,700hp
Weight (operational)	105 tonnes	Power at Rail	2,070hp
Height	12ft 10in	Tractive Effort	55,000lb
Width	8ft 9$\frac{1}{2}$in	Cylinder Bore	10in
Length	69ft 6in	Cylinder Stroke	12in
Min Curve negotiable	4 chains	Main Generator Type	EE 840/1B
Maximum Speed	90mph	Aux Generator Type	EE 911/5C
Wheelbase	58ft 6in	Number of Traction Motors	6
Bogie Wheelbase	13ft 6in	Traction Motor Type	EE 538A
Bogie Pivot Centres	45ft	Gear Ratio	53:18
Wheel Diameter	3ft 7in	Fuel Tank Capacity	900gal
Brake Type	Vacuum	Cooling Water Capacity	gal
Sanding Equipment	Pneumatic	Lub Oil Capacity	gal
Route Availability	6	Boiler Water Capacity	620gal
Heating Type	Steam – Clayton RO 2000		

Born at the time of BR's quest for second generation Type 4 power, *Diesel Prototype 2* or DP2 was a remarkable machine. The locomotive was constructed by English Electric at Vulcan Foundry using a production 'Deltic' body, but internally the machine was nothing like a 'Deltic' and contained an EE 16CSVT power unit developing 2,700hp. DP2 was constructed during late 1961/early 1962 and was wheeled out for the first time in mid February, thorough testing then took place and it was 2nd May before the locomotive operated a light engine test on BR tracks. On 8th May, after BR acceptance tests, DP2 painted in BR Brunswick green livery operated between Crewe and Penrith and during the following weeks commenced driver training. By the end of June DP2 was operating main line passenger services on the Euston–Carlisle route on a six day week cycle, and gave little trouble with technical equipment.

By May 1963 the locomotive was redeployed on Euston–Blackpool diagrams. Both BR and the builders were delighted with the EE prototype and on several occasions the locomotive was placed in traffic without any EE or engineering staff on board! In June 1963 DP2 was returned to Vulcan Foundry for bogie and traction motor attention, and when returned to BR was shedded at Finsbury Park where, after shed and driver training had been completed, it was placed on 'Deltic' diagrams, giving a weekly mileage of around 5,270. In September 1963 DP2 was called by EE to the RSH works at Darlington where bogie attention was effected. During 1964 and 1965 DP2 was deployed on numerous ER diagrams, until May 1965 when called to Vulcan Foundry for a classified overhaul, emerging during late August with the only physical change being a revised two-tone green livery. Once back on BR DP2 was again deployed on the ECML.

During 1965-66 the English Electric Co. had been developing advanced electronic traction equipments, and in 1966 DP2 was called to Vulcan Foundry for this equipment to be installed. This included electronic tractive effort and automatic wheelslip control components, and after fitting and works testing, DP2 operated various controlled test trains over the arduous Shap incline formed of 16 Mk 1 vehicles. Such was the advances in the electronics installed that on one test DP2 started a 16 vehicle train on an upward gradient and obtained 30mph in just 575 yards. By late 1966 DP2 was returned to the ER and continued to be deployed on Type 4 and 5 diagrams. This remarkable locomotive, which was of course the forerunner to the Class 50s, came to grief on 31st July 1967 at Thirsk while hauling a passenger service. It collided with derailed cement wagons, the damage being so severe that after removal to its owner's works the decision was taken to scrap the locomotive, dismantling being effected in 1968.

Posed on the multi-gauge tracks outside Vulcan Foundry, DP2 is seen in June 1962 while minor alterations were being carried out following its initial testing. The locomotive's No. 2 end is nearest in this view, and the livery shown is Brunswick green with small yellow warning panels.

GEC Traction

After its release from Vulcan Foundry, DP2 was used on driver training prior to commencing passenger duties on WCML expresses. By Summer 1963 the locomotive was a regular performer on the Euston–Blackpool line and it is on one of these duties that the locomotive is seen in this illustration.

GEC Traction

After its Summer 1965 overhaul at Vulcan Foundry DP2 was repainted into two-tone green livery and used on East Coast Main Line (ECML) services, where the locomotive was usually operated on Type 5 schedules. DP2 is illustrated at King's Cross in its two-tone paint scheme.

J. Tandy

If it was not for the number being visible, this illustration could have been of a production 'Deltic'. This close resemblance is not surprising as a production line 'Deltic' bodyshell was used in the construction of DP2. The locomotive slowly pulls out of King's Cross with an Edinburgh service in 1965.

GEC Traction

No. 2 End

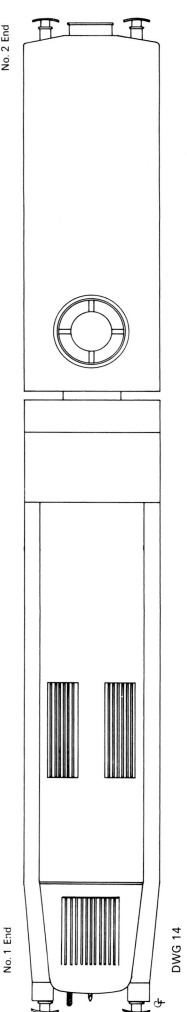

No. 1 End

DWG 14

No. 2 End

No. 1 End

DWG 15

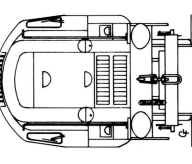

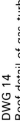

DWG 16

DWG 14
Roof detail of gas-turbine 'prototype' No. GT3.

DWG 15
Side elevation of gas-turbine No. GT3.

DWG 16
Front (locomotive) end detail of gas-turbine No. GT3.

GT3

Number	GT3	Brake Type	Vacuum
Built by	EE Vulcan Foundry	Sanding Equipment	Pneumatic
Introduced	1961	Route Availability	Not issued
Wheel Arrangement	4-6-0	Heating Type	Steam – Spanner
Weight (operational)	123$^1/_2$ tonnes	Multiple Coupling Restriction	Not fitted
Height	13ft	Brake Force	65 tonnes
Width	8ft 10in	Gas Turbine Type	EM27L
Length	68ft 0$^1/_2$in	Turbine Horsepower	2,700hp
Min Curve negotiable	4$^1/_2$ chains	Tractive Effort	36,000lb
Maximum Speed	90mph	Fuel Tank Capacity	gal
Wheelbase	55ft 4in	Cooling Water Capacity	gal
Wheel Diameter (driving)	5ft 9in	Lub Oil Capacity	gal
Bogie Wheel Diameter	3ft	Boiler Water Capacity	gal

During English Electric's quest to advance rail traction the company designed and built a gas-turbine powered locomotive, No. GT3 between 1959-61. The physical appearance of the design very closely resembled a 4-6-0 steam locomotive, the tender of which carried diesel fuel in place of coal!

Over the years other gas-turbine traction has been built, but GT3 was significant in having a mechanical transmission. GT3 emerged from Vulcan Foundry in May 1961 painted in a red oxide livery, with a cast GT3 numberplate on the cab side, and an English Electric roundle replacing the BR lion and wheel logo on the tender. Once the locomotive was mobile from its builder's yard it was moved to Marylebone and displayed in the Institute of Locomotive Engineers exhibition. After the locomotive was accepted by BR for operation, GT3 was transferred to the Rugby testing station where stringent proving and comparison tests were carried out. This included taking the locomotive through its paces up to 97mph on the famous Rugby test rollers. After departing from Rugby the locomotive was deployed on further track testing which included gradient and brake evaluation, and during the course of these a number of problems were found. This led to the locomotive operating 'tests' on the Leicester–Woodford Halse line. In early 1962 GT3 was used for testing over the arduous Shap incline with trains of up to 16 coaches. These tests proved very successful and on one run a speed of 43mph was recorded at the summit. By the time GT3's testing was almost complete the decision had been taken by the BTC to invest in diesel and electric traction and thus the interesting gas-turbine principle had no place in the modernisation of the railways. By late 1962 GT3 was returned to English Electric and many components removed, with the chassis eventually being sold to Wards of Salford for scrap.

On a number of official English Electric papers of the time, GT3 was referred to as BR No. 19000 and on one artist's impression of the locomotive, dated August 1958 the name *Lord of the Isles* was added!

Plate 'B'
GT3 in as built condition.

GEC Traction Ltd

One of the most unusual 'prototype' modern traction locomotives built was the gas-turbine propelled GT3, built by English Electric. The locomotive, based on a 4-6-2 steam locomotive chassis is seen under construction at Vulcan Foundry in December 1960.

Author's Collection

After GT3 was completed it was hauled to London for display at the Institute of Locomotive Engineers exhibition at Marylebone, along with other 'new generation' rolling stock. Sporting its EE roundel on the tender, GT3 is seen at Marylebone along with 'Hymek' No. D7000, an AL5 and SR Bo-Bo straight electric locomotive.

J. Tandy

At various times during 1962, GT3 was deployed on controlled road tests on different sections of line, the most significant being carried out in March and October over Shap Summit. The top illustration, taken on 6th October 1962 shows the locomotive hauling train No. 1279 at Shap Wells while en-route from Crewe to Carlisle, while the lower illustration taken the previous day, shows the train passing 'Shap Summit'.

Both: The Late Derek Cross

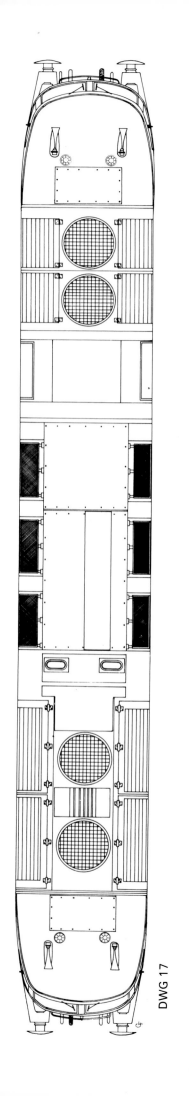

DWG 17

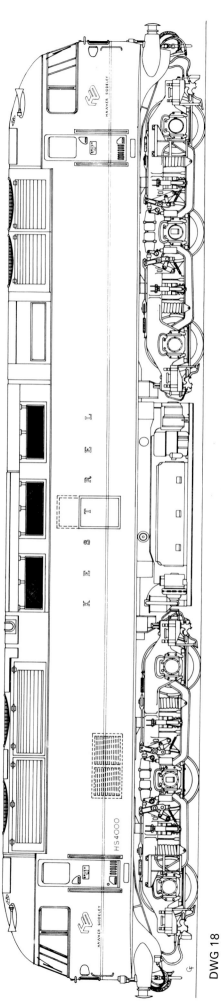

DWG 18

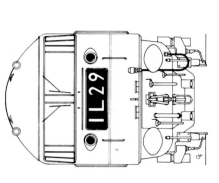

DWG 19

DWG 17
General roof arrangement of Brush 'prototype' *Kestrel* No. HS4000.

DWG 18
Side elevation of Brush 'prototype' *Kestrel*, showing the original design of bogies.

DWG 19
Front end detail of *Kestrel* No. HS4000.

HS4000

Number	HS4000	Engine Horsepower	4,000hp
Built by	Brush	Power at Rail	3,412hp
Introduced	1968	Tractive Effort	70,000lb
Wheel Arrangement	Co-Co	Cylinder Bore	9.45in
Weight (operational)	133 tonnes	Cylinder Stroke	11.02in
Height	13ft 0$\frac{1}{2}$in	Main Alternator Type	Brush BA
Width	8ft 9$\frac{3}{4}$in	Aux Alternator Type	Brush BAA
Length	66ft 6in	Number of Traction Motors	6
Min Curve negotiable	4 chains	Traction Motor Type	Brush TM
Maximum Speed	125mph	Gear Ratio	53:18 (Note: 2)
Wheelbase	51ft 8$\frac{1}{2}$in	Fuel Tank Capacity	1,000gal
Bogie Wheelbase	14ft 11in (Note: 1)	Cooling Water Capacity	gal
Bogie Pivot Centres	37ft 2in	Lub Oil Capacity	gal
Wheel Diameter	3ft 7in	Boiler Water Capacity	Not fitted
Brake Type	Dual		
Sanding Equipment	Pneumatic		
Route Availability	9		
Heating Type	Electric		
Multiple Coupling Restriction	Not fitted		
Brake Force	tonnes		
Engine Type	Sulzer 16LVA24		

1. When built the bogie wheelbase was 14ft 11in; this was later changed to 14ft 6in after Class 47 style bogies were fitted.

2. When built the gear ratio was 60:19.

During 1966 it became apparent that Brush had designed and were in the course of building a 4,000hp diesel-electric locomotive at Loughborough. The design was intended as a possible for the BR market and suitable for the export field. The locomotive was given the name *Kestrel* and the number HS4000, derived from the Hawker Siddeley ownership of the Brush Company and the power output of 4,000hp. Whilst *Kestrel* was a private venture BR engineers were involved with detailed design work, and were obviously interested in its operational potential.

After construction and on works testing, HS4000 painted in distinctive brown and yellow livery, was handed over to BR at Marylebone on 29th January 1968. BR were very interested to test the revolutionary new locomotive but problems were encountered with a too heavy axle loading, which considerably restricted its operation on BR. The high performance of HS4000 was tested on various freight diagrams in early 1968, but it was not until 8th May 1968 that the locomotive really showed what it could do, when it hauled a train of 20 Mk 1 coaches weighing over 665 tons up Shap incline surmounting the summit at 46mph. After this test period the locomotive was sent to the ER at Shirebrook depot from where it was deployed on heavy coal and freight traffic. A regular duty for the locomotive was a daily Shirebrook–March diagram formed of 32 hoppers loaded to around 1,600 tons.

On 4th August 1968 a special train was formed weighing 2,028 tons headed by HS4000 between Mansfield and Lincoln. Reports show that the train was driven in a low power notch to keep speed to within the limits for the wagons and route! The immense power that HS4000 had available was clearly shown. In late August 1968 HS4000 went to Derby and was the subject of extensive testing involving constant power output and dynamic braking, the route used for tests being: Derby–Nuneaton–Stoke–Derby. By late September HS4000 was returned to Shirebrook, again for coal train operation. Brush were very keen to see HS4000 at the head of a passenger train, but BR engineers were adamant that the axle loading was far too high. Brush decreed that re-bogieing was the only answer and in January 1969 HS4000 was re-bogied with modified Class 47 units.

Following its return to traffic and acceptance by BR for passenger operation, driver training commenced on the ECML. From 20th October 1969 HS4000 started working the 07.55 King's Cross–Newcastle and 16.45 return service. Performance was superb with speeds in excess of 100mph being recorded on more than one occasion. On 5th June 1970 HS4000 was called to Vickers Works at Barrow for an engine overhaul, and whilst at the works negotiations were ripe between Brush and authorities in Russia, for the sale of the machine to the USSR railways.

After its power unit overhaul HS4000 was returned to the Shirebrook area from where it was withdrawn in March 1971. After visiting BREL Crewe for minor alterations HS4000 was exported via Cardiff to Russia and displayed at the railway exhibition at Scherbinka in the Summer of 1971. From that date little has been known of the locomotive.

Early 1968 saw the emergence of Brush prototype *Kestrel* painted in its distinctive brown and yellow livery. On 8th May the locomotive was used on a 20 coach test train between Crewe and Carlisle, and for the first time engineers saw the locomotive performing at nearly full potential. This illustration shows the train at Crewe prior to departure.

Brush Ltd

After alterations had been carried out to its bogies to reduce axle loading, HS4000 was deployed on ECML express services between King's Cross and Newcastle. With stock to form the 16.45 Newcastle–King's Cross service, HS4000 stands in Heaton carriage sidings on 28th October 1969.

Ian Carr

One of the few times that HS4000 was put on public display was at the 1970 Barrow Hill Open Day, when the locomotive was the star attraction alongside LNER steam locomotive No. 532 *Blue Peter*. Indicative of its last freight working. HS4000 displays the train reporting number 8P55, as well as 'Little Midland Society' headboard.

Roger Kaye

After being sold to the USSR, *Kestrel* passed through BREL Crewe Works for various modifications, including the removal of BR AWS equipment. The locomotive was then hauled to Cardiff Docks, where it was loaded on board the Russian ship *Kpachokamck* for its journey to the Soviet Union.

Author's Collection

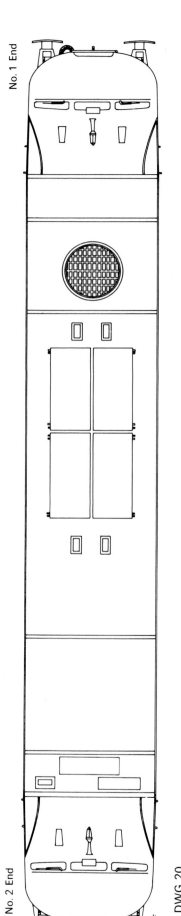

No. 1 End

No. 2 End

DWG 20

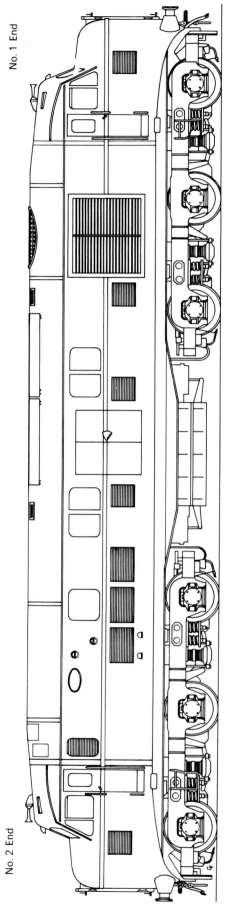

No. 1 End

No. 2 End

DWG 21

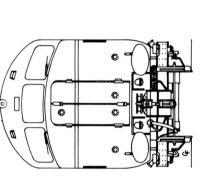

DWG 22

DWG 20
Roof detail of LMS/BR 'prototype' 1,600hp locomotives.

DWG 21
Side elevation of LMS/BR 'prototype' 1,600hp locomotives, the No. 1 end being on the right.

DWG 22
Front end elevation of LMS/BR 'prototype' locomotives in original condition.

10000–10001

Class	D16/1, later 16/8	Heating Type	Steam – Clarkson
Number Range	10000–10001	Multiple Coupling Restriction	Special
Built by	LMS/BR Derby	Brake Force	89 tonnes
Introduced	1947–48	Engine Type	EE 16SVT
Wheel Arrangement	Co-Co	Engine Horsepower	1,600hp
Weight (operational)	131 tonnes	Power at Rail	hp
Height	12ft 11¼in	Tractive Effort	41,400lb
Width	9ft 3in	Cylinder Bore	10in
Length	61ft 2in	Cylinder Stroke	12in
Min Curve negotiable	4½ chains	Main Generator Type	EE 823A
Maximum Speed	93mph	Aux Generator Type	EE 909A
Wheelbase	51ft 2in	Number of Traction Motors	6
Bogie Wheelbase	15ft 8in	Traction Motor Type	EE 519/1B
Bogie Pivot Centres	35ft 6in	Gear Ratio	55:18
Wheel Diameter	3ft 6in	Fuel Tank Capacity	900gal
Brake Type	Vacuum	Cooling Water Capacity	40gal
Sanding Equipment	Not fitted	Lub Oil Capacity	gal
Route Availability	8	Boiler Water Capacity	900gal

About a year prior to Railway Nationalisation, the LMS announced they were keen to investigate the advantages of diesel traction, and were going to construct two prototype locomotives. The prime mover to be used was an English Electric unit able to develop 1,600hp, power for traction being electric, provided by a generator coupled to the diesel engine.

Construction of the two LMS prototypes was carried out at Derby Works where the first locomotive carrying the number 10000 emerged in November 1947. The livery applied was black with silver waist height band, roof and bogies, together with the letters LMS mid height on the bodyside. After No. 10000 was completed it underwent a considerable testing period at Derby, but on 18th December was operated to London for display to senior LMS officials at Euston. After its first day of glory the machine was returned to Derby Works where a number of adjustments were carried out. By mid January 1948, No. 10000 was operating various main line specials and on 14/15th January operated from Derby to St Pancras, spent the night at Camden, and the following day worked through to Manchester via Peak Forest. In February No. 10000 was released to general service on the Midland route.

The second of the prototypes, No. 10001 was not completed until July 1948 emerging without the LMS legend. After this machine had completed essential tests it replaced No. 10000 on Midland line services, this locomotive being called to Derby Works for inspection. By September 1948 both locomotives were available for operation and commenced driver training on the Euston-Carlisle route, being allocated to Camden shed. From 5th October the 1.00pm Euston–Glasgow (as far as Carlisle) and a balancing 'up' service became their regular duty, operating in multiple. Whilst working the train during the second week of the month No. 10000 suffered a power unit failure which necessitated Derby Works attention. Whilst this was being carried out No. 10001 was utilised on Midland line services from St Pancras. Between 1949 and 1953 the machines were either used singly or in multiple on a variety of St Pancras and Euston line services, visiting Derby at various times for inspection and modification. During one of No. 10000's visits to Derby in November 1951 the LMS legend on the sides was removed and the then standard lion and wheel motif applied.

During March 1953 both locomotives were reallocated to the Southern Region, based at Nine Elms from where they were used on Waterloo–Bournemouth and West of England services. The locomotives' operation on the SR continued until Spring 1955 when both were returned to the LMR. During early 1956 both locomotives were given classified overhauls at Derby Works and emerged painted in standard locomotive green livery. From then until their final withdrawal in March 1966 and December 1963 respectively, both operated on the London Midland Region at the head of freight and passenger duties. It must not pass without note that the EE power units used in these prototypes were developed and refined, and the design has seen use in many production designs of BR locomotive, including the Class 40 and Class 50.

During the summer of 1947 the LMS prototype locomotive No. 10000 was taking shape at LMS Derby Works, prior to its emergence the following November. The illustration, left shows the boiler roof section being lowered into position while the view, right is of the main locomotive body being lowered onto its Co-Co bogies under the watchful eye of many construction and design staff.

Both: Author's Collection

Following the delivery of No. 10001 in July 1948, the two LMS 'prototype' locomotives operated on a number of services in multiple, this being the first occasion in this country that more than one diesel locomotive could be operated by one driver. This illustration shows the pair led by No. 10001 departing from Rugby with an Anglo-Scottish express.

Author's Collection

During 1950 selected freight services were operated by both locomotives in an attempt to evaluate performance. Still sporting its LMS legend, No. 10000 heads a down fitted freight past Bushey in March 1950.

Author's Collection

In the later years of their lives both locomotives were repainted by Derby works into green livery, with small yellow warning panels. No. 10001 is shown sharing depot space at Willesden on 12th September 1964 with BR Type 2 locomotives Nos D5007 and D5092.

R.C. Riley

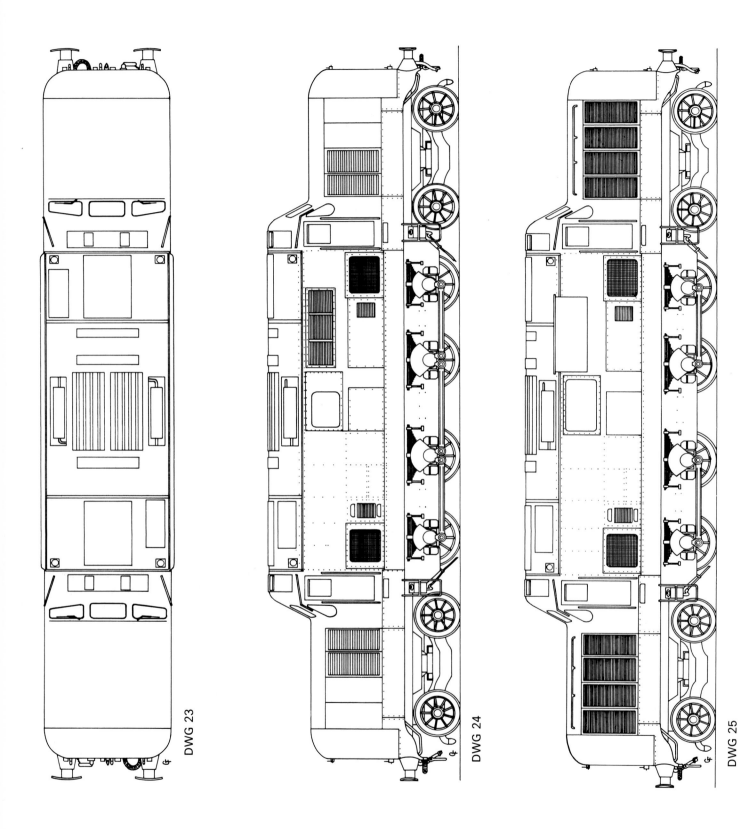

DWG 23

DWG 24

DWG 25

34

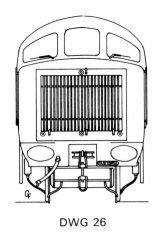

DWG 26

DWG 23
Roof detail of 'Fell' 'prototype' No. 10100.

DWG 24
Side elevation of 'Fell' 'prototype' showing the original layout.

DWG 25
Side elevation of 'Fell' 'prototype' showing revised layout with 4–4–4–4 wheel arrangement.

DWG 26
Front end elevation of 'Fell' 'prototype' No. 10100.

10100

Number	10100	Heating Type	Steam
Built by	BR Derby	Multiple Coupling Restriction	Not fitted
Built	1950	Brake Force	tonnes
Sold to BR	1955	Engine Type (Main)	4 x Paxman 12RPH
Wheel Arrangement	4–8–4 (2–D–2)	(Aux)	2 x AEC 6 cylinder
	(Note: 1)	Engine Horsepower (Total)	2,400hp
Weight (operational)	120 tonnes	Power at Rail	hp
Height	13ft	Tractive Effort	25,000lb
Width	9ft	Cylinder Bore	7in
Length	50ft	Cylinder Stroke	$7^3/4$in
Min Curve negotiable	5 chains	Transmission	Vulcan Sinclair
Maximum Speed	84mph		SCRD fluid
Wheelbase	41ft 4in	Fuel Tank Capacity	720gal
Wheel Diameter (Driving)	4ft 3in	Cooling Water Capacity	60gal
(Pony)	3ft 3in	Lub Oil Capacity	gal
Brake Type	Vacuum	Boiler Water Capacity	500gal
Sanding Equipment	Not fitted		
Route Availability	Not issued	1. Wheel arrangement altered to 4–4–4–4	

In the months just after Nationalisation in early 1948 the LMS received permission to build a diesel-mechanical locomotive for main-line operation. Design and building was effected at Derby locomotive works, with its transmission system developed by Lt Col L.F.R. Fell. The prototype soon became known as the 'Fell' locomotive and incorporated some novel features.

The 'Fell' was propelled by four 500hp Paxman engines which powered the two intermediate axles of the four coupled main set. The four engines, each coupled to a common gearbox by fluid couplings, 'came in' at differing road speeds; between 0–6mph only No.1 engine was used; between 7–17mph engines Nos 1 and 2 were used; for speeds between 18–24mph three engines operated and for all speeds above 25mph four power units developing the full 2,000hp were required. Unlike conventional practice the four power units were housed in the nose or bonnet part of the locomotive, with the fluid couplings and gearbox being housed in the main body section. In addition to the four main power plants two further 150hp engines were provided for auxiliaries and train heating power.

The 'Fell' locomotive, given the number 10100, emerged in July 1950 but was the subject of extensive testing, and did not commence main-line operation until January 1951. Even then it was only light engine and empty stock services in the Derby area. In May 1951 the machine was hauled to London and displayed at Marylebone, returning to Derby the following day where extensive modification and testing recommenced. By the autumn the machine was operating St Pancras–Manchester line services but often made visits to Derby Works for repairs. In 1954 No. 10100 suffered a major failure and lay in Derby Works for the next twelve months, before being repaired. After return to active operation it was used for performance tests over the Settle & Carlisle route, which apparently proved very successful. From 1955 the 'Fell' returned to St Pancras–Manchester line services where its reliability was reasonable but still frequent visits had to be made to Derby. On 15th October 1958 after working in on a St Pancras service No. 10100 caught fire at Manchester Central and was severely damaged. 'Fell' was stored at Derby and eventually cut up during 1960. The livery of the 'Fell' locomotive was black with silver lining until 1955 when repainted at Derby Works in standard locomotive green with centrally positioned crests.

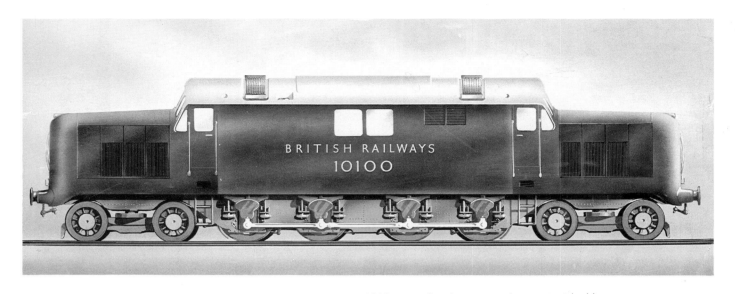

Artist's impression of the 'Fell' locomotive published by BR in late 1948, soon after the construction contract had been placed.

Author's Collection

After its modification into a 4-4-4-4 locomotive, the machine did not operate on the Midland route on any regular basis, as either technical malfunction or trials took the machine to various parts of the railway network. No. 10100 is seen dumped at Derby Works after its fire at Manchester in 1958 which eventually led to its withdrawal.

A. Ross

Showing its 4-4-4-4 wheel arrangement, and other later body modifications No. 10100 is seen at Manchester Central, whilst running round its coaches when deployed on main-line passenger work.

L. Price

Whilst deployed on Derby–St Pancras line services No. 10100 is seen passing Kibworth North Signal Box on 12th July 1952 with the 12.15pm Derby–St Pancras. On the right an LMS 0-6-0 tender locomotive No. 58928 is seen with a short freight, the driver of which is taking a keen interest in the 'new' traction.

A. Ross

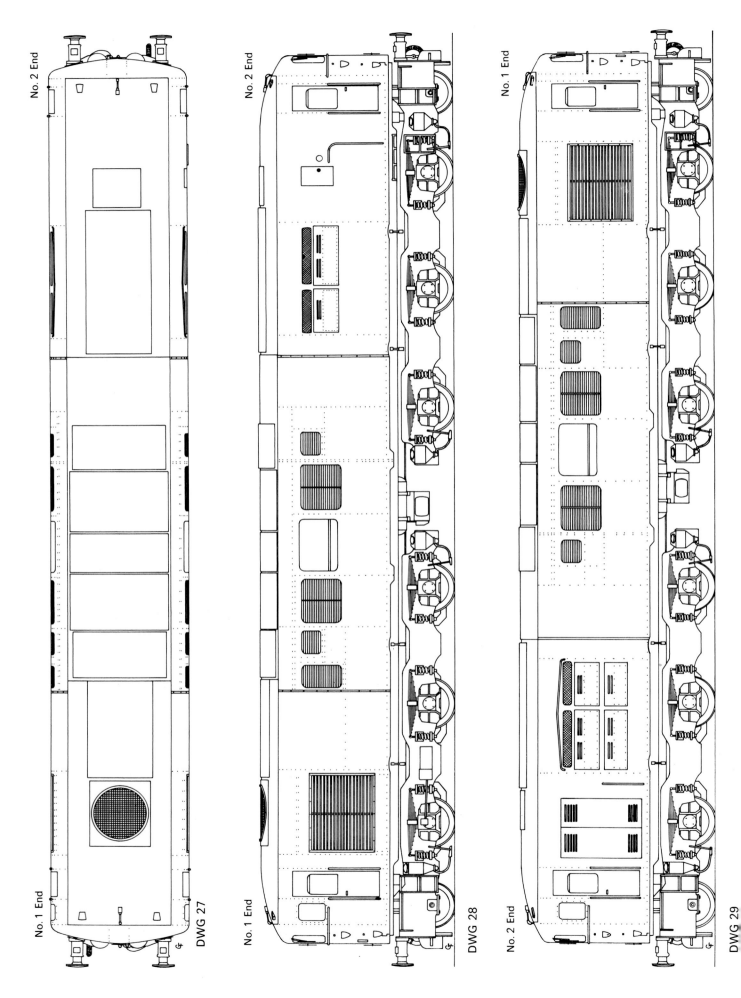

No. 2 End

No. 1 End

DWG 27

No. 2 End

No. 1 End

DWG 28

No. 1 End

No. 2 End

DWG 29

38

No. 2 End

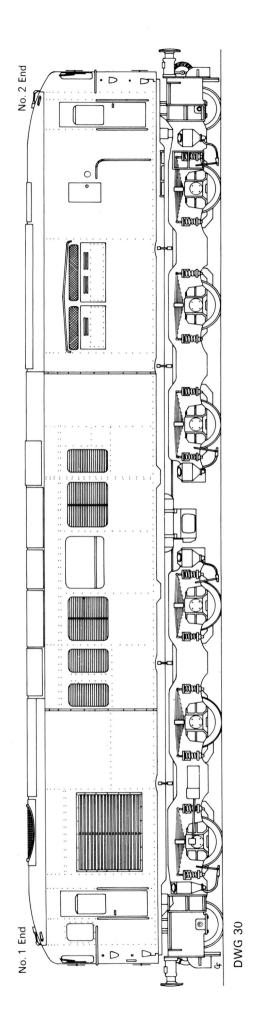

No. 1 End

DWG 30

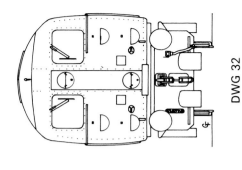

DWG 32

10201–10203

DWG 27
Roof detail of SR designed 'prototype' main-line loco-motives.

DWG 28
Side elevation of Nos 10201 and 10202, the No. 1 end being on the left.

DWG 29
Side elevation of Nos 10201 and 10202, the No. 1 end being on the right.

DWG 30
Side elevation of No. 10203, showing the different grille layout, the No. 1 end being on the left.

DWG 31
Front end detail of SR 'prototypes' with original layout.

DWG 32
Front end detail of SR 'prototype' design with revised front, incorporating door position.

DWG 31

10201–10203

Class	D16/2, later 16/9	D16/2 later 16/9
Number Range	10201–10202	10203
Built by	BR Ashford	BR Brighton
Introduced	1950–51	1954
Wheel Arrangement	1Co-Co1	1Co-Co1
Weight (operational)	135 tonnes	132 tonnes
Height	13ft 1in	13ft 1in
Width	9ft 3in	9ft 3in
Length	63ft 9in	63ft 9in
Min Curve negotiable	4$^1/_2$ chains	4$^1/_2$ chains
Maximum Speed	90mph	90mph
Wheelbase	55ft 6in	55ft 6in
Bogie Wheelbase (Rigid)	16ft 0in	16ft
Bogie Wheelbase (Total)	21ft 6in	21ft 6in
Bogie Pivot Centres	28ft 6in	28ft 6in
Wheel Diameter (Driving)	3ft 7in	3ft 7in
Wheel Diameter (Pony)	3ft 1in	3ft 1in
Brake Type	Vacuum	Vacuum
Sanding Equipment	Pneumatic	Pneumatic
Route Availability	6	6
Heating Type	Steam – Spanner	Steam – Laidlaw-Drew
Multiple Coupling Restriction	Not multiple fitted	Not multiple fitted
Brake Force	tonnes	tonnes
Engine Type	EE 16 SVT	EE 16 SVT Mk 2
Engine Horsepower	1,750hp	2,000hp
Power at Rail	1,300hp	1,550hp
Tractive Effort	48,000lb (Note: 1)	50,000lb
Cylinder Bore	10in	10in
Cylinder Stroke	12in	12in
Main Generator Type	EE 823A	EE 822-1B
Aux Generator Type	EE	EE
Number of Traction Motors	6	6
Traction Motor Type	EE 519-4D	EE 519-4D
Gear Ratio	19:61 (Note: 2)	19:61
Fuel Tank Capacity	1,150gal	1,180gal
Cooling Water Capacity	280gal	280gal
Lub Oil Capacity	16gal	16gal
Boiler Water Capacity	880gal	840gal
Boiler Fuel Capacity	From main supply	From main supply

1. When introduced the tractive effort figure was 31,200lb, this was later amended to the figure given.

2. Gear ratio when built was 17:65.

In 1949 the Southern Region made its first move towards main-line diesel traction when the frames for a 1Co–Co1 locomotive, eventually to become No. 10201 were laid at Ashford Works under the supervision of Mr O.V.S. Bulleid the SR CME. Before the first locomotive was completed the frames for a second were assembled. The third locomotive of the fleet was not constructed until 1953–4 and then at Brighton Works.

No 10201 was completed in November 1950 and commenced tests, firstly on the SR, and in January 1951 on the London Midland Region between St Pancras and Derby. After return to the SR No. 10201, resplendent in its main-line black and silver livery, was displayed at the Festival of Britain exhibition. The second of the build, carrying the number 10202 was completed in July 1951 and allocated to Nine Elms for driver and fitter training before taking up regular duties on the South Western Division following the return of No. 10201 from exhibition duty. Regular passenger duties commenced, from 15th October 1951 with both locomotives operating the SR's crack West of England services. On various occasions the machines were taken out of service for testing and modification work, but on the whole performed to a very high standard.

In early 1952 both locomotives were called to Brighton Works for a check up, returning to the West of England route within a short period. During April 1952 a series of controlled road tests were carried out on the Waterloo–Salisbury route using No. 10202 hauling 11 bogies plus a dynamometer coach. In November 1952 both locomotives were again taken out of service and sent to Brighton Works where a number of modifications were carried out, including re-gearing to increase tractive effort. By Spring 1953 both were returned to the Western section and continued main line operations.

During February 1953 Brighton Works commenced construction of the third member of the fleet No. 10203, which was completed in March 1954. A number of technical differences were incorporated in this locomotive, the most significant being the installation of a higher powered engine now developing 2,000hp. After its commissioning trials No. 10203 joined her sisters on the Waterloo–Exeter route where she soon showed off her superior power output. After only twelve months of all three SR diesels operating together Nos. 10201–2 were reallocated to the LMR at Camden for use alongside Nos. 10000–1. No. 10203 continued to operate on the SR until July 1955 when she too was reallocated to the LMR.

After Midland training had been completed Nos. 10201-2 found work double heading such services as the "Royal Scot", while No. 10203 was deployed on more mundane Euston–Bletchley workings, but did however on occasions make trips to Manchester, Carlisle and Glasgow. By the end of the 1950s the locomotives saw less and less work, being used on secondary passenger and freight duties. In November 1962 Nos. 10201 and 10203 were taken out of service and stored at Derby Works, being joined by No. 10202 in early 1963. At the end of 1963 all three locomotives were withdrawn and later offered for scrap.

When constructed all three locomotives were painted in black livery with silver lining, and this remained until the locomotives were allocated to the LMR, when Derby Works outshopped them in locomotive green livery.

Resplendent in its main-line black and silver livery, No. 10201 is shown from the No. 1 end in this official illustration, dated February 1951.

BR

41

Commencing on 15th October 1951 the two available 'SR' prototype locomotives were diagrammed for Waterloo–West of England line services, as far as Exeter. On the first day of operation No. 10202 is seen at Woking with the 11.00 departure from Waterloo, while in the adjacent platform SR Class N15 No. 30454 *Queen Guinevere* is seen on a Waterloo–Basingstoke service.

Author's Collection

The third and most powerful of the 'SR' main-line locomotives, No. 10203 emerged from Brighton Works in March 1954, being immediately deployed on the Waterloo–Bournemouth/West of England line. In early 1955 No. 10203 is seen departing from Waterloo with a West of England express. The locomotive has its No. 2 end leading. Note the engine room window in the open position.

GEC Traction

For a period during 1954-55 all three locomotives operated on the South Eastern section, often at the head of the "Golden Arrow" service. No. 10202 passes Herne Hill with the down service on a gloomy 17th June 1955.

L. Price

After Nos 10201-02 had been reallocated to the London Midland Region, repainting into green livery was effected by BR Derby Works, after which both were used on Euston–Glasgow line services. On 17th January 1957 the up "Royal Scot" is seen awaiting departure from Carlisle headed by both locomotives.

I.M. Wainwright

No. 2 End

No. 1 End

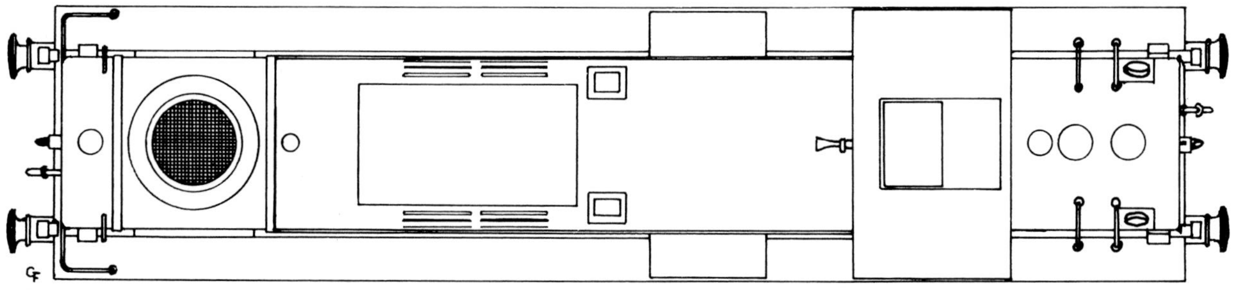

DWG 33

No. 2 End

No. 1 End

DWG 34

No. 2 End

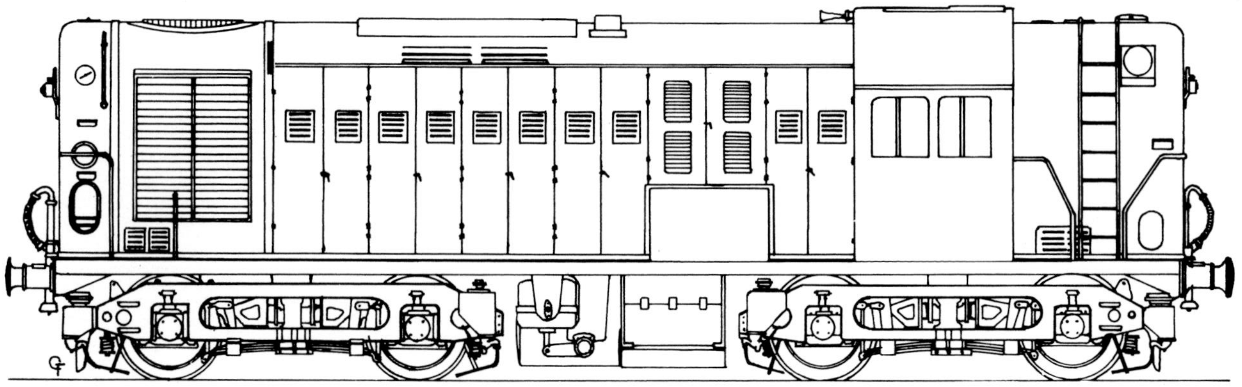

DWG 36

No. 1 End

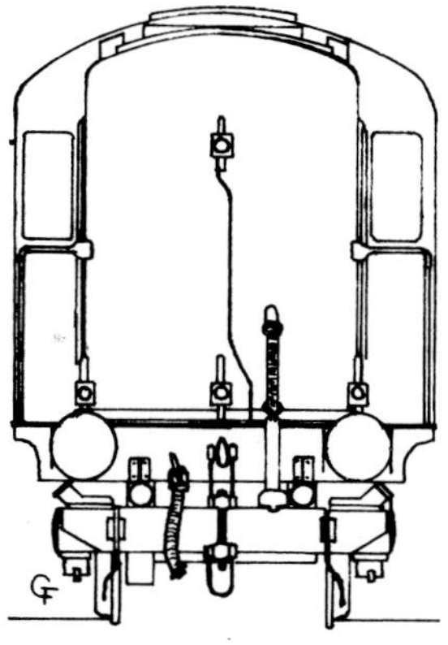

DWG 35

DWG 33
No. 10800 roof detail.

DWG 34
Side elevation of No. 10800 in original condition.

DWG 35
Front end detail of No. 10800 No. 1 end in original condition.

DWG 36
Front end detail of No. 10800 No. 2 end in original condition.

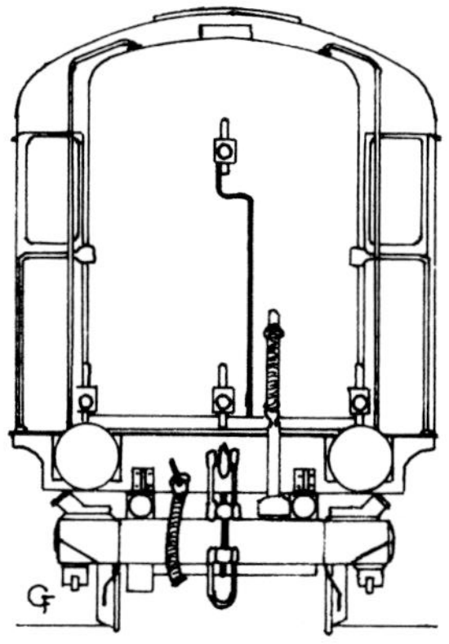

44

10800

Number		10800	Engine Horsepower	(As built)	827hp
Built by		NBL Ltd		(Rebuilt)	1,400hp
Rebuilt by		Brush	Power at Rail		hp
Introduced		1950	Tractive Effort	(As built)	34,500lb
Rebuilt		1961		(Rebuilt)	lb
Wheel Arrangement		Bo-Bo	Cylinder Bore	(As built)	7in
Weight (operational)		70 tonnes		(Rebuilt)	7¹/₄in
Height		12ft 9⁵/₁₆in	Cylinder Stroke	(As built)	7¹/₄in
Width		9ft 2in		(Rebuilt)	8¹/₄in
Length		41ft 10¹/₂in	Main Generator Type	(As built)	BTH
Min Curve negotiable		3³/₄ chains	Main Alternator Type	(Rebuilt)	Brush
Maximum Speed		70mph	Aux Generator Type	(As built)	BTH
Wheelbase		31ft	Aux Alternator Type	(Rebuilt)	Brush
Bogie Wheelbase		8ft 6in	Number of Traction Motors		4
Bogie Pivot Centres		22ft 6in	Traction Motor Type	(As built)	BTH 159
Wheel Diameter		3ft 6in		(Rebuilt)	Modified BTH 159
Brake Type		Vacuum	Gear Ratio		66:15
Sanding Equipment		Pneumatic	Fuel Tank Capacity		300gal
Route Availability		4	Cooling Water Capacity		85gal
Heating Type	(As built)	Steam– Clarkson	Lub Oil Capacity		gal
	(Rebuilt)	Not fitted	Boiler Water Capacity	(As built)	300gal
Multiple Coupling Restriction		Not Fitted		(Rebuilt)	Not fitted
Brake Force		46 tonnes	Boiler Fuel Capacity	(As built)	90gal
Engine Type	(As built)	Paxman 16PHXL Mk 2		(Rebuilt)	Not fitted
	(Rebuilt)	Maybach MD655			

Note: This locomotive was rebuilt as a Brush test locomotive and named *Hawk*. Rebuilt data above applies.

In 1945 the London Midland & Scottish Railway (LMSR) engineer Mr H.G. Ivatt decided to produce a basic design for an 800hp diesel-electric locomotive for comparison with similar output steam locomotives on secondary and branch line usage. In 1946 the LMSR placed an order with the North British Locomotive Co. (NBL) of Glasgow to produce a locomotive to their specification. The design adopted was like an elongated shunter, but mounted on a Bo-Bo wheel configuration with the cab slightly set in at one end. The cab was arranged to enable the driver to face the direction of travel and for this, duplicate controls were fitted. The power unit installed was a Davey Paxman 16RPH diesel engine which drove BTH electrical equipment.

The locomotive was constructed during 1948–50 and when completed carried the BR number 10800. The livery applied was black with silver bogies. After release from the builder's works No. 10800 underwent testing in Scotland, making frequent return trips to NBL for modification or repair. After a few months the locomotive was allocated to the LMR at Willesden and operated various tests in the London area. In March 1952 the locomotive was reallocated to Brighton on the SR from where it operated on the Victoria–Oxted line and various Central and South Eastern routes to gauge branch line operation. No. 10800's Southern operations did not last long and in July 1952 was reallocated to Plaistow shed on the ER for further trials, eventually being returned to the LMR in 1954 and deployed on such workings as Birmingham–Norwich before being withdrawn from operational service in August 1959. After withdrawal the locomotive was taken to Doncaster Works where it lay for many months awaiting a decision on its future.

In 1961 Brush Ltd of Loughborough were seeking a locomotive for experimental traction purposes and No. 10800 filled the role adequately, the locomotive being sold to Brush in 1962. Once with its new owner the Paxman power unit was replaced by a Maybach, MD655 which drove a Brush 3-phase brushless ac generator. The generator output was then passed through sophisticated electronics. Like all Brush 'prototype' locomotives it was allocated a name; *Hawk* being bestowed upon this locomotive but no plates were ever carried. After modification at Brush No. 10800 was put through a test programme for most of 1963–64, prior to receiving major body attention and repainting into a green and brown livery. In early 1965 the locomotive was inspected by BR and transferred to the Rugby Testing Station for performance tests to be carried out. After further static trials No. 10800 was accepted onto BR tracks for active operation over the GC Leicester– Nottingham route. Although basically successful the locomotive suffered a number of technical problems, and by 1968 Brush decided not to continue with the 10800 *(Hawk)* project and the machine was stored at Loughborough. The body of the locomotive was finally broken up in 1972–3.

The LMS designed NBL built 827hp Bo-Bo locomotive No.10800 was, like her more powerful main-line sisters painted in black and silver livery. This broad side official illustration shows the cab end on the right, with the bonnet section including the cooler group on the left.

BR

After only a short period in service the silver bogies had become rather discoloured, and were later re-painted black. This view showing the opposite end of the locomotive to the previous photograph was taken in May 1957.

L. Price

Illustrations of No.10800 working trains are quite hard to find, however this 1958 view shows the locomotive entering Oxford with a goods from the LMR. This was only a short period before the locomotive was finally taken out of service.

R. Simpson

After No. 10800's rebuilding by Brush as a trial locomotive its appearance was drastically altered, with the area to the rear of the cab fitted-out with sophisticated electronics. New louvres were positioned in the main bonnet area, and after body attention by Brush a 'mid' green livery complete with lion and wheel emblem was applied. No. 10800 in its final form is seen at the Brush works in Loughborough.

Brush Ltd

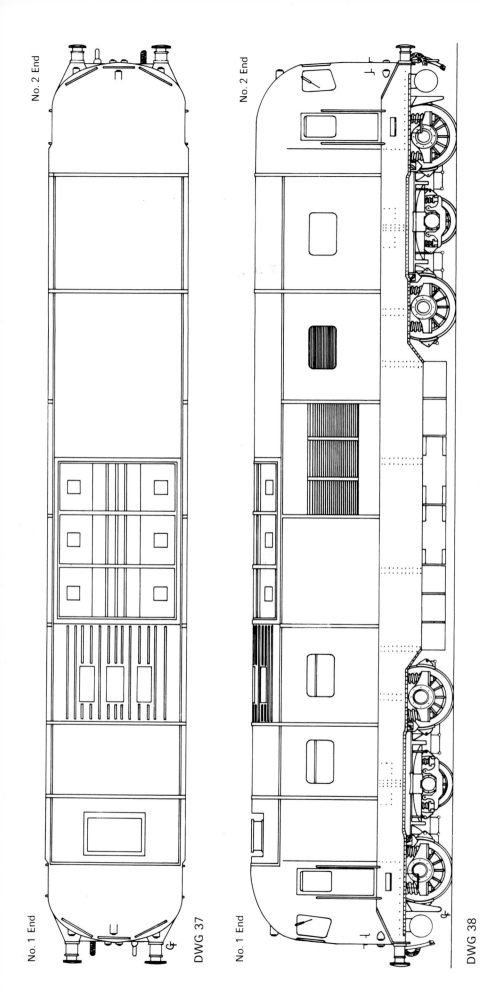

No. 2 End

No. 1 End

DWG 37

No. 2 End

No. 1 End

DWG 38

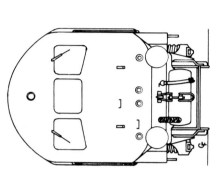

DWG 39

DWG 37
Gas-turbine No. 18000 roof detail.

DWG 38
Gas-turbine No. 18000 side elevation.

DWG 39
Front end detail of gas-turbine locomotive No. 18000.

18000

Number	18000	Sanding Equipment	Pneumatic
Built by	Brown Boveri	Route Availability	Not issued
Introduced	1950	Heating Type	Steam
Wheel Arrangement	A1A-A1A	Multiple Coupling Restriction	Not fitted
Weight (operational)	115 tonnes	Brake Force	tonnes
Height	13ft 4in	Gas Turbine Type	Brown Boveri
Width	9ft 2^1/$_2$in	Turbine Horsepower	2,500hp
Length	63ft 0^1/$_2$	Tractive Effort	60,000lb
Min Curve negotiable	chains	Main Generator Type	Brown Boveri
Maximum Speed	90mph	Traction Motor Type	Brown Boveri
Wheelbase	49ft 10in	Number of Traction Motors	4
Bogie Wheelbase	11ft 9^3/$_4$in	Fuel Tank Capacity	gal
Bogie Pivot Centres	38ft 0^3/$_4$in	Cooling Water Capacity	gal
Wheel Diameter (Driving)	4ft 0^1/$_2$in	Lub Oil Capacity	gal
(Pony)	3ft 2in	Boiler Water Capacity	gal
Brake Type	Vacuum		

Britain's first main-line gas-turbine locomotive was ordered by the Great Western Railway (GWR) in June 1940 from the Swiss company of Brown Boveri. Although ordered some eight years prior to Nationalisation No. 18000 was not delivered until 1949.

The British order for the gas-turbine powered locomotive was to established Swiss design and incorporated a number of European features which had to be modified for its British operation. After shipment to England No. 18000, painted in BTC main-line black and silver livery, was put through its paces at Swindon Works under the watchful eye of its builders, before main-line running could commence. Whilst at Swindon the locomotive was weighed, turning the scales at 115 tons, thus determining the same operating restriction being imposed as a 'King' class steam locomotive. In early 1950 No. 18000 took to the main-line, firstly for local tests, but in June more adventurous running commenced when selected Paddington-Plymouth duties were operated.

In late June No. 18000 was deployed on performance tests over the arduous Devon banks which identified that the locomotive was unable to haul a 350 ton train over the 1:42 Hemerdon incline from a standing start without assistance, the maximum weight that could be satisfactorily moved being 297 ton. Although a number of technical failures befell the locomotive in the autumn of 1950, the machine was kept in service, normally operating the Paddington-Bristol/West of England route. In April 1951 a fire developed in the heat exchanger which necessitated the locomotive to be out of service at Swindon Works until late August, as parts had to be obtained from the locomotive's builders.

Between 1952 and 1960 No. 18000 operated on the WR main-line with good availability, on numerous occasions being deployed on controlled road tests. In December 1960 No. 18000 was returned to Swindon Works where the decision was taken to withdraw the locomotive from any further active testing. Between January 1961 and January 1964 the locomotive lay at Swindon Works awaiting its final fate; however, in late 1963 No. 18000 was sold back to its builders in Switzerland, being shipped via the Harwich-Zeebrugge train ferry on 8th January 1964.

After arrival in Switzerland the machine was the subject of further research and was then placed on display outside the works. During the early 1990s a number of BR engineers and enthusiasts set about the task of bringing the locomotive back to the UK, and in 1994 their efforts came to fruition when it returned by road to Tinsley depot with sponsorship from the then Railfreight Distribution. It was later handed over to the private preservation sector and is now on display in its 1950s black livery at The Railway Age, Crewe.

No. 18000 passes Iver during 1951, with an up Plymouth–Paddington express. The locomotive has its No. 2 end leading in this view.

C.R.L. Coles

Ordered by the GWR, but delivered to BR was the Brown-Boveri gas-turbine No. 18000, which like other main-line 'modern' traction was painted in black and silver livery. This side elevation shows the machine with its No. 1 end on the left.

BR

On New Year's Day 1952 No. 18000 is seen passing Didcot with the noon service from Bristol Temple Meads to London. As the driving controls of this locomotive were unlike anything else in service, only selected drivers were trained on its operation, principally those based at Old Oak Common and Bristol.

BR Workshops

Whilst the gas-turbine prototype No. 18000 was basically successful, a few problems were encountered and this superb picture shows GWR 'King' No. 6021 *King Richard II* piloting No. 18000 near Swindon on 4th March 1958 after the latter had failed on a Bristol–Paddington express.

K. Leech

After restoration at Tinsley depot near Sheffield, No. 18000, returned to its 1950s black and silver livery, took part in a line up of traction at Willesden EuroTerminal where this illustration was taken on 27th June 1994.

Colin J. Marsden

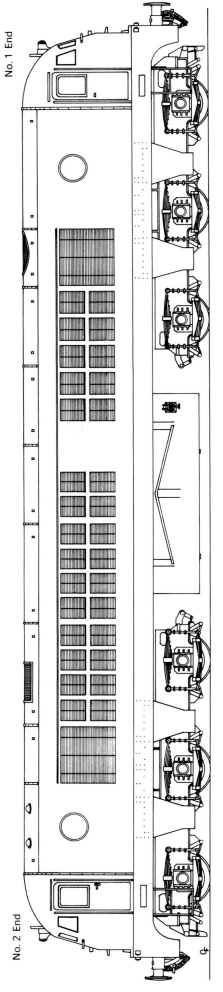

No. 1 End

No. 2 End

DWG 40

No. 1 End

No. 2 End

DWG 41

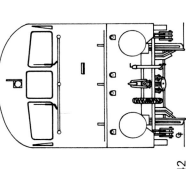

DWG 42

DWG 40
Gas-turbine No. 18100 roof detail.

DWG 41
Gas-turbine No. 18100 side elevation.

DWG 42
Front end detail of gas-turbine locomotive No. 18100.

18100

Number	18100	Route Availability	Not issued
Built by	Metropolitan Vickers	Heating type	Steam– Spanner
		Multiple Coupling Restriction	Not fitted
Introduced	1952	Brake Force	tonnes
Wheel Arrangement	Co-Co	Gas Turbine Type	Metropolitan Vickers
Weight (operational)	129$^1/_2$ tonnes		
Height	12ft 10in	Turbine Horsepower	3,000hp
Width	9ft	Power at Rail	2,450hp
Length	66ft 9$^1/_4$in	Tractive Effort	60,000lb
Min Curve negotiable	4 chains	Main Generator Type	MV
Maximum Speed	90mph	Number of Traction Motors	6
Wheelbase	53ft	Traction Motor Type	MV271
Bogie Wheelbase	15ft	Fuel Tank Capacity	995gal
Bogie Pivot Centres	37ft 6in	Cooling Water Capacity	620gal
Wheel Diameter	3ft 8in	Lub Oil Capacity	gal
Brake Type	Vacuum	Boiler Water Capacity	From main supply
Sanding equipment	Not fitted		

A second gas-turbine powered locomotive was ordered by the GWR during the mid 1940s, the constructional contract being placed with the Metropolitan–Vickers Co. of Manchester. Building of the locomotive was effected during 1949–51, with the locomotive delivered to Swindon in December 1951.

In common with the earlier WR gas-turbine (18000) No. 18100 was mounted on 6-wheel bogies, however on this locomotive all were powered, providing extra rail power which the WR required. During the locomotive's design period a number of stipulations were imposed by the BTC in terms of output and projected performance, which in broad terms equated to the requirement to haul an 18 coach train weighing around 650 tons over the Devon banks. Other requirements stated that good ride qualities had to be obtained at speeds up to 90mph, and that the driving controls had to be of a 'simple nature' to enable non technical staff to operate the machine. Train heating was provided by an oil fired steam boiler.

After delivery to the WR No. 18100 underwent a series of performance tests over a number of routes with differing train formations. Unlike her Swiss sister No. 18100 was able to haul 300+ton trains over Hemerdon Bank and start an 18 coach formation on the incline without any difficulty. By 1952 No. 18100 was taken into the general traffic fleet and commenced operating many Paddington–Bristol/West of England services. Between 1952 and 1958 the locomotive operated successfully with few major problems and clocked up some 450,000 miles prior to being withdrawn from service and stored at Swindon Works. After a short period at Swindon No. 18100 was sent to Metropolitan–Vickers at their Bowsfield Works near Stockton-on-Tees where it was converted into the prototype 25kV electric locomotive, No. E1000 (E2001). This machine was then used for equipment testing and staff training before the production electric locomotives for the Crewe–Manchester/Liverpool service were completed.

No E1000 (E2001) did not last long on the LMR once the production fleet was in service and during 1960 commenced a series of tests into the effect of wind resistance on locomotives. By 1962 the locomotive was at the Rugby Testing Station being used for instructional purposes. After being dumped at various locations around the Midlands No. E2001 was eventually returned to Rugby from where it was sold to J. Cashmore of Great Bridge for scrap in November 1972, being finally dismantled in January 1973. When built the locomotive was painted in main-line black livery with silver lining and bogies and this remained throughout its life even after conversion to an electric locomotive.

The second of the WR gas-turbine powered locomotives was constructed by Metropolitan Vickers of Manchester and is shown in this illustration under construction during September 1951. When handed over to the WR the livery was 'main-line' black and silver.

GEC Traction

After arriving at Bristol Temple Meads at the head of a test train from London, No. 18100 attached to a recording vehicle, awaits the signal to depart for Bristol depot, where the locomotive will be prepared for its return journey to the Capital.

L. Price

Sporting the steam style headboard "The Merchant Venturer" as well as oil headlamps and stencil reporting numbers, No. 18100 passes Iver on 5th April 1952 with the prestigious Paddington–Bristol express.

C.R.L. Coles

Front end detail of the locomotive after conversion to electric prototype No. E1000. Note that the steam heat pipe has been removed, and the buffers 'trimmed' to keep the locomotive to the required gauge.

BR

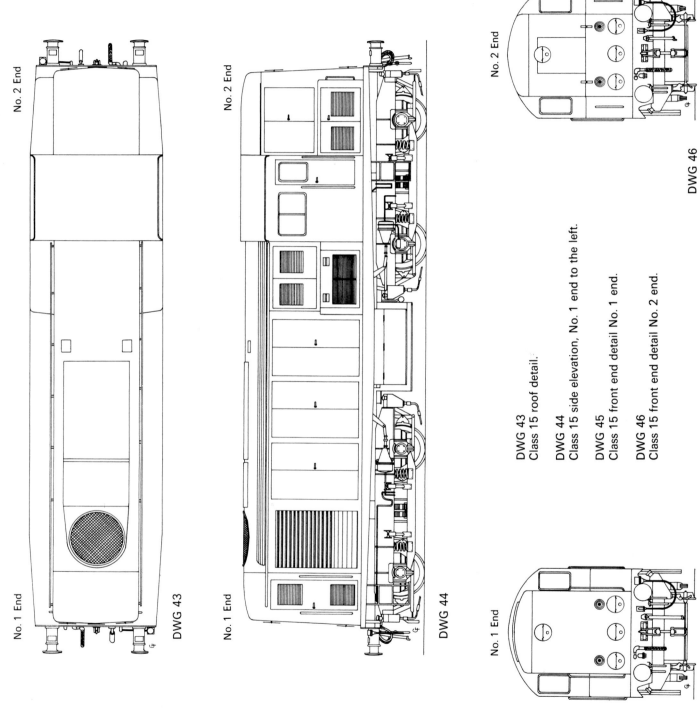

No. 2 End

No. 1 End

DWG 43

No. 2 End

No. 1 End

DWG 44

No. 2 End

DWG 46

No. 1 End

DWG 45

DWG 43
Class 15 roof detail.

DWG 44
Class 15 side elevation, No. 1 end to the left.

DWG 45
Class 15 front end detail No. 1 end.

DWG 46
Class 15 front end detail No. 2 end.

Class 15 (D8200–D8243)

Class	15	Heating Type	Not fitted (Through steam pipe)
Former Class Codes	D8/1, later 8/5		
Number Range	D8200–D8243	Multiple Coupling Restriction	Blue Star
Built by	Yorkshire Eng Co & BTH Ltd	Brake Force	31 tonnes
		Engine Type	Paxman 16YHXL
Introduced	1957–61	Engine Horsepower	800hp
Wheel Arrangement	Bo-Bo	Power at Rail	627hp
Weight (operational)	68 tonnes	Tractive Effort	37,500lb
Height	12ft 6in	Cylinder Bore	7in
Width	9ft 2in	Cylinder Stroke	$7^3/4$in
Length	42ft	Main Generator Type	BTH RTB10858
Min Curve negotiable	$3^1/2$ chains	Aux Generator Type	BTH RTB7420
Maximum Speed	60mph	Number of Traction Motors	4
Wheelbase	31ft	Traction Motor Type	BTH
Bogie Wheelbase	8ft 6in	Gear Ratio	
Bogie Pivot Centres	22ft 6in	Fuel Tank Capacity	400gal
Wheel Diameter	3ft 3in	Cooling Water Capacity	gal
Brake Type	Vacuum	Lub Oil Capacity	gal
Sanding Equipment	Pneumatic	Boiler Water Capacity	Not Fitted
Route Availability	4		

Of the many orders placed under the Modernisation Plan pilot scheme, one was a contract awarded to Clayton Equipment Co. to construct a fleet of ten (subsequently increased to 44) Type A (Type 1) 800hp locomotives for local freight and branch line operation.

The locomotives were powered by a Paxman 16YHXL engine which drove British Thomson-Houston (BTH) electrical equipment. The original order for ten locomotives, allocated BR running numbers D8200-D8209, was placed during November 1955 with construction being effected by the Yorkshire Engine Co. during 1956-57. Subsequent orders were placed for identical locomotives during 1958-59 which led to an eventual production fleet of 44, running numbers for subsequent locomotives being D8210-D8243.

Construction of locomotives D8210-D8243 was carried out by Clayton. The first locomotive of the build was handed over to the BTC at Euston station on 18th November 1957; after initial testing and proving the locomotive was allocated to Devons Road (Bow) shed and commenced operation in and around East London. However, after only a short time their operating range was extended by taking over many cross-London freights. It is interesting to note that when ordered this fleet was to be deployed in East Anglia, but due to several London authorities demanding the implementation of the newly passed Clean Air Act, it was decided to use the fleet in London, enabling steam to be phased out from several areas.

In less than a year from the introduction of No. D8200 the initial fleet of ten pilot order locomotives was in service and providing a good miles-per-casualty figure. The order for locomotives Nos D8210-D8243 began to appear in October 1959, with the final locomotive taking to the rails in February 1961. The complete fleet of BTH Type 1s, as they became known, was deployed on ER London area freights and some empty stock duties for many years, until the gradual decline in freight traffic in the late 1960s/early 1970s led to their withdrawal. Two machines soldiered on during the early 1970s for empty stock working in the Stratford-Liverpool Street area but the majority of locomotives were sold for scrap. Under the BR numerical classification the fleet became Class 15, but none survived to receive their five figure TOPS numbers. When built the fleet was painted in all over BR green livery, which was later altered to accommodate yellow warning ends.

After withdrawal from operational service, four locomotives were taken into departmental service as carriage pre-heating units. All have now been withdrawn. Luckily one example, No. D8233, has been saved by enthusiasts and is presently under restoration at The Railway Age, Crewe.

Official side elevation view of the first locomotive of the build. No. D8200, finished in Brunswick green livery, displaying its number and lion emblem on the cab side. This illustration was taken just prior to the locomotive being handed over to the BTC in November 1957.

Author's Collection

Front (nose) 3/4 view of BTH Type 1, showing the locomotive in 'as built' condition. Buffer beam connections consisting of centre screw coupling, vacuum pipe, through steam pipe, multiple control jumper and receptacle, and air control pipes.The left bottom train identification disc is in the upper position revealing the light below.

Author's Collection

After introduction the first ten locomotives were allocated to the LM at Devons Road shed, from where the fleet was used on freight diagrams on the former LMS main line. On 8th May 1958 locomotives Nos D8202 and D8201 are seen at the head of a southbound freight at Rugby.

GEC Traction

Following the completion of the first locomotive of the fleet, performance tests were carried out over the southern end of the Settle and Carlisle route, for which the locomotive was finished in grey undercoat. Sporting this short lived livery No. D8200 is seen at Appleby on 2nd November 1957.

Author's Collection

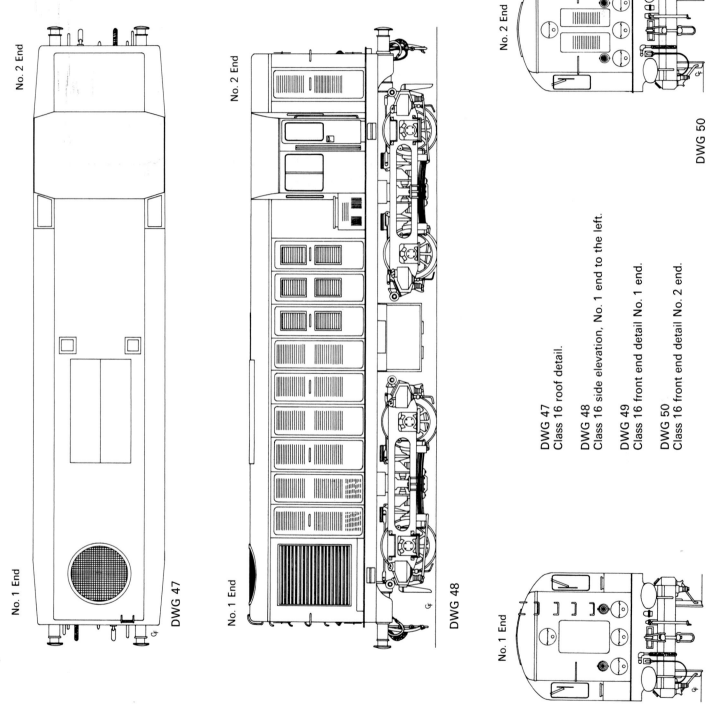

No. 2 End

No. 1 End

DWG 47

No. 2 End

No. 1 End

DWG 48

No. 2 End

DWG 50

No. 1 End

DWG 49

DWG 47
Class 16 roof detail.

DWG 48
Class 16 side elevation, No. 1 end to the left.

DWG 49
Class 16 front end detail No. 1 end.

DWG 50
Class 16 front end detail No. 2 end.

Class 16 (D8400–D8409)

Class	16	Heating type	Not fitted (Through steam pipe)
Former Class Codes	D8/2, later 8/4		
Number Range	D8400–D8409	Multiple Coupling Restriction	Red Circle
Built by	NBL Ltd	Brake Force	tonnes
Introduced	1958	Engine Type	Paxman 16YHXL
Wheel Arrangement	Bo-Bo	Engine Horsepower	800hp
Weight (operational)	68 tonnes	Power at Rail	627hp
Height	12ft 6in	Tractive Effort	42,000lb
Width	8ft 8½in	Cylinder Bore	7in
Length	42ft 6in	Cylinder Stroke	7¾in
Min Curve negotiable	3½ chains	Main Generator Type	GEC WT 881
Maximum Speed	60mph	Aux Generator Type	GEC
Wheelbase	28ft 6in	Number of Traction Motors	4
Bogie Wheelbase	8ft 6in	Traction Motor Type	GEC WT 441
Bogie Pivot Centres	20ft	Gear Ratio	
Wheel Diameter	3ft 7in	Fuel Tank Capacity	400gal
Brake Type	Vacuum	Cooling Water Capacity	gal
Sanding Equipment	Pneumatic	Lub Oil Capacity	gal
Route Availability	4	Boiler Water Capacity	Not fitted

Another of the orders placed under the pilot scheme of the Modernisation Plan was for a small fleet of ten type A (Type 1) Bo-Bo locomotives for which the construction contract was awarded to the North British Locomotive Co. (NBL) of Glasgow. This company had previously built the LMSR Bo-Bo prototype No. 10800, and this fleet showed a remarkable resemblance to this locomotive. The power plant adopted was the Paxman 16YHXL which drove GEC traction equipment. Running numbers allocated to the fleet were D8400–D8409.

Construction of the first locomotive commenced in late 1956 at the NBL Queen's Park Works in Glasgow, emerging for active road testing in July 1958. This was initially carried out around Glasgow, and later, after acceptance at Doncaster, in London where the entire fleet was originally shedded at Devons Road in Bow. The ten examples of the fleet all emerged in just under a year, but before the last of the class entered service some of the earlier delivered examples were suffering major technical problems and failure, leading to some of them spending lengthy periods out of service, usually at Stratford Works.

The main problem was the diesel engine, which although the same as that fitted to the D8200 fleet, had the tendency to seize in the D8400s, caused by inadequate ventilation of the power unit due to fundamental design deficiencies. Another problem identified was water contamination of the oil, caused by cylinder head failure. Another problem area which caused concern was the electro-magnetic control equipment which was not only non-standard but prone to failure. This also prevented the locomotives from operating in multiple with the more commonly found electro-pneumatic types.

After a short period of service the entire fleet was concentrated at Stratford depot in East London from where they could be found operating light weight cross-London freights and trip working in the East London area – so, as to be close to Stratford repair shops for urgent attention if required! With the decline of freight traffic in the late 1960s and their poor operating history these locomotives were deemed as surplus to requirements during 1968. All were subsequently sold for scrap, with none being saved for preservation.

The livery applied when built was standard locomotive green, which remained with the addition of yellow warning ends until their withdrawal. Under the BR classification system this fleet were deemed as Class 16.

The first of the North British Type A (Type 1) locomotives looking very similar to the LMS ordered prototype, No. 10800 emerged in May 1958 being allocated to the ER at Stratford depot. Displaying Brunswick green livery, as applied to the entire fleet upon construction, is No. D8402 which is seen outside its home depot in 1959.

Author's Collection

Front end detail, showing the nose end door in the open position, and the ladder rungs to the right giving access to the locomotive roof, a feature that would not be considered safe today. Similar to the BTH Type 1 fleet a through steam heat pipe was fitted.

Author's Collection

The usual deployment for this fleet was on secondary freight and empty coaching stock duties on the ER, however on 22nd May 1960 No D8408 made a trip to the South Coast when it operated a special from Loughton to Brighton and return. Seen here departing from Patcham Tunnel.

E. Arthur

Unfortunately due to their non-standard and problematic equipment the life span of the D84xx or Class 16 fleet was short, with the BTC only obtaining 10 years service from most machines. On 20th October 1962, No D8403 passes Canning Town with a freight from Temple Mills.

John Faulkner

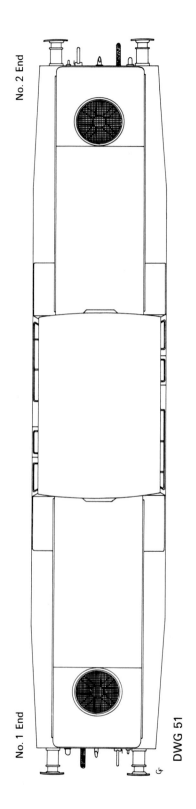

No. 2 End

No. 1 End

DWG 51

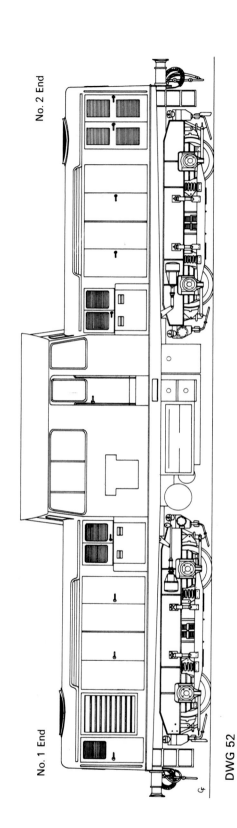

No. 2 End

No. 1 End

DWG 52

DWG 53

DWG 51
Class 17 'Clayton' roof detail.

DWG 52
Class 17 'Clayton' side elevation, No. 1 end on left.

DWG 53
Class 17 'Clayton' front end layout.

Class 17 (D8500–D8616)

Class	17	Multiple Coupling Restriction	
Former Class Codes.		(D8500–D8587)	Red Diamond
(D8500–87)	9/18	(D8588–D8616)	Blue Star
(D8588–616)	9/19	Brake Force	35 tonnes
Number Range	D8500–D8616	Engine Type.	
Built by	Clayton & Beyer	(D8500–85/88–616)	2 x Paxman 6ZHXL
	Peacock	(D8586–87)	2 x Rolls Royce 'D'
Introduced	1962–65	Engine Horsepower (Total)	900hp
Wheel Arrangement	Bo-Bo	Power at Rail	602hp
Weight (operational)	68 tonnes	Tractive Effort	40,000lb
Height	12ft 8in	Cylinder Bore	7in
Width	8ft 9½in	Cylinder Stroke	7¾in
Length	50ft 7in	Main Generator Type.	
Min Curve negotiable	3½ chains	(D8500–87)	GEC WT800
Maximum Speed	60mph	(D8588–616)	Crompton
Wheelbase	36ft 6in		Parkinson
Bogie Wheelbase	8ft 6in	Aux Generator Type. (D8500–87)	GEC WT
Bogie Pivot Centres	28ft	(D8588–616)	Crompton
Wheel Diameter	3ft 3½in		Parkinson
Brake Type	Vacuum	Number of Traction Motors	4
Sanding Equipment	Pneumatic	Traction Motor Type	GEC WT421
Route Availability	4	Gear Ratio	
Heating Type	Not fitted (Through steam pipe)	Fuel Tank Capacity	500gal
		Cooling Water Capacity	gal
		Lub Oil Capacity	gal
		Boiler Water Capacity	Not fitted

Ordered as a successor to the pilot scheme Type 1s, was this fleet of centre cab locomotives which were probably the least successful of any type. Not only was this in respect of having a central cab, whereby the driver had to look over a bonnet in either direction, but the power units, which for the bulk of the fleet were Paxman 6ZHXL units, giving dubious performance. Electrical equipment was provided by Clayton for the first 88 locomotives and Crompton Parkinson for the remainder.

After the design and order became public in 1961, considerable Union pressure was placed on the BTC after they had suggested that the new design would assist with eliminating the need for two men in the cab. Whilst most agreed that all-round visibility was good, the Union were not going to agree to staff cuts, claiming that the secondman would be required for shunting operations and safety. The initial order was for 88 locomotives, all for use in Scotland and with this in mind most were fitted with single-line token exchange equipment. During late 1961 a second order for 29 locomotives was placed, giving a total of 117 locomotives on order at the end of 1961, running numbers allocated being D8500–D8616. Construction of the first order of locomotives was awarded to the Clayton Equipment Co, from where the first locomotive emerged in September 1962, being handed over to the BTC at Marylebone. After only a short period major technical problems were identified, mainly involving the power units; this included cylinder head trouble, crankshaft movement, and oil contamination. In an attempt to overcome engine problems the final two locomotives of the initial build were fitted with Rolls Royce power units, and whilst these proved more successful, the type was not adopted for further use. The second batch of 29 locomotives was constructed by Beyer Peacock of Gorton, Manchester with delivery commencing in March 1964, continuing until April 1965. Ironically the BP built locomotives proved far more successful, but did not return a reliability figure satisfactory to the BTC who in subsequent years had to invest considerable finance in modification work to all locomotives.

The 'Claytons' as the fleet was usually known were given the classification 17 under the BR numerical system. Most of their work was performed either north of the border or in the North East where reliability figures were around 60%. With this in mind BR invested in further BR Type 1 locomotives (Class 20). The 'Claytons' being gradually phased out of service during the late 1960s with the final examples being withdrawn in 1971.

After withdrawal by BR one member of the class saw industrial use, No. D8568, and this is now preserved on the North Yorkshire Moors Railway by the Diesel Traction Group. Two others, Nos D8521 and D8598 passed to the Research Department at Derby where No. D8521 was modified as a mobile power plant and No. D8598 deployed as power on a variety of test trains in the Midlands. Regrettably both were disposed of for scrap in 1978.

When constructed the locomotives emerged in green livery with small yellow warning ends; these were later enlarged to fill the full nose end. After the adoption of BR blue as the standard livery many examples were outshopped in this style, again retaining the full yellow end.

Deemed to be the 'Standard Type 1' locomotive the Clayton fleet of Bo-Bos was not totally successful and some of the shortest lived main-line locomotives. No. D8501 is shown in this broad side illustration, with its No. 1 end being on the left. Note the token exchange equipment space on the body side.

Author's Collection

The first 88 locomotives of this type were allocated from new to Scotland, and by 1971 the entire fleet was operating north of the border. No. D8561 is seen heading a Bathgate coal train from Belverday Colliery on 7th September 1971, just a few weeks prior to the entire fleet being eliminated.

The late Derek Cross

Whilst the single cab 'Clayton' locomotives main diagrams were confined to freight operation, some passenger duties were performed, but mainly with the locomotives coupled in pairs, as the 900hp available on a single locomotive was insufficient. On 10th July 1965 No. D8526 piloting No. D8520 is seen passing Shotts with a summer Saturday holiday relief.

The late Derek Cross

When delivered locomotives Nos D8588–D8616 were allocated to the North Eastern Region for freight operation, normally operating singly on trip workings. In 1968 No. D8588 is seen passing Pelaw signal box with a freight off the South Shields line.

Geoff Lendon

After its demise from BR operation one locomotive, No. D8568, saw industrial use, firstly for Hemelite at Hemel Hempstead and subsequently at the Ribblesdale Cement Works at Clitheroe. After its useful life was over the machine was purchased by the Diesel Traction Group which keeps the locomotive on the Princes Risborough Railway. Displaying Ribblesdale livery, the locomotive is seen on the North Yorkshire Moors Railway at Grosmont on 1st October 1983.

Tony Aloszko

Class 20 (D8000–D8199/D8300–D8327) 20001–20228

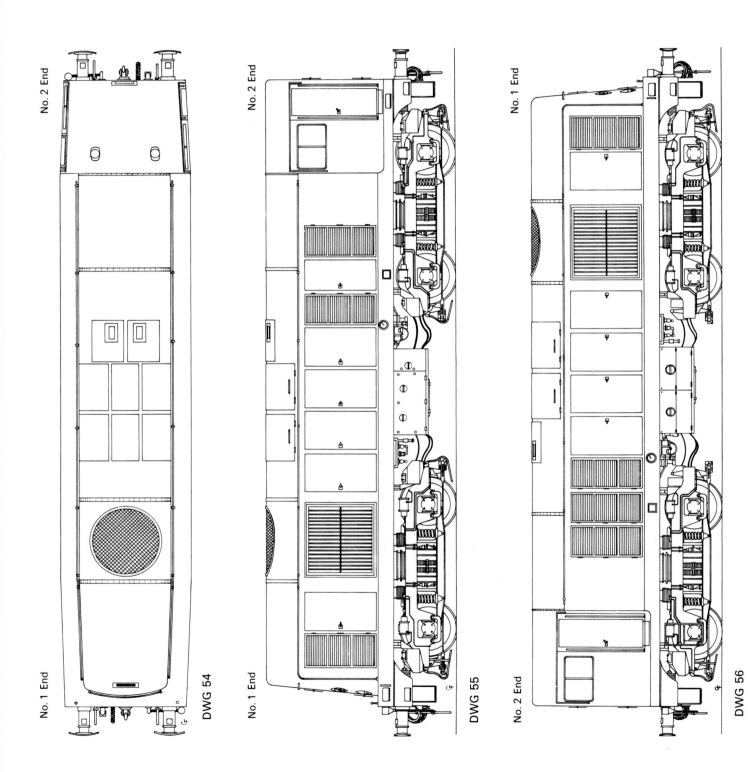

No. 2 End / No. 1 End — DWG 54

No. 2 End / No. 1 End — DWG 55

No. 1 End / No. 2 End — DWG 56

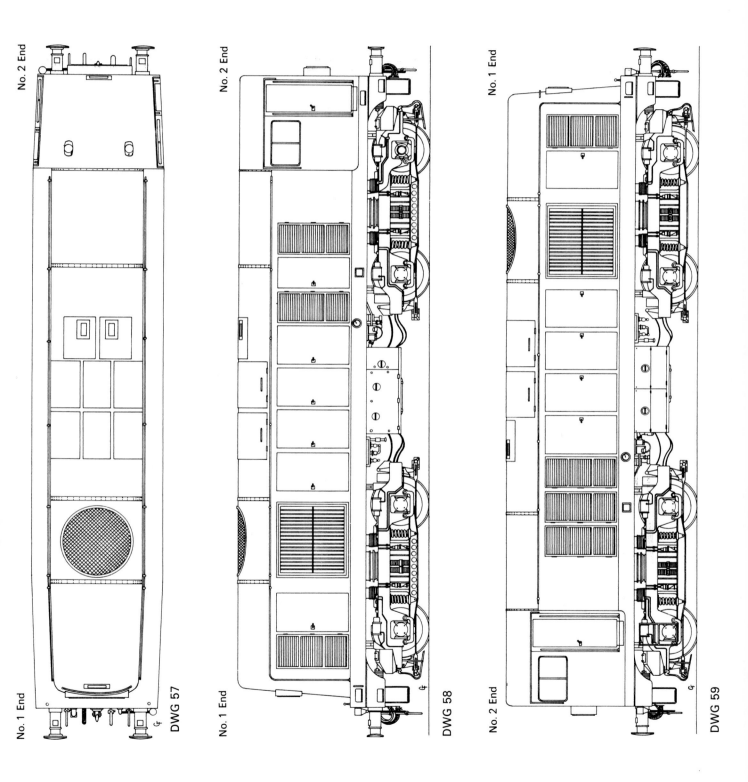

No. 2 End

No. 1 End

DWG 57

No. 2 End

No. 1 End

DWG 58

No. 1 End

No. 2 End

DWG 59

69

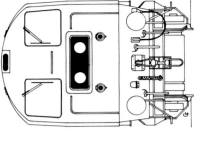

DWG 63

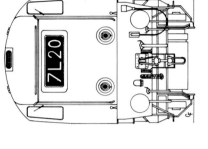

DWG 62

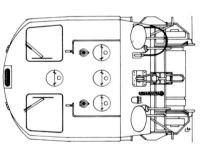

DWG 61

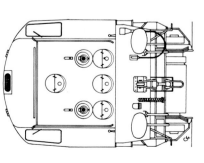

DWG 60

DWG 54
Class 20 roof detail, for locomotives Nos D8000–D8128 (20001–128) fitted with disc route indicators.

DWG 55
Class 20 side elevation side 'A', with the No. 1 end to the left. Layout for locomotives Nos D8000–D8128 (20001–128).

DWG 56
Class 20 side elevation side 'B', with the No. 1 end to the right. Layout for locomotives Nos D8000–D8128 (20001–128).

DWG 57
Class 20 roof detail, for locomotives Nos D8129–D8327 (20129–227) fitted with 4-character route indicator boxes.

DWG 58
Class 20 side elevation side 'A', with the No. 1 end to the left. Layout for locomotives Nos D8129–D8327 (20129–227).

DWG 59
Class 20 side elevation side 'B', with the No. 1 end to the right. Layout for locomotives Nos D8129–D8327 (20129–227).

DWG 60
Class 20 nose end layout for D8000–D8128 (20001–128) series, showing oval buffers with vacuum brake connections.

DWG 61
Class 20 cab end layout for D8000–D8128 (20001–128) series, showing oval buffers with vacuum brake connections.

DWG 62
Class 20 nose end layout for Nos D8129–D8327 (20129–227) showing round buffers and dual brake connections.

DWG 63
Class 20 cab end layout for Nos D8129–D8327 (20129–227) showing round buffers and dual brake connections.

DWG 64
Class 20 nose end layout for refurbished locomotives showing marker lights in place of headcode box.

DWG 64

Class	20/0	20/3	20/9
Former Class Codes	D10/3, later 10/3	-	-
Number Range TOPS	20001-20228	20301-20315	20901-20906
Former Number Range	D8000-D8199, D8300-D8327	20/0 series	20/0 series
Built by	EE & RSH Ltd	EE & RSH Ltd	EE & RSH Ltd
Introduced	1957-68	1995	1989
Wheel Arrangement	Bo-Bo	Bo-Bo	Bo-Bo
Weight (operational)	73 tonnes	76 tonnes	73 tonnes
Height	12ft 7⅝in	12ft 7⅝in	12ft 7⅝in
Width	8ft 9in	8ft 9in	8ft 9in
Length	46ft 9¼in	46ft 9¼in	46ft 9¼in
Min Curve negotiable	3½ chains	3½ chains	3½ chains
Maximum Speed	75mph (Note: 2)	75mph	60mph
Wheelbase	32ft 6in	32ft 6in	32ft 6in
Bogie Wheelbase	8ft 6in	8ft 6in	8ft 6in
Bogie Pivot Centres	24ft	24ft	24ft
Wheel diameter	3ft 7in	3ft 7in	3ft 7in
Brake Type	Dual (Note: 3)	Air	Air
Sanding Equipment	Pneumatic	Pneumatic	Pneumatic
Route Availability	5	5	5
Multiple Coupling Restriction	Blue Star	Special DRS	Blue Star
Brake Force	35 tonnes	31 tonnes	35 tonnes
Engine Type	English Electric 8SVT Mk11	English Electric 8SVT Mk11	English Electric 8SVT Mk11
Engine Horsepower	1,000hp	1,000hp	1,000hp
Power at Rail	770hp	770hp	770hp
Tractive Effort	42,000lb	42,000lb	42,000lb
Cylinder bore	10in	10in	10in
Cylinder Stroke	12in	12in	12in
Main Generator Type	EE819-3C	EE819-3C	EE819-3C
Aux Generator Type	EE911-2B	EE911-2B	EE911-2B
Number of Traction Motors	4	4	4
Traction Motor Type (20001-049)	EE526-5D	EE526-8D	EE526-8D
(20051-228)	EE526-8D		
Gear Ratio	63:17	63:17	63:17
Fuel Tank Capacity	380gal (Note: 1)	640gal (Note: 4)	380/640gal
Cooling Water Capacity	130gal	130gal	130gal
Lub Oil Capacity	100gal	100gal	100gal

Remote control radio equipment was installed on Nos 20058/087.

Transponder coding equipment was installed on Nos 20001/4/6/16/ 20/6/41/9/52/3/65/72/3/80-2/99/101/5/13.

Snowplough brackets were fitted on Nos 20028-34/70-127/9-88/90-228.

Notes

1. No. 20084 was fitted with additional fuel tanks, giving a capacity of 1,040gal.

2. The maximum speed of the Class 20s was 75mph until 5/87.

3. When built vacuum brakes were fitted as standard, dual brakes being fitted over the years.

4. Nos 20301-305 have 640gal capacity, 20306-315 have 1,080gal capacity

Main body differences:
Locomotive Nos 20001-128 were built with disc type train reporting equipment, while locomotives Nos 20129-228 were built with four-position headcode boxes.

Refurbishment of some examples in the 1970s and '80s led to marker lights being installed in place of discs and headcodes.

The final and most successful batch of Type A (Type 1) locomotives ordered under the Modernisation Plan were the English Electric series, later classified Class 20. The initial order placed in 1956 was for just 20 locomotives; however, following subsequent orders a total production run of 228 locomotives ensued.

After receiving the contract for 20 pilot scheme locomotives (allocated numbers D8000-D8019), the English Electric Co. sub-contracted mechanical assembly to the Vulcan Foundry works at Newton-le-Willows, where construction commenced during mid 1957. The body styling followed the other pilot scheme Type A locomotives, having a single cab at one end, but was far more streamlined in appearance, which closely followed previous EE constructed locomotives for New Zealand and Tasmania. After the first locomotive was completed, testing was carried out in the Penrith area before the locomotive was handed over to the BTC at Euston. The allocation of all 20 pilot locomotives was to Devons Road, Bow, from where freight and local passenger duties were operated. The design was an immediate success and, before all 20 were available, running and testing trials were being carried out all over the LMR and even in Scotland. Before the final locomotive of the pilot order was delivered a subsequent order had been placed for 30 locomotives for delivery at the end of 1959. These 30, intended for use on the Eastern and Scottish Regions, were constructed equally by Vulcan Foundry and Robert Stephenson & Hawthorns.

During the ensuing months other repeat orders were placed with English Electric for identical locomotives until 128 were in traffic by July 1962. Production then ceased in favour of the 'Standard' Type 1 or 'Clayton' locomotives then on order. As time proved the new 'Standard' Type 1 was to be little less than disastrous and subsequently a further 100 English Electric Type 1s were ordered in the mid 1960s with delivery from mid 1966, construction of this batch being awarded to Vulcan Foundry. With the delivery of the 100 additional locomotives, insufficient straight numbering in the D80xx and D81xx range remained, and as the D82xx series was already in use the additional locomotives carried on in the D83xx series. The prime mover installed in the EE Type 1s was the well established English Electric 8SVT Mk 111 with electric equipment also provided by English Electric. When built all locomotives were fitted with vacuum-only train brake equipment; however, over the years dual brake equipment was fitted to most examples.

A number of detail differences have existed within the fleet. The first 128 locomotives were constructed with disc style train reporting equipment, while all subsequent locomotives sported four-character alpha/numerical reporting equipment. Locomotives built for Scottish operation were fitted with space for token exchange apparatus, while round and oval buffers were fitted at various times during the build. Once the entire fleet of BR Class 20s was in service, allocation was shared between the London Midland, Eastern and Scottish

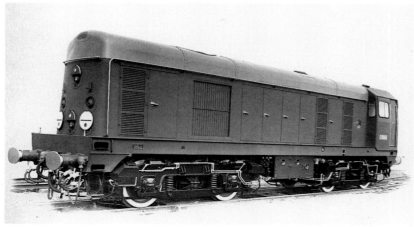

All 20 of the pilot order Type A (Type 1) locomotives were allocated to Devons Road shed at Bow, London, from where they were used on LM local passenger and freight duties. No. D8005 is shown from its cab end in this 1959 illustration.

BR

The entire fleet of pilot order Type A locomotives were finished in Brunswick green livery, with a grey roof, underframes were finished in black with air pipes picked out in white. No. D8006 in 'as built' condition is illustrated prior to delivery to the LMR.

GEC Traction

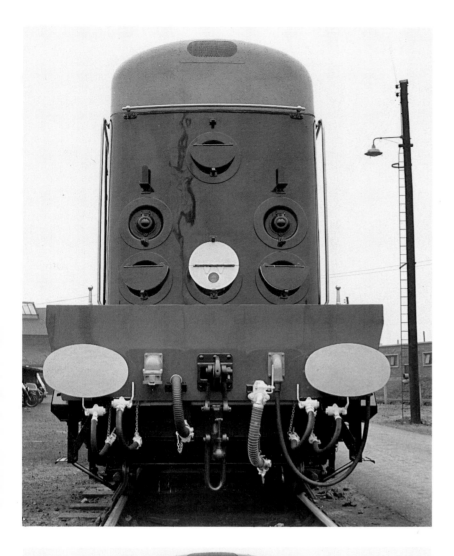

Regions, with the class visiting both Western and Southern Regions.

Under 1970-80s rationalisation of BR motive power the Class 20s were among the few types that underwent major refurbishing to keep them 'on the road' until the 1990s. A considerable number passed through BREL works in the 1980s for major refurbishing, mainly emerging without train reporting equipment, frontal identification being provided by sealed beam marker lights. Much work was also carried out internally. Withdrawal of life-expired machines commenced in the mid 1980s, with only a handful remaining in traffic at the time of privatisation, mainly working for the BR Telecom arm.

The Class 20s were the first class to enter main line private ownership when six locomotives were sold to Hunslet Barclay for contract hire work in 1989. These were reclassified as Class 20/9 and renumbered 20901-906. In 1995 a new company called Direct Rail Services (DRS) was formed by British Nuclear Fuels Ltd (BNFL) for the movement of waste and raw commodities associated with the nuclear industry. DRS originally purchased five locomotives which were given a massive rebuild by Brush, emerging as Class 20/3; subsequent purchases and rebuilds have created a fleet of 15 Class 20/3s. In early 1999 the Hunslet Barclay fleet of six locomotives was sold to DRS to supplement their fleet. Three of these later went to Kosovo on the Train for Life special and at the end of 1999 were working under NATO control in Kosovo.

A number of Class 20s were sold by BR to private engineering operators for use during the construction of the Channel Tunnel; these mostly came under the remit of Doncaster based RFS. A large number of Class 20s have now entered the preservation movement.

When constructed, the entire fleet was painted in BR standard green livery, yellow warning panels and later full yellow ends being progressively applied. After blue was adopted as the standard livery, the entire class was repainted into this scheme with, of course, full yellow warning ends. With the implementation of the operating sectors in the 1980s and the Class 20 fleet being allocated primarily to the Railfreight sector, a number of machines emerged in the Railfreight grey livery with wrap around yellow ends, giving a somewhat different appearance to these 25-30 year old workhorses. In July 1988 No. 20088 was outshopped in new Railfreight sub-sector colours. Locomotives sold for use on Channel Tunnel construction traffic were repainted in RFS grey, while those operated by Hunslet Barclay were painted in that company's house colours. Locomotives now operated for DRS are painted in dark blue livery.

Front end, and rear end layouts of English Electric Type A locomotive, in 'as built' condition. Both ends were fitted with four hinged discs, with white lights behind, red tail indicators being positioned above the two bottom outer discs. Buffer beam connections consist of a centre screw coupling, multiple control jumper cable and socket, vacuum pipe, through steam pipe, and air control connections.

Both: Author's Collection

During the early 1960s following the BTC decision to adopt the yellow warning end as standard to all locomotives, small half height panels were applied to both ends of the Type 1 fleet. At around the same time the round BR lion and wheel logo was adopted and applied to the bonnet just in front of the cab. Locomotives Nos D8121 and D8124 are seen at Linwood with an automotive special formed of Hillman Imps on 12th March 1966.

Author's Collection

As detailed in the introductory text, later Type 1 locomotives were built with alpha/numeric route identification boxes, which did look rather ugly on the cab end. Painted in blue livery Nos 20158 and 20178 with white disc in the former indicator box, depart from Peak Forest on 11th July 1986 with the 15.45 to Walton Old Junction.

Colin J. Marsden

For ease of operation it is usual for pairs of Class 20s to be coupled nose to nose, thus providing a cab at the outer end of the motive power unit. Locomotives Nos 20187 and 20007 approach Chinley on 11th July 1987 with the 11.24 Oakleigh–Great Rocks empty ICI hopper train.

Colin J. Marsden

Under the privatisation of Britain's railways a new company to come on the scene was Direct Rail Services, a subsidiary of British Nuclear Fuels Ltd. The company first introduced a fleet of five Class 20s, heavily rebuilt by Brush or RFS Doncaster and reclassified Class 20/3. This fleet had grown to 15 machines by mid 1999. The company also has six ex-EPS Class 37/6s. The locomotives are all painted in dark blue with DRS branding and normally operate BNFL traffic as well as contract hire freight services. No. 20307 is illustrated.

Colin J. Marsden

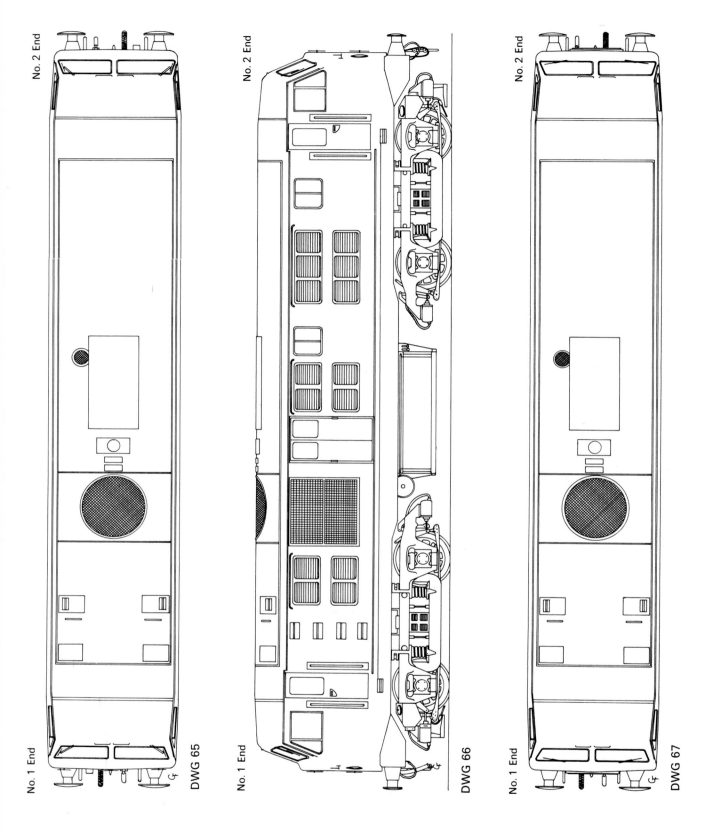

No. 2 End

No. 1 End

DWG 65

No. 2 End

No. 1 End

DWG 66

No. 2 End

No. 1 End

DWG 67

76

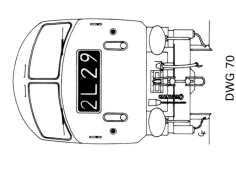

DWG 70

Class 21/29 (D6100–D6157)

DWG 65
Class 21 roof detail.

DWG 66
Class 21 side elevation, with No. 1 end on the left.
Showing modified drop light cab side windows.

DWG 67
Class 29 roof detail.

DWG 68
Class 29 side elevation, with No. 1 end on the left.

DWG 69
Class 21 end elevation.

DWG 70
Class 29 end elevation.

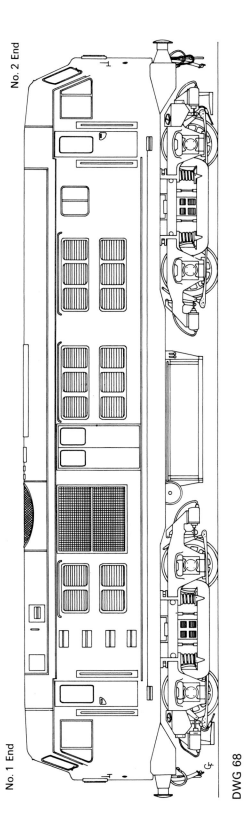

DWG 68

DWG 69

Class 21/29 (D6100–D6157)

Class	21	29
Former Class Codes (as built)	D11/2, later 11/4	13/4
(de-rated)	D10/1, later 10/4	13/4
Number Range	D6100–D6157	See Note: 1
Built by	NBL Ltd	Rebuilt by BR Glasgow
Introduced	1958-60	1965
Wheel Arrangement	Bo-Bo	Bo-Bo
Weight (operational)	73 tonnes	73 tonnes
Height	12ft 6⁷/₈in	12ft 6⁷/₈in
Width	8ft 8in	8ft 8in
Length	51ft 6in	51ft 6in
Min Curve negotiable	4¹/₂ chains	4¹/₂ chains
Maximum Speed	75mph	80mph
Wheelbase	37ft	37ft
Bogie Wheelbase	8ft 6in	8ft 6in
Bogie Pivot Centres	28ft 6in	28ft 6in
Wheel Diameter	3ft 7in	3ft 7in
Brake Type	Vacuum	Vacuum
Sanding Equipment	Pneumatic	Pneumatic
Route Availability	5	5
Heating Type	Steam – Spanner Mk 1	Steam – Spanner Mk 1
Multiple Coupling Restriction	See Note: 2	See Note: 2
Brake Force	tonnes	tonnes
Engine Type	NBL/MAN L12V18/21	Paxman 12YJXL
Engine Horsepower	1,100hp (Note: 3)	1,350hp
Power at Rail	816hp	925hp
Tractive Effort	45,000lb	47,000lb
Cylinder Bore	7in	7in
Cylinder Stroke	8¹/₄in	7³/₄in
Main Generator Type	EE WT880	EE WT880
Aux Generator Type	EE WT761	EE WT761
Number of Traction Motors	4	4
Traction Motor Type	EE WT440	EE WT440
Gear Ratio		
Fuel Tank Capacity	360gal	375gal
Cooling Water Capacity	146gal	146gal
Lub Oil Capacity	gal	gal
Boiler Water Capacity	600gal	600gal
Boiler Fuel Capacity	100gal	From main supply

1. Twenty Class 29s were rebuilt from Class 21s in 1965, locomotives rebuilt being Nos D6100–03/06–08/12–14/16/19/21/23–24/29–30/32–33/37.

2. When introduced Red Circle (electro-magnetic) restrictions applied. In later years Nos D6104/22/35/38–57 were fitted with Blue Star (electro-pneumatic) equipment.

3. When built the installed HP was 1,100, however this was later reduced to 1,000hp.

Under the BTC pilot scheme of traction modernisation the North British Locomotive Co. of Glasgow was contracted to build a fleet of ten Type B (later Type 2) locomotives for main-line passenger and freight operation. During the construction of the original contract, a subsequent order for a further 48 like locomotives was placed. The number range allocated being D6100–D6151.

The power unit adopted for this build was the German design, British built MAN L12V18/21 developing 1,100hp. Coupled to this unconventional 4-stroke engine was GEC electrical equipment. The first locomotive was constructed at the NBL Queen's Park Works during 1958, commencing active testing during December in Scotland and arriving in London during January 1959, where it was allocated to Hornsey depot. In a period of just under four months all ten pilot scheme locomotives were delivered, all being allocated to Hornsey from where GE suburban-line duties were operated. During May 1959 the 'production' fleet commenced delivery, also going to ER London division sheds. By early 1960 major technical difficulties were identified, mainly involving the coupling between the power unit/generator group, and the overhaul performance of the engine. In September 1960 the BTC decided to reallocate the entire fleet to Scotland where more suitable duties were available for them, and close to the manufacturer's works where major repair work could be effected if required.

Such were the problems with the engines that in early 1963 No. D6123 was despatched to Davey Paxman's works in Colchester where a Paxman 'Ventura' power unit was installed. The locomotive was then thoroughly tested in Scotland and a decision made that this power unit was more reliable than the original type, culminating in a fleet of 20 locomotives being re-engined, with refurbishing being carried out by Paxman. The new engines gave the locomotives slightly increased power, 1,350hp compared to the 1,000hp of the original ten locomotives and 1,100hp of the production fleet. After locomotives had been fitted with Paxman power units they were reclassified 29.

The locomotives that retained their original power units were, to say the least, totally unreliable, and withdrawn during 1968. Under the National Traction Plan those re-engined examples were permitted to carry on operating in Scotland, remaining active until late 1971. All locomotives were sold for scrap, with no examples being preserved.

When constructed the locomotives were in all over BR standard green livery, small yellow ends being added in the early 1960s. Locomotives rebuilt as Class 29 emerged in two-tone green with yellow panels/ends. A handful of machines did emerge painted in BR standard rail blue in the late 1960s and did of course sport full yellow warning ends.

The ten pilot order NBL Type 2 locomotives, outshopped in Brunswick green livery were all shedded at Hornsey depot when new, and used on London area mixed traffic duties. No. D6101 is seen outside the shed on 4th October 1959.

B.J. Hemming

The production batch of NBL Type 2 locomotives was allocated between the Eastern and Scottish Regions when delivered, but was concentrated entirely in the Scottish Region from 1960. No. D6112 is seen in July 1961 at Holehouse with a Waterside–Ayr coal duty.

L. Price

In the early years of the 1960s when the entire fleet was allocated to the Scottish Region, major problems were identified in power units. However the class managed to soldier on and a number of passenger duties were performed by the class – often doubleheaded. On 8th September 1962 Nos D6120 and D6105 are seen approaching Perth with a Glasgow–Aberdeen working.

The late Derek Cross

The power unit problems were so serious that during the early 1960s when re-engining was being considered, a sizeable proportion of the fleet was stored at various locations around Scotland. On 2nd May 1963 two machines, Nos D6120 and D6109 were captured passing Bridge of Allan near Stirling with a mixed freight train.

L. Price

Following trials in 1963 with No. D6123 it was decided to invest in refurbishment of 20 locomotives, this included the installation of Paxman 'Ventura' engines, and other technical alterations. Externally the front end was fitted with 4-character route indicators and the livery altered to two-tone green. Refurbished No. D6121 is seen at Corpach with a Fort William–Mallaig working.

The late Derek Cross

Clearly displaying its 4-character route indicator – although not being used correctly, Class 29 No. D6130 pulls away from Stirling on 15th August 1966 with a Glasgow–Aberdeen service formed entirely of maroon liveried Mk 1 stock.

The late Derek Cross

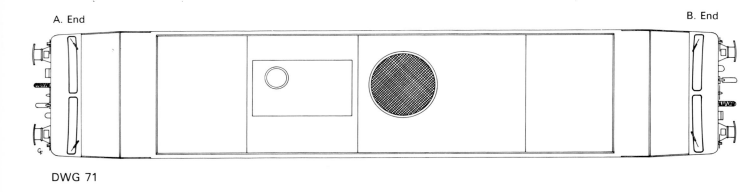

A. End   B. End

DWG 71

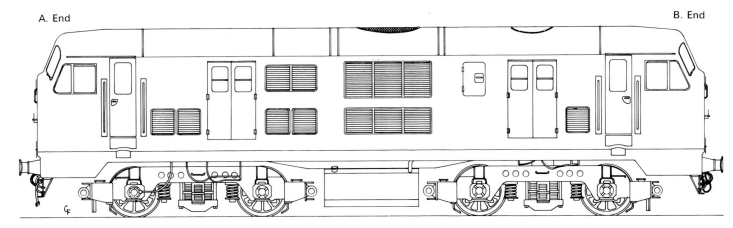

A. End   B. End

DWG 72

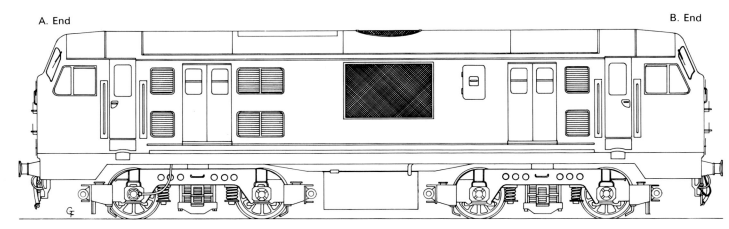

A. End   B. End

DWG 73

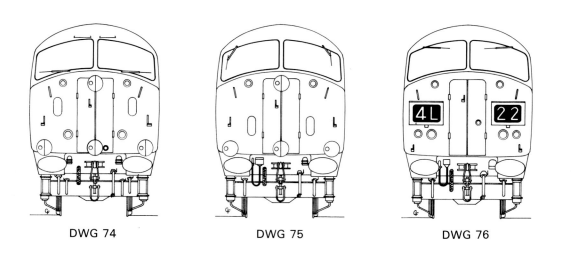

DWG 74   DWG 75   DWG 76

DWG 71
Class 22 roof detail.

DWG 72
Class 22 side elevation, showing original design bodywork as for D6300–D6305.

DWG 73
Class 22 side elevation, showing production D11/5 type.

DWG 74
Class 22 front end layout, showing the original disc reporting equipment. D6300–D6305

DWG 75
Class 22 Front end layout, showing production batch disc layout (D6306–D6357).

DWG 76
Class 22 front end layout, showing the split box route indicator, as modified on D6306–D6357.

Class 22 (D6300 – D6357)

Class	22
Former Class Codes (D6300–05)	D10/2A, later 10/4A
(D6306–57)	D11/5, later 11/4A
Number Range	D6300–D6357
Built by	NBL
Introduced	1959–62
Wheel Arrangement	B-B
Weight (operational)	65–68 tonnes
Height	12ft 10in
Width	8ft 8in
Length	46ft 8^1/$_2$in
Min Curve negotiable	4^1/$_2$ chains
Maximum Speed	75mph
Wheelbase	34ft 6in
Bogie Wheelbase	8ft 6in
Bogie Pivot Centres	23ft
Wheel Diameter	3ft 7in
Brake Type	Vacuum
Sanding Equipment	Pneumatic
Route Availability	4

Heating Type (D6300–05)	Steam-Spanner MkI
(D6306–57)	Steam – Clayton or Stones
Multiple Coupling Restriction	
(D6300–05)	Orange Square
(D6306–57)	White Diamond
Brake Force	29 tonnes
Engine Type (D6300–05)	MAN L12V18 21A
(D6306–57)	MAN L12V18 21B
Engine Horsepower (D6300–05)	1,000hp
(D6306–57)	1,100hp
Power at Rail	hp
Tractive Effort (D6300–05)	40,000lb
(D6306–57)	38,000lb
Cylinder Bore	7^3/$_4$in
Cylinder Stroke	8^1/$_4$in
Transmission Type	Voith LT306r
Fuel Tank Capacity	450gal
Cooling Water Capacity	135gal
Lub Oil Capacity	38gal
Boiler Water Capacity	500gal
Boiler Fuel Supply	From main tank

The North British Locomotive Co. (NBL) also won a contract to build six diesel-hydraulic locomotives fitted with the same MAN L12V18/21 engine but this time coupled to Voith-North British transmission as part of the BTC pilot scheme order. Similar in appearance to the previously detailed diesel-electric class, this fleet was also mounted on two 4-wheel bogies. Further repeat orders for this design were placed in the late 1950s which gave a fleet total of 58. The locomotives formed part of the Type 'B' power classification which was later amended to Type 2. Under the numerical classification, the fleet became Class 22.

The first locomotive of the diesel-hydraulic design was delivered to Swindon Works in December 1958, after operating several proving trials in Scotland. Once at Swindon the machine was put through its paces and performed satisfactorily. Once in service all six of the pilot order, allocated running numbers D6300–D6305 were deployed on secondary passenger and freight duties as well as banking duties over the South Devon hills. The production order of locomotives commenced delivery in February 1959 (carrying numbers D6306–D6357) at a rather leisurely pace until the final locomotive was delivered in the spring of 1962.

This protracted delivery schedule was due to a considerable number of modifications required by BR in experience of the pilot scheme locomotives, and because NBL were also constructing the 2,200hp 'Warship' locomotives in the

same shop at Glasgow. The power unit installed in the pilot scheme locomotives was set to provide 1,000hp, while those on the production fleet provided 1,100hp. Other differences between the two types included the fitting of electro-pneumatic control equipment to the pilot order, while an all electric control system was fitted to the production batch. All locomotives up to No. D6334 were built with the disc train identification system, whereas subsequent locomotives were installed with 4-character alpha/numeric boxes and in the fullness of time a number of earlier examples were similarly treated. During their careers the fleet operated to virtually all corners of the WR except South Wales, and gave a good return to the BTC for their investment. Their main duties consisting of freight and secondary passenger, however on a number of occasions, main-line duties were performed, usually double-headed. Towards the end of the locomotives' lives several were deployed on London area ecs duties.

Due to their non-standard equipment, and the Railways' decision to adopt diesel-electric transmission as their standard system, the fleet was phased out of service from 1968 with the final locomotive being withdrawn in 1971. All locomotives were broken up for scrap.

When built all locomotives were painted in BR green livery, yellow warning panels being added in the mid 1960s. After the adoption of BR blue livery in 1967 several locomotives were so treated.

The D6300 fleet or NBL Type 2 diesel-hydraulics were introduced for WR operation from December 1958, when the first of six pilot order locomotives was delivered. No. D6302, the third of the build, is seen outside Swindon Works with its body side doors open. The pilot order locomotives were fitted with the disc train identification system.

Author's Collection

Following the pilot order came a 'production' contract which led to 58 locomotives being built with slightly different body styling. After construction in Glasgow, testing was carried out on the Scottish Region prior to delivery to the WR. No. D6335 is seen at Dumfries whilst operating a Glasgow-Carlisle test train. Note the oil headlights on the front.

NBL Ltd

The production fleet of NBL Type 2 diesel-hydraulic locomotives, later to become Class 22 were slightly different from the pilot order as all electric multiple control equipment was fitted and route indicator boxes installed to all locomotives after No. D6334. Most earlier examples were modified with route boxes in later years. No. D6310 painted in green livery with small yellow warning panels is seen at Bristol in October 1969.

Geoff Lendon

Locomotives of the Class that survived to pass through Swindon Works for classified attention after January 1968 emerged in blue livery with full yellow ends, which whilst looking smart, was not as appealing as the original green. Displaying the final livery choice, No. D6308 (of the pilot order) is illustrated at Bristol in 1969.

Geoff Lendon

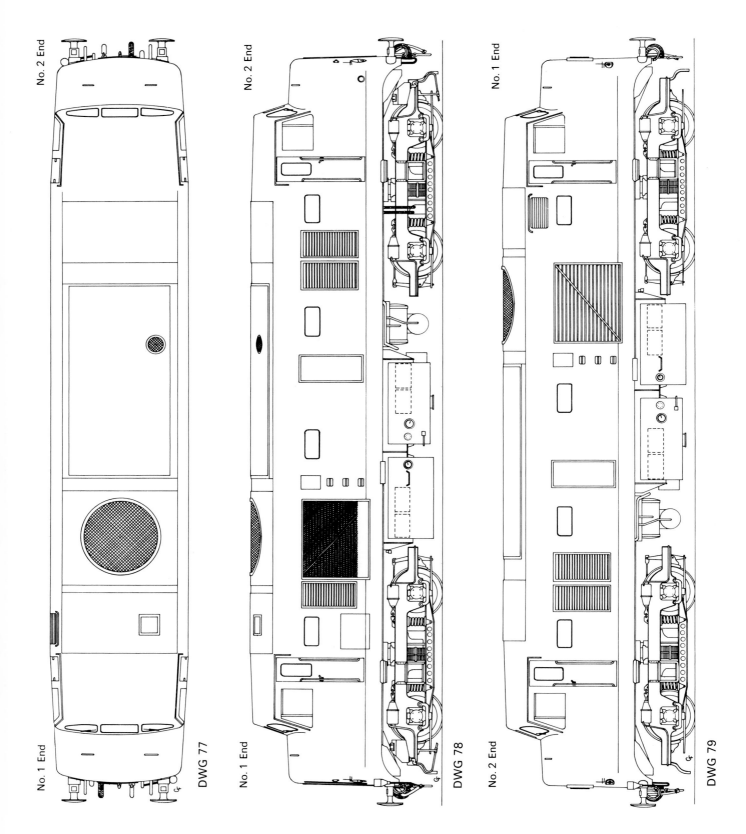

No. 2 End

No. 1 End

DWG 77

No. 2 End

No. 1 End

DWG 78

No. 1 End

No. 2 End

DWG 79

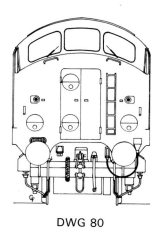
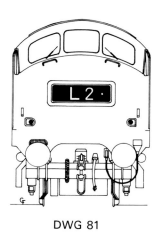

DWG 80   DWG 81

DWG 77
Class 23 'Baby Deltic' roof detail.

DWG 78
Class 23 'Baby Deltic' side elevation, showing the original layout with the No. 1 end on the left.

DWG 79
Class 23 'Baby Deltic' side elevation, showing the refurbished layout with the No. 1 end on the right.

DWG 80
Class 23 'Baby Deltic' front end layout, showing original design.

DWG 81
Class 23 'Baby Deltic' front end layout, showing refurbished design.

Class 23 (D5900–D5909)

Class	23	Multiple Coupling Restriction	Blue Star
Former Class Codes	D11/1, later 11/3	Brake Force	36 tonnes
Number Range	D5900–D5909	Engine Type	Napier 'Deltic'
Built by	EE Vulcan Foundry		T9-29
Introduced	1959	Engine Horsepower	1,100hp
Wheel Arrangement	Bo-Bo	Power at Rail	768hp
Weight (operational)	74 tonnes	Tractive Effort	47,000lb
Height	12ft 8in	Cylinder Bore	$5^{1}/_{8}$in
Width	8ft $10^{3}/_{4}$in	Cylinder Stroke	$3^{1}/_{2}$in
Length	52ft 6in	Main Generator Type	EE 835D
Min Curve negotiable	$4^{1}/_{2}$ chains	Aux Generator Type	EE 912
Maximum Speed	75mph	Number of Traction Motors	4
Wheelbase	40ft 6in	Traction Motor Type	EE 533A
Bogie Wheelbase	8ft 6in	Gear Ratio	62:17
Bogie Pivot Centres	32ft	Fuel Tank Capacity	450gal
Wheel Diameter	3ft 7in	Cooling Water Capacity	gal
Brake Type	Vacuum	Lub Oil Capacity	gal
Sanding Equipment	Pneumatic	Boiler Fuel Capacity	100gal
Route Availability	5	Boiler Water Capacity	500gal
Heating Type	Steam – Stone OK 4616		

The least successful of any English Electric built locomotives was this fleet of ten 'Baby Deltics' ordered under the pilot scheme of the Modernisation Plan, and using a single 'Deltic' power unit, powering English Electric control equipment. The external design was a 'very' scaled down version of the 2,000hp EE build. The number series allocated to the 'Baby Deltic' fleet was D5900–D5909.

After the order was placed with English Electric, Vulcan Foundry was awarded the constructional contract, from where the first completed locomotive was ready in early 1959. Unfortunately when the BTC visited the works for a pre-delivery inspection a number of problems were identified, the most serious being the locomotive was heavier than that stipulated, preventing the machine from being accepted onto BR tracks. By April remedial action had been taken and No. D5903 was sent to Doncaster Works for further inspection. Although accepted by BR the weight was still in excess of that required, which prevented the machines from operating over the desired routes. By the end of 1959 all locomotives had been accepted, and allocated to Hornsey shed for work on King's Cross suburban services. After only a short period, serious power unit problems led to most of the fleet being relegated to local and shunting duties, and by February 1963 over half the fleet had been stored at Stratford Works pending a solution to the problem.

By July 1963 the complete fleet was taken out of service and after rapid negotiations with English Electric the complete fleet was taken back to Vulcan Foundry for major rebuilding work. This operation took about a year, with the first 'new' locomotive, No. D5905 emerging in June 1964, when it was hauled to Doncaster Works for testing. By mid 1965 all ten locomotives were back in Eastern Region stock, this time allocated to the new Finsbury Park diesel depot. After their rebuilding at Vulcan Foundry the locomotives emerged with conventional 4-character alpha/numerical train reporting boxes. Once the complete fleet was back in traffic their performance was considerably improved, and they were now deployed on King's Cross–Hitchin, Peterborough and Cambridge line duties.

Under the 1960s traction rationalisation plan the 'Baby Deltic' fleet, which under the numerical classification system became Class 23, were deemed as non-standard and identified for early withdrawal. The first locomotive to be withdrawn was No. D5906 in September 1968, with the complete fleet being eliminated by March 1971. One locomotive, No. D5901 was retained for several years being operated by the Research Division at Derby as motive power for their Tribology test train.

When constructed all locomotives were in standard green livery with a grey sole bar. After rebuilding a two tone green scheme was applied with small yellow and later full yellow ends, some locomotives still in service after 1969 did receive BR blue livery.

The ten English Electric 'Baby Deltic' locomotives were plagued with problems right from the start, and regrettably were the least successful of any English Electric locomotive. In original condition No. D5908 is illustrated from the No. 2 end. Note the front end ladder.

Author's Collection

After only a short time in traffic all locomotives were causing problems, mainly involving the power unit. Problems were such that the entire fleet was relegated to secondary usage until remedial action could be taken. Whilst still performing passenger diagrams No. D5902 is seen heading for the Capital with a set of 'quad-arts' in the summer of 1959.

Author's Collection

The major 1963–4 rebuilding programme led to the locomotives being returned to the ER in a fully refurbished state, the most noticeable external alteration being the installation of 4-character alpha/numeric train identification boxes. Refurbished No. D5905 is seen arriving at Hitchin on 13th February 1970 with a down local freight.

John Cooper-Smith

After its useful days in BR revenue earning service No. D5901 was taken over by the Research Division at Derby as motive power for test trains, where it retained its green livery and small yellow warning ends. No. D5901 is seen at Derby in 1973.

Richard L. Charlson

Class 24 (D5000–D5150)
24001–24150

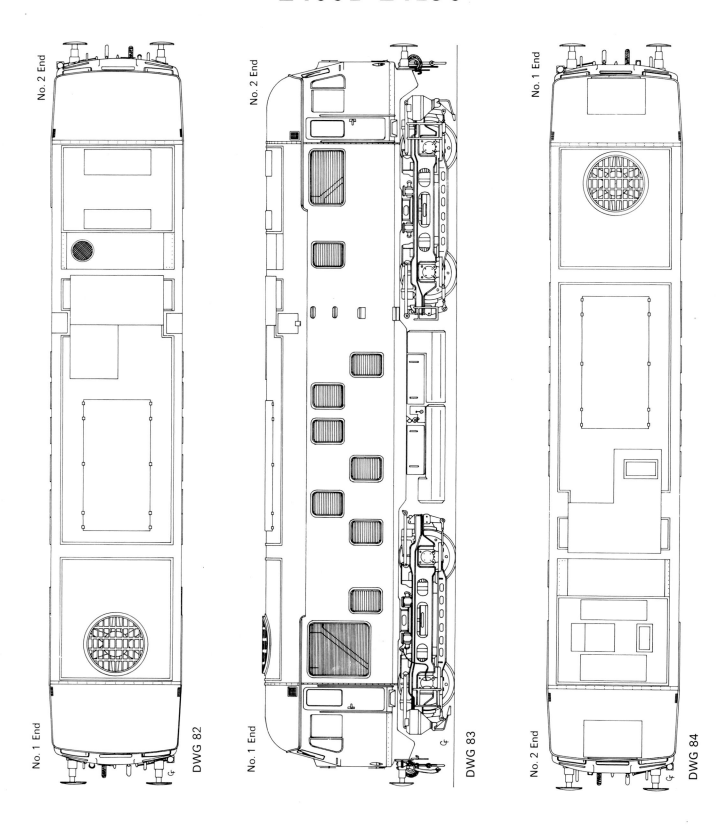

No. 2 End

No. 1 End

DWG 82

No. 2 End

No. 1 End

DWG 83

No. 1 End

No. 2 End

DWG 84

No. 1 End

No. 2 End

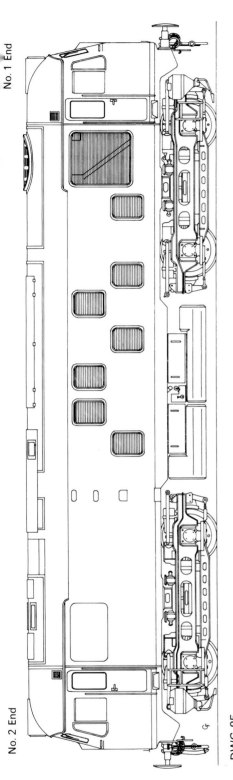

DWG 85

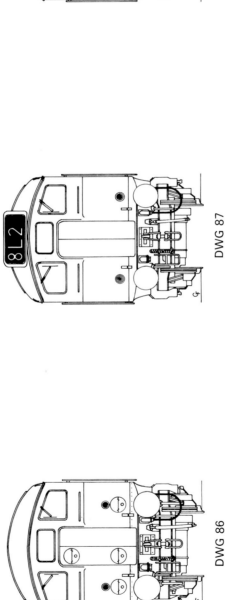

DWG 86

DWG 87

DWG 88

DWG 82
Class 24 roof detail as fitted to locomotives Nos D5000–D5113 (24001–113) with disc train reporting equipment.

DWG 83
Class 24 side elevation of side 'A' with No. 1 end on the left for locomotives Nos D5000–D5113 (24001–113), carrying disc train reporting equipment.

DWG 84
Class 24 roof detail as fitted to locomotives Nos D5114–D5150 (24114–150) with 4-character train reporting equipment.

DWG 85
Class 24 side elevation of side 'B' with No. 1 end on the right for locomotives Nos D5114–D5150 (24114–150), carrying the 4-character train reporting system.

DWG 86
Class 24 front end layout showing disc headcode arrangement as fitted to locomotives Nos D5000–D5113 (24001–113).

DWG 87
Class 24 front end layout showing 4-character route indicator box and front communicating doors.

DWG 88
Class 24 front end layout showing 4-character route indicator box with front doors sealed and two fixed beam headlights fitted.

Class 24 (D5000–D5150)
24001–24150

	24/0	24/1
Class	24/0	24/1
Former Class Codes	D11/1, later 11/1	D11/3, later 11/1A
Number Range	24001–24049	24050–24150
Former Number Range	D5000–D5049	D5050–D5150
Built by	BR Derby, Crewe	BR Crewe, Derby and Darlington
Introduced	1958–59	1959–1961
Wheel Arrangement	Bo-Bo	Bo-Bo
Weight (operational)	77–79 tonnes	71–73 tonnes
Height	12ft 8in	12ft 8in
Width	8ft 10in	8ft 10in
Length	50ft 6in	50ft 6in
Min Curve negotiable	4^1/2 chains	4^1/2 chains
Maximum Speed	75mph	75mph
Wheelbase	36ft 6in	36ft 6in
Bogie Wheelbase	8ft 6in	8ft 6in
Bogie Pivot Centres	28ft	28ft
Wheel Diameter	3ft 9in	3ft 9in
Brake Type	Vacuum	Vacuum
Sanding Equipment	Pneumatic	Pneumatic
Route Availability	6	6
Heating Type	Steam – Stones OK 4616 or 4610	Steam – Stones OK 4610
Multiple Coupling Restriction	Blue Star	Blue Star
Brake Force	38 tonnes	38 tonnes
Engine Type	Sulzer 6LDA28A	Sulzer 6LDA28A
Engine Horsepower	1,160hp	1,160hp
Power at Rail	843hp	843hp
Tractive Effort	40,000lb	40,000lb
Cylinder Bore	11in	11in
Cylinder Stroke	14in	14in
Main Generator Type	BTH RTB15656	BTH RTB15656
Aux Generator Type	BTH RTB7440	BTH RTB7440
Number of Traction Motors	4	4
Traction Motor Type	BTH 137BY	BTH 137BY
Gear Ratio	16:81	16:81
Fuel Tank Capacity	630gal	630gal
Cooling Water Capacity	187gal	187gal
Lub Oil Capacity	100gal	100gal
Boiler Water Capacity	600gal	600gal
Boiler Fuel Capacity	From main supply	From main supply

BR Derby Works was awarded a contract under the pilot scheme to construct 20 Type B (Type 2) locomotives. Subsequent orders eventually led to a fleet of 151 machines of the same type, with minor technical differences, being constructed prior to all resources being placed on a similar design, later classified 25. The number range allocated to the original fleet being D5000–D5150, and under the BR classification system the machines became Class 24.

Building of the first locomotive (No. D5000) commenced at Derby Works in August 1957, it being completed in July 1958 when it was displayed at Marylebone station. All 20 locomotives of the pilot order were in traffic by July 1959 and operating satisfactorily. Although destined for the

London Midland Region, when first introduced the locomotives were deployed on the Southern Region to cover for the late delivery of their Type 3 'Crompton' locomotives. Concurrent with the construction of the first 20 locomotives, repeat orders were placed with BR Derby, Crewe and Darlington workshops to produce almost identical machines but with minor technical and structural modifications, the most significant being the installation of a 4-character alpha/numerical headcode system from No. D5114. By the time all 151 locomotives were in traffic the class was to be found operating on the Eastern, North Eastern, Scottish and Southern Regions.

The power unit installed in these locomotives was the

Sulzer 6LDA28A, set to develop 1,160hp. Traction equipment was provided by British Thomson-Houston (BTH). The performance obtained from these small locomotives was excellent, with availability figures of around 85% being recorded.

Under the BR computer based Total Operations Processing System (TOPS) the locomotives became Class 24, being numbered 24001–24150. Due to the rationalisation of BR traction the Class 24s started to be phased out during the late 1960s, with the final locomotive being withdrawn from capital stock in October 1980. After withdrawal several locomotives were retained for carriage pre-heating duties, while one, No. 24061 was handed over to the Research Division at Derby. Thankfully the modern traction preservationists have saved three locomotives of the fleet.

When built the locomotives emerged in all over green livery, small yellow panels and later full yellow ends being added as time progressed. After the adoption of BR blue as the standard livery from 1967, locomotives were progressively repainted into this scheme.

The BR standard Type 2, to emerge under the Modernisation Plan was later classified Class 24. One of the production locomotives, No. D5030 is illustrated from its No. 2 end. The livery shown is Brunswick green with a grey roof and off white sole bar band.

Author's Collection

Front end layout of BR standard Type 2 showing the nose end communicating doors, the four train identification discs, two tail marker lights, and standard buffer beam equipment. When this official works illustration was taken most of the draw gear connections had been painted in workshop grey.

BR

The first 113 BR Type 2 locomotives were built with the disc train identification system, this being standard at the time of construction. In ex-works condition, but still retaining some of its original non-standard paintwork No. D5000 (the prototype locomotive) is seen outside Derby shed in February 1963.

Alec Swain

After their initial introduction to the LMR, a number of locomotives were reallocated 'on loan' to the SR to assist with a shortage of traction. Nos D5011 and D5009 are seen passing Bromley South in June 1959 at the head of a Charing Cross—Dover service.

The late Derek Cross

Locomotives built after No. D5114 were fitted with 4-character alpha/numeric train reporting boxes, which cleaned up the front end appearance. However the body side louvres still gave the machines a rather cluttered look. In green livery, sporting a yellow warning panel No. D5136 is seen at Manchester Piccadilly with an empty stock train.

GEC Traction

During the late 1960s/early 1970s the entire BR Type 2 Class 24 fleet emerged from classified overhaul painted in standard rail blue livery with full yellow ends. No. 24077 the former D5077 is seen near Amlwch on Anglesey with a chemical train bound for Ellesmere Port in July 1976.

B. Wynne

After withdrawal from revenue earning service No. 24061 became the property of the Research Division at Derby, where it was used for test train operation. In later years the locomotive was numbered 97201 and painted in the section's blue and red livery.

Colin J. Marsden

Class 25 (D5151–D5299/D7500–D7677) 25001–25323

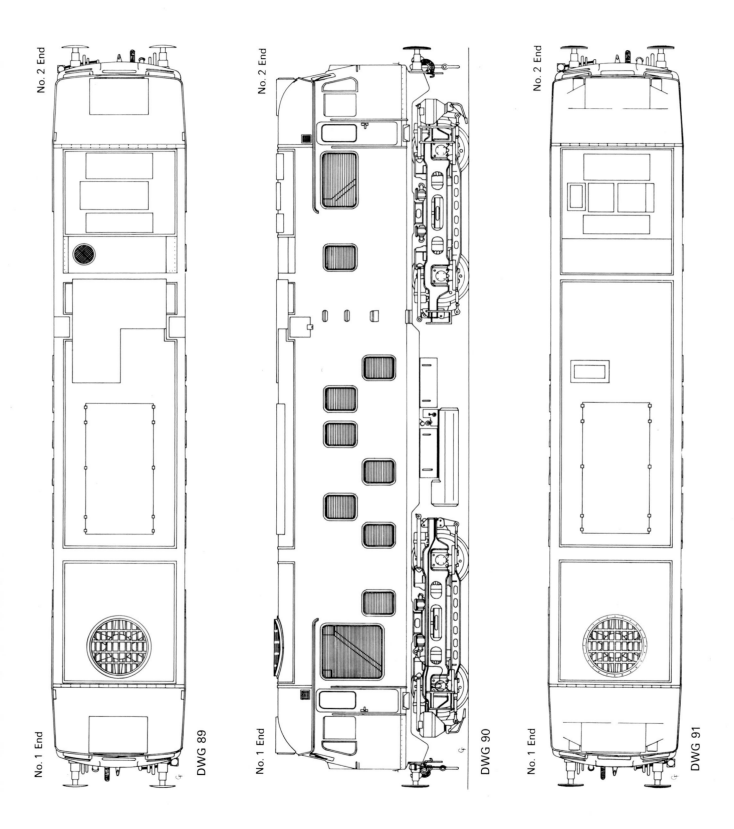

No. 2 End

No. 1 End

DWG 89

No. 2 End

No. 1 End

DWG 90

No. 2 End

No. 1 End

DWG 91

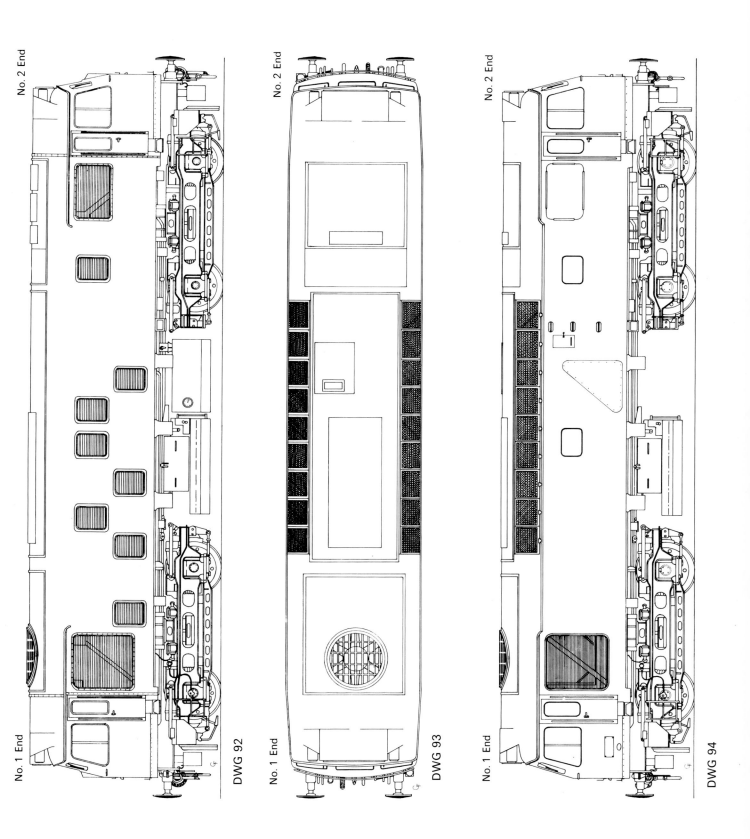

No. 2 End

No. 1 End

DWG 92

No. 2 End

No. 1 End

DWG 93

No. 2 End

No. 1 End

DWG 94

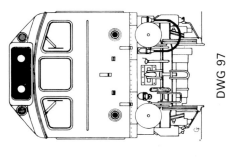

DWG 97

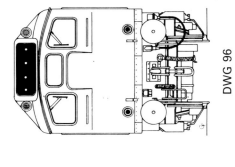

DWG 96

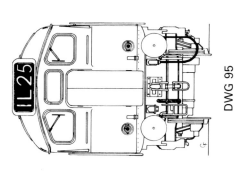

DWG 95

DWG 89
Class 25 roof detail as applicable to locomotives Nos D5151–D5175 (25001–025) fitted with 4-character route indicator and air horns on the buffer beam.

DWG 90
Class 25 side elevation showing original design front end as fitted to Nos D5151–D5175 (25001–025). The No. 1 end is on the left.

DWG 91
Class 25 roof detail as applicable to locomotives Nos D5176–D5232/D7568–D7597 (25026–082/218–247) fitted with 4-character route indicator box, adjacent air horns and nose end communicating doors.

DWG 92
Side elevation of Class 25 as applicable to locomotives Nos D5176–D5232/D7568–D7597 (25026–082/218–247) fitted with 4-character route indicator box, adjacent air horns and nose end communicating doors. The No. 1 end is on the left.

DWG 93
Class 25 roof detail as applicable to locomotives Nos D5233–D5299/D7500–D7567 (25083–217) and Nos D7598–D7677 (25248–327) fitted with revised front end.

DWG 94
Side elevation of Class 25 as applicable to locomotives Nos D5233–D5299/D7500–D7567 (25083–217) and Nos D7598–D7677 (25248–327) fitted with revised front end.

DWG 95
Class 25 front end showing original design as fitted to locomotives Nos D5151–D5175 (25001–025).

DWG 96
Class 25 front end showing horns adjacent to route indicator box as fitted to locomotives Nos D5176–D5232/ D7568–D7597 (25026–082/218–247). The front communicating doors are shown sealed.

DWG 97
Class 25 front end design as fitted to locomotives Nos D5233–D5299/D7500–D7567 (25083–217) and Nos D7598–D7677 (25248–327).

98

Class 25 (D5151–D5299/D7500–D7677) 25001–25323

Class	25/0	25/1	25/2	25/3	25/9
Former Class Codes	D12/1, later 12/1	D12/1, later 12/1	D12/1, later 12/1	D12/1, later 12/1	–
Number Range TOPS	25001–25025	25026–25082	25083–25247	25248–25327	25901–25912
Former Number Range	D5151–D5175	D5176–D5232	D5233–D7597	D7598–D7677 (Note: 1)	(Note: 2)
Built by	BR Darlington	BR Darlington, Derby	BR Derby, Darlington	BR Derby, Beyer Peacock	BR Derby, Beyer/ Peacock
Introduced	1961–62	1963	1963–66	1965–67	1965–67
Wheel Arrangement	Bo-Bo	Bo-Bo	Bo-Bo	Bo-Bo	Bo-Bo
Weight (operational)	72 tonnes	72 tonnes	76 tonnes	76 tonnes	76 tonnes
Height	12ft 8in	12ft 8in	12ft 8in	12ft 8in	12ft 8in
Width	9ft 1in	9ft 1in	9ft 1in	9ft 1in	9ft 1in
Length	50ft 6in	50ft 6in	50ft 6in	50ft 6in	50ft 6in
Min Curve Negotiable	4 Chains	4 Chains	4 Chains	4 Chains	4 Chains
Maximum Speed	90 mph	90 mph	90 mph	90 mph	60 mph
Wheelbase	36ft 6in	36ft 6in	36ft 6in	36ft 6in	36ft 6in
Bogie Wheelbase	8ft 6in	8ft 6in	8ft 6in	8ft 6in	8ft 6in
Bogie Pivot Centres	28ft	28ft	28ft	28ft	28ft
Wheel Diameter	3ft 9in	3ft 9in	3ft 9in	3ft 9in	3ft 9in
Brake Type	Vacuum	Vacuum, later Dual	Vacuum, later Dual	Vacuum, later Dual	Dual
Sanding Equipment	Pneumatic	Pneumatic	Pneumatic	Pneumatic	Pneumatic
Heating Type	Steam (Note: 3)	Steam (Note: 3)	Steam (Note: 4)	Not fitted	Not fitted
Boiler Type	Stone 4610	Stone 4610	Stone 4610	Not fitted	Not fitted
Route Availability	5	5	5	5	5
Coupling Restriction	Blue Star	Blue Star	Blue Star	Blue Star	Blue Star
Brake Force	38 tonnes	38 tonnes	38 tonnes	38 tonnes	38 tonnes
Engine Type	Sulzer 6LDA–28B	Sulzer 6LDA–28B	Sulzer 6LDA–28B	Sulzer 6LDA–28B	Sulzer 6LDA–28B
Engine Horsepower	1,250hp	1,250hp	1,250hp	1,250hp	1,250hp
Power at Rail	949hp	949hp	949hp	949hp	949hp
Tractive Effort	45,000lb	45,000lb	45,000lb	45,000lb	45,000lb
Cylinder Bore	11in	11in	11in	11in	11in
Cylinder Stroke	14in	14in	14in	14in	14in
Main Generator Type	AEI RTB 15656	AEI RTB 15656	AEI RTB 15656	AEI RTB 15656	AEI RTB 15656
Aux Generator Type	AEI RTB 7440	AEI RTB 7440	AEI RTB 7440	AEI RTB 7440	AEI RTB 7440
Number of Traction Motors	4	4	4	4	4
Traction Motor Type	AEI 137BX	AEI 253AY	AEI 253AY	AEI 253AY	AEI 253AY
Gear Ratio	67.18	67.18	67.18	67.18	67.18
Fuel Tank Capacity	500gal	500gal	500gal	500gal	500gal
Cooling Water Capacity	187gal	187gal	187gal	187gal	187gal
Boiler Water Capacity	580gal	580gal	580gal	Not fitted	Not fitted
Lub Oil Capacity	100gal	100gal	100gal	100gal	100gal
Boiler Fuel Capacity	From main supply	From main supply	From main supply	Not fitted	Not fitted

1. Locomotives Nos. D7598–D7617 (25248–25267) were classified 12/1A.

2. Class 25/9 locomotives were modified from Class 25/3 in 1986.

3. Steam heat equipment in later years was largely isolated.

4. Steam heat was only fitted to Nos. D7568–7597 (25218–25247).

The Class 25/9 locomotives were operated by 'Railfreight' for use on Chemical and Industrial Mineral operations.

Main body differences
Two different body designs were used in the Class 25 build, the main differences being:

D5151–D5176 (25001–25026) Front gangway, bodyside grilles, no horns on front.

D5177–D5232 (25027–25082) Front gangway, with bodyside grilles.

D5233–D7567 (25083–25217) No gangway, cant height grilles.

D7568–D7597 (25218–25247) Front gangway, with bodyside grilles.

D7598–D7677 (25248–25327) No gangway, cant height grilles.

Following the previously detailed Class 24 locomotives came the Class 25s, which were almost identical except for detail and power unit alterations. This fleet, which eventually ran to 323 locomotives, was ordered subsequent to the pilot scheme, and commenced delivery in April 1961.

The first batch of BR standard Type 2s as they became known was constructed by BR Darlington Works, with repeat orders going to Darlington, Derby and the private sector. One of the main differences between this class and the Class 24s was the installation of the higher powered Sulzer 6LDA28B unit giving an output of 1,250hp. The first 25 locomotives of the build retained the same electrical equipment as the Class 24s, but subsequent locomotives were given AEI equipment, which gave an increased road speed of 90mph.

During the course of production a number of modifications were incorporated into these locomotives in terms of front end layout and side ventilation louvres, and is detailed at the end of the technical description. The first standard Type 2 No. D5151 (25001) was allocated to the North Eastern Region, but after some 32 locomotives the area of allocation was changed to the London Midland Region who received all locomotives up to No. D7597. Nos D7598–D7610/D7624–D7649 went to the Eastern, while the Scottish Region received Nos D7611–D7623. Locomotives above No. D7649 all being allocated to the LMR. Of course a considerable amount of re-allocation has taken place over the years, including a number of locomotives allocated to the WR to replace diesel-hydraulic types.

When the order for locomotives Nos D7624–D7677 was placed, Beyer Peacock & Co. of Manchester were awarded the contract, who produced some very fine locomotives. Unfortunately, due to company problems, construction of the final 17 locomotives was handed back to BR at Derby, from where the last locomotive entered service on 17th May 1967.

Under the TOPS 5-figure classification system the Class 25 fleet was divided into four sub-classes 25/0–25/3, this was mainly to identify different electrical equipment. In 1986 a further sub-class, 25/9 was formed, when a fleet of 12 locomotives were selected for dedicated 'Railfreight' operation by the Chemical and Industrial Mineral sub-sector.

When delivered all locomotives except the final 17 were painted in various configurations of green, the last batch emerging in BR rail blue. As time progressed all locomotives were repainted into standard blue with full yellow warning ends.

With the decline of freight traffic and the rationalisation of the BR traction fleet, the Class 25s were doomed with withdrawals commencing in the late 1970s, the final locomotive being withdrawn in 1987. Thankfully several members of the fleet have been preserved.

Subsequent orders for BR Type 2 locomotives from No. D5151 were fitted with the slightly more powerful 'B' series power unit, and identified as a separate class, but for the first few the physical appearance was identical to their lower powered sisters. No. D5155 is shown from the No. 1 end.
Author's Collection

During the course of the build the decision was taken to remove the front end communicating doors, permitting a tidying up of the front end, and at the same time the side louvres were grouped at cant rail height. The first of the revised body styled locomotives is shown, from the No. 1 end.
Author's Collection

Due to various locomotives being constructed concurrently at more than one works the numbering of redesigned locomotives was not in straight sequence, (details of body designs are given under the technical data). In pristine condition No. D7544 is seen on display at the Institute of Locomotive Engineers exhibition at Marylebone in April 1965.

Alec Swain

The original allocation of this class was to the North Eastern Region, but subsequent batches were allocated to the London, Midland and Eastern Regions. Photographed just days after delivery, No. D5152 is seen with a rake of LNER stock during trial running from Thornaby in May 1961.

GEC Traction

After only a short time in service the Type 2 fleet, which became the second largest of any production type, was found to perform to a high standard with few failures and were thus liked by the train crews. On 30th May 1969 Nos D5255 and D5248 head a long rake of coal empties through Long Eaton.

John Faulkner

Following the demise of diesel-hydraulic traction on the WR the type 2 or Class 25s as they were by then classified, were allocated to the WR and became regular performers on secondary passenger and freight duties. On 30th July 1973 No. D7577 enters Radipole Halt with a Bristol–Weymouth service.

Colin Caddy

Locomotives constructed with the nose end communciating doors had this fitment sealed out of use from the mid 1960s as it was a constant cause of cab draughts. No. 25042 is seen light engine at Crewe on 25th September 1985 from the No. 2 end showing the sealed up layout.

Colin J. Marsden

For the final years of Class 25 activity the fleet was concentrated on the London Midland Region, where they were widely used on freight operations. On 2nd March 1984 No. 25175 approaches Walsall with an empty HBA coal train.

Colin J. Marsden

In far from ideal conditions, and with snow still falling, Class 25 No. 25054 passes Horton with a Carlisle–Ribblehead empty stone train on 7th February 1983. This train was routed via Horton to run round as no crossover facilities were in existence at Ribblehead.

Colin J. Marsden

Following withdrawal from BR service a number of Class 25s have entered preservation and have now been restored for heritage railway operation. Sporting two-tone green livery but with later BR 'dots' as frontal identification No. D7628 is seen at Pickering on the North Yorkshire Moors Railway on 28th May 1994 with the 13.50 service from Grosmont.

Colin J. Marsden

In 1986 a fleet of twelve Class 25 locomotives were overhauled and formed into a new sub-class, 25/9 for use by the Railfreight Chemical and Industrial Mineral sector. The former No. 25323 now sporting No. 25912 is illustrated. The Class 25/9 locomotives were restricted to 60mph.

Colin J. Marsden

After withdrawal three redundant Class 25 locomotives were converted into ETHEL's (Electric Train Heat Ex Locomotives), being used to provide an electric train supply to coaching stock where steam heat locomotives were in use. The three machines were first used in Scotland, and later throughout the country. *ETHEL 1* No. ADB 97250 is illustrated.

Colin Boocock

Class 26 (D5300–D5346)
26001–26046

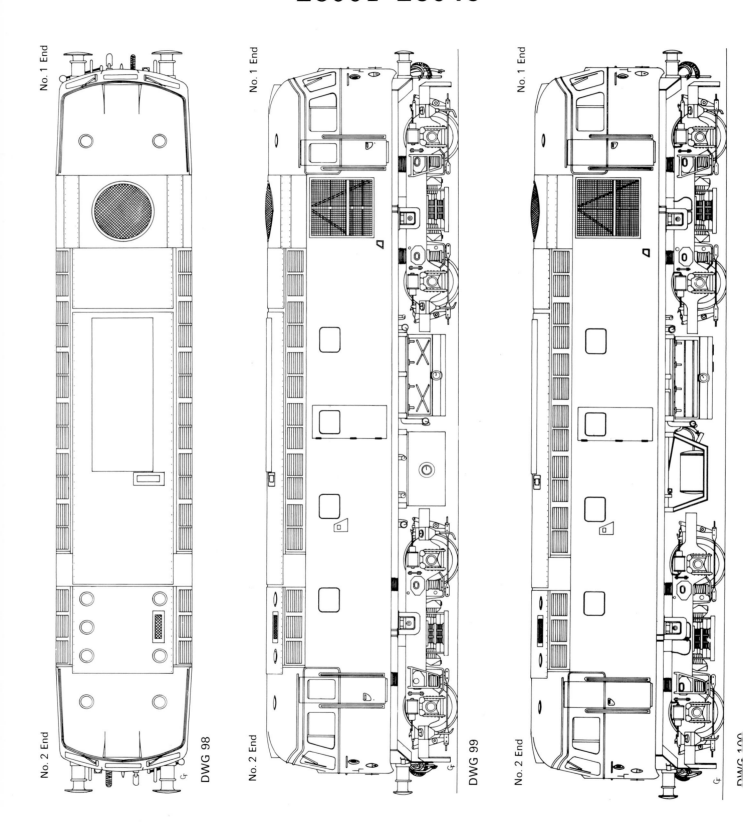

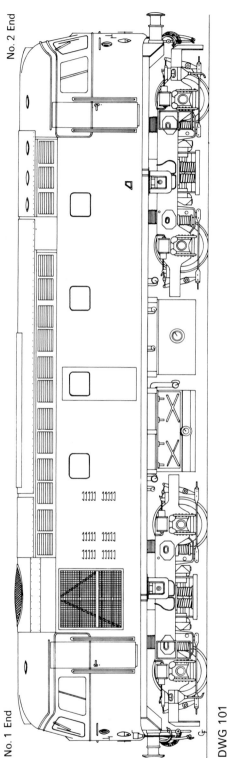

DWG 101

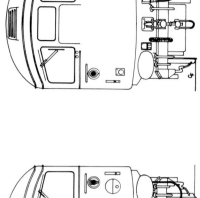

DWG 105

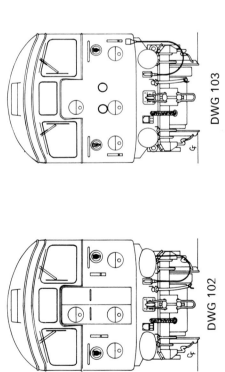

DWG 104

DWG 103

DWG 102

DWG 98
Class 26 roof detail.

DWG 99
Class 26 side elevation showing original condition with No. 1 end on the right.

DWG 100
Class 26 side elevation showing Class 26/0 locomotive with additional air compressor mounted on the underframe. The No. 1 end is on the right.

DWG 101
Class 26 side elevation showing the No. 1 end on the left with slide type cab windows and sealed front communicating doors.

DWG 102
Class 26 front end showing original condition with discs and communicating doors.

DWG 103
Class 26 front end showing the disc train reporting equipment as well as two sealed beam headlights. Drawing shows vacuum braking, steam heating and round style buffers.

DWG 104
Class 26 front end showing sealed up front doors, dual brake fitting and with steam heat pipe removed.

DWG 105
Class 26 front end showing fully refurbished layout, doors sealed, no discs, no heat and dual brakes.

Class 26 (D5300–D5346)
26001–26046

Class	26	Route Availability	
Former Class Codes		(26/0)	5 (Note: 4)
(D5300–19)	D11/4, later 11/6	(26/1)	6
(D5320–46)	11/6A	Heating Type	Steam (Note: 2)
Number Range TOPS		Multiple Coupling Restriction	Blue Star
(26/0)	26001–26020	Brake Force	35 tonnes
(26/1)	26021–26046	Engine Type	Sulzer 6LDA28A
Former Number Range	D5300–D5346		(Note: 3)
Built by	Birmingham R.C.W.	Engine Horsepower	1,160hp
Introduced	1958–59	Power at Rail	900hp
Wheel Arrangement	Bo-Bo	Tractive Effort	42,000lb
Weight (operational)	75–79 tonnes	Cylinder Bore	11in
Height	12ft 8in	Cylinder Stroke	14in
Width	8ft 10in	Main Generator Type	CG391–A1
Length	50ft 9in	Aux Generator Type	CAG193–1A
Min Curve negotiable	5 chains	Number of Traction Motors	4
Maximum Speed	75mph	Traction Motor Type	
Wheelbase	39ft	(26/0)	CP171–A1
Bogie Wheelbase	10ft	(26/1)	CP171–D3
Bogie Pivot Centres	29ft	Gear Ratio	63:16
Wheel Diameter	3ft 7in	Fuel Tank Capacity	500gal
Brake Type	Dual (Note:1)	Cooling Water Capacity	190gal
Sanding Equipment	Pneumatic	Lub Oil Capacity	100gal
		Boiler Water Capacity	550gal

1. All Class 26 locomotives were built with vacuum brake equipment, dual brakes being installed over the years.

2. Originally, Class 26 locomotives were fitted with Stones steam heat generators, but during later years these were isolated.

3. When constructed locomotives were fitted with the Sulzer 6LDA-28A type power unit, but when refurbished Sulzer 6LDA-28B type units were fitted.

4. RA reclassified to 6 for all locomotives from 1987.

Main body differences

Two sub-classes existed within Class 26:

26/0. Nos 26001-020. Within this sub-class two distinct groups existed: Nos 26001-07, which weighed 75 tonnes and were fitted with slow speed control equipment, and Nos 26008-20 which were the standard locomotive, weighing 79 tonnes. All 26/0s were originally fitted with leaf secondary springing, but following refurbishment most had coil springing and modified bogies. On Class 26/0 locomotives the multiple control jumper cable had its housing on the buffer beam.

26/1. Nos 26021-046. This locomotives weighed 79 tonnes and were fitted with later-design traction motors. Class 26/1 locomotives had their multiple control jumper cable housed on the locomotive body front (driver's side).

This fleet was another owing its inception to the 1955 BR Modernisation Plan pilot scheme, when the BTC placed an order with Birmingham Railway Carriage & Wagon Co. (BRCW) to build a batch of 20 Type 2 locomotives, the number range allocated being D5300-D5319. The finished design was very pleasing with a far more eyecatching style than the other Type 2s ordered under the scheme. During the course of producing the 'Pilot' order a subsequent order for 27 identical locomotives was placed, allocated running numbers D5320-D5346.

Construction of the first 20 locomotives commenced in late 1957, with the first example arriving at Hornsey depot in London during July 1958. In a period of just eight months all 20 locomotives were in traffic, operating King's Cross suburban and semi-fast duties. Performance was good, with no serious problems reported. In April 1959 the 'production' batch of 27 BRCW Type 2s commenced delivery, all this series being allocated to Scotland. Progressively from early 1960 the Eastern Region examples were reallocated to Scotland, from where the entire fleet operated until withdrawal.

The power unit used in this build was the Sulzer 6LDA28A, set to provide a continuous output of 1,160hp, power for traction being provided by Crompton Parkinson electrical equipment. In common with a number of pilot scheme locomotives, front end communicating doors were provided to enable footplate staff to change over en route. This equipment was only ever used under test conditions and removed in later years.

When constructed the entire order was finished in BR Brunswick green livery with off-white cab window lining and grey waist-height band and roof; yellow warning panels and latterly full yellow ends were applied. From the late 1960s, when BR corporate blue was made the norm, all members of the fleet carried this scheme. From the mid 1980s, when sectorisation was introduced, grey livery was applied to a numbers.

The first seven locomotives of the build, Nos 26001-007, were in the 1980s dedicated to Lothian coal traffic and for this operation fitted with an additional air compressor on the underframe in place of the boiler water tank. Other detail differences between the pilot and production order are tabulated under the technical description.

Following traction rationalisation the Class 26 fleet was withdrawn from traffic in the early 1990s. Many locomotives have thankfully been obtained by the preservation movement, but by early 2000 none had been recertified for main line Railtrack operation.

The BRCW Co designed and built Type 2 locomotives, ordered under the Modernisation Plan, also incorporated front end communicating doors, but on this class they blended in with the general front design more effectively. In ex works condition the first locomotive of the build, No. D5300 is illustrated from its No. 2 end.

BR

By early 1959, the 20 pilot scheme locomotives were all in traffic, allocated to Hornsey depot being used on ER suburban services. On 8th November 1958 No. D5301 is seen at Enfield Chase with the 12.41pm Hertford North–King's Cross.

John Faulkner

Although the entire 47 locomotives of this BRCW build were constructed with disc train reporting equipment, by the early 1980s the discs were being progressively removed, and the redundant nose end doors sealed up. This view shows the fully refurbished front end on No. 26021, the first locomotive of the production batch. The lower two front lamps are marker lights, while those below the cab windows are tail indicators. Buffer beam equipment is standard, with air and vacuum brake pipes, coupling and multiple control equipment.

Tom Noble

Painted in Railfreight triple grey livery with coal sub-sector markings, No. 26004 is seen at the Bo'ness Railway in late 1999, fully restored to its early 1990s condition as used on Lothian coal services. Note the front connecting doors have been sealed up and that an Eastfield depot logo has been applied to the non-driving cab side.

Colin J. Marsden

Today the Class 26s are almost entirely relegated to freight operations, being seldom recorded on passenger duties. In days when pairs could be regularly seen on Aberdeen–Inverness trains Nos 26041 and 26034 stand at Elgin on 16th November 1984 with the 13.40 Aberdeen–Inverness.

Colin J. Marsden

With a fully refurbished front end, showing no signs of the former central door or disc indicators, No. 26015 with its No. 2 end leading passes Princes Street Gardens, Edinburgh on 13th November 1984 with a southbound ballast train.

Colin J. Marsden

Class 27 (D5347–D5415)
27001–27212

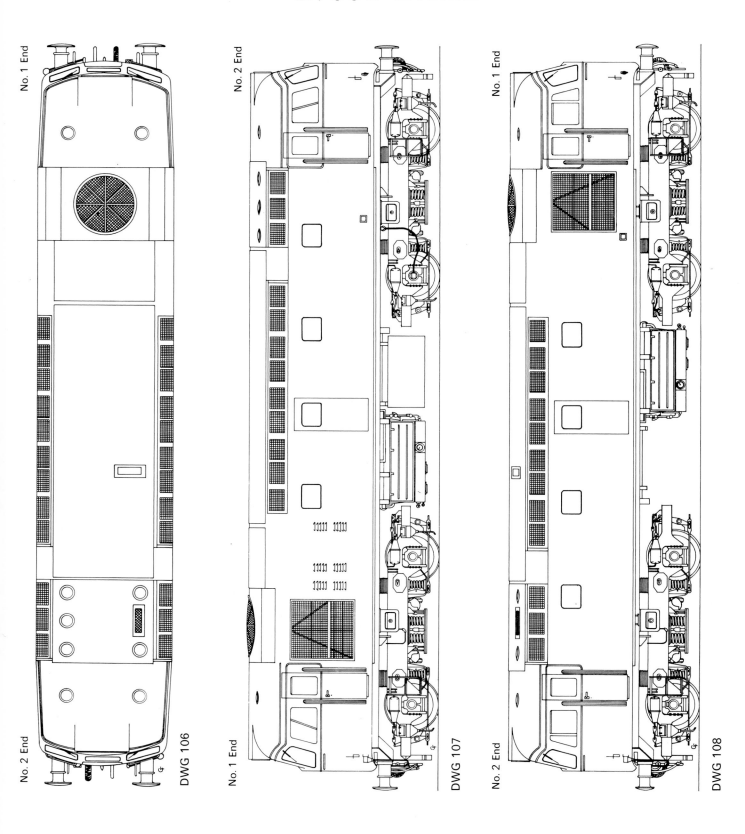

No. 1 End

No. 2 End

DWG 106

No. 2 End

No. 1 End

DWG 107

No. 1 End

No. 2 End

DWG 108

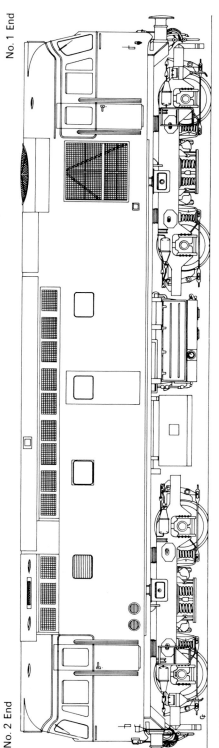

No. 1 End

No. 2 End

DWG 109

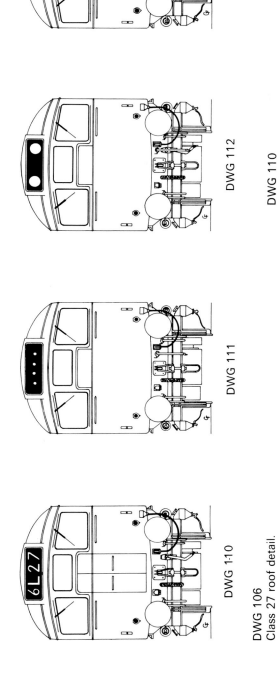

DWG 1·10

DWG 111

DWG 112

DWG 113

DWG 106
Class 27 roof detail.

DWG 107
Class 27 side elevation showing slide style cab windows, and underslung boiler water tank. The No 1 end is on the left.

DWG 108
Class 27 side elevation showing droplight style cab windows, no underslung boiler water tank as applicable to D5370–78 (27024–031). No 1 end is on the right.

DWG 109
Class 27/2 side elevation.

DWG 110
Class 27 front end layout showing original design with communicating doors.

DWG 111
Class 27 front end showing front doors sealed up, dual brakes installed but with steam heat pipe removed.

DWG 112
Class 27 front end showing front doors sealed up, dual brakes installed but retaining steam heat pipes.

DWG 113
Class 27/2 (push-pull and ETH fitted) front end.

Class 27 (D5347–D5415)
27001–27212

Class	27	Route Availability	5
Former Class Codes	D12/3, later 12/6	Heating Type	Steam, later removed
Number Range TOPS	27001–27066 (Note: 1)	Multiple Coupling Restriction	Blue Star
Former Number Range	D5347–D5415	Brake Force	35 tonnes
Built by	Birmingham R.C. & W. Ltd	Engine Type	Sulzer 6LDA28B
Introduced	1961–62	Engine Horsepower	1,250hp
Wheel Arrangement	Bo-Bo	Power at Rail	933hp
Weight (operational)	74–77 tonnes	Tractive Effort	40,000lb
Height	12ft 8in	Cylinder Bore	11in
Width	8ft 10in	Cylinder Stroke	14in
Length	50ft 9in	Main Generator Type	GEC WT981
Min Curve negotiable	5 chains	Aux Generator Type	GEC WT782
Maximum Speed	90mph (Note: 2)	Number of Traction Motors	4
Wheelbase	39ft	Traction Motor Type	GEC WT459
Bogie Wheelbase	10ft	Gear Ratio	60:17
Bogie Pivot Centres	29ft	Fuel Tank Capacity	Note: 4
Wheel Diameter	3ft 7in	Cooling Water Capacity	190gal
Brake Type	Dual (Note: 3)	Lub Oil Capacity	100gal
Sanding Equipment	Pneumatic	Boiler Water Capacity	300gal

1. In 1970 24 Class 27 locomotives were converted for push-pull operation on the Edinburgh – Glasgow route. Twelve locomotives became Class 27/1 (Nos 27101–112) and were fitted with push-pull equipment while retaining steam heating equipment. The other twelve became Class 27/2 and were fitted with electric train heating, provided by a 130kW generator powered by a Deutz diesel-engine, renumbering was 27201–212. Most locomotives were later converted back to Class 27/0.

2. A 45mph speed restriction was imposed on the surviving members of this fleet in May 1987 for departmental operation.

3. When constructed vacuum brakes were fitted, dual brakes being progressively fitted.

4. Due to various internal modifications, the fuel tank capacity varied thus:

27001–23/32–42	500gal
27024–31	600gal
27043–56	685gal
27057–66	970gal

Main body differences

When constructed locomotives D5370–78 (27024–031) were built for North Eastern Region operation and were not fitted with an underslung fuel tank.

The first 23 members of the fleet were fitted with slide type cab windows, a number of which has been replaced by the drop light type.

Class 27/2 locomotives had additional ventilation grilles in the body sides.

Following the complete success of the BRCW (Class 26) locomotives the BTC decided that they would continue with the same basic design for a subsequent locomotive fleet, but that extra power would be an advantage. To provide this the Sulzer 6LDA28B unit was employed giving an output of 1,250hp, electrical equipment was this time supplied by GEC as Crompton Parkinson were unable to take on the additional work load. The number range allocated to this fleet was D5347–D5415, and under the numerical classification system the fleet became Class 27.

Construction of the locomotives was again carried out at the BRCW works at Smethwick from where the first locomotive emerged during June 1961, being allocated to Scotland. Again performance was very good, with only minor teething troubles being experienced. Locomotives up to No. D5369 all went to Scotland but the next batch, Nos D5370–D5378 went to the North Eastern Region for freight duties. These were not fitted with train heating equipment, leaving a space on the underframe where the boiler water tank would have been fitted. Locomotives Nos D5379–D5415 were allocated to the London Midland Region operating St Pancras line services, the final locomotive of the build being handed over to BR during October 1962.

By the time this class of locomotives was constructed the disc train identification system was being dispensed with, and all examples were fitted with roof mounted alpha/numeric 4-character displays. This considerably cleaned up the front end appearance, but the centre doors for en-route crew changes were retained.

After operating quite satisfactorily in England it was decided during 1967–68 to concentrate the entire fleet in Scotland where more suitable work could be found for the machines.

During 1970 when BR were keen to capture the lucrative Edinburgh – Glasgow market from the road haulier, a high speed service was planned. Various classes of locomotive were tried, and the decision taken to use two Class 27 locomotives either end of a rake of Mk II coaches. For this duty a fleet of 24 locomotives were modified; 12 at Derby Works and 12 at Glasgow Works. The work involved was considerable with the Derby modifications being fitted with electric train supply (ETS) equipment in place of the steam heating boiler. Other new fittings included dual braking, automatic fire fighting equipment and a driver-guard communication system. The twelve locomotives rebuilt by Glasgow were not given ETS equipment but retained their steam heating boilers. After conversion locomotives retaining steam heat became Class 27/1, those with ETS were 27/2, while conventional locomotives became 27/0. After only a short period of operating the intensive Edinburgh – Glasgow service a number of technical problems were identified, but with a high standard of maintenance the service was kept going until replacement was made with Class 47s and Mk III coaches.

After introduction of the Class 47s on the Edinburgh – Glasgow service the Class 27/1 and 27/2s were converted back to conventional locomotives, being renumbered into the Class 27/0 range.

Due to altering traffic demands, and the presence of blue asbestos the Class 27 fleet was deemed for withdrawal during the 1980s, with the last locomotive being withdrawn in 1987.

When constructed all locomotives were painted in Brunswick green livery, the last few emerging with small yellow warning panels, which were progressively applied to the remainder of the fleet by mid 1964. Following the adoption of BR blue as the standard livery all locomotives were repainted into this scheme.

Thankfully several Class 27 locomotives have been preserved by modern traction preservationists, enabling enthusiasts to observe these interesting and versatile machines first hand.

Whilst the construction of the previously described Class 26s was progressing, the BTC placed an order for what was latterly the Class 27 fleet. The locomotives were very similar to the Class 26s but incorporated 4-character route indicator boxes, and a more powerful 'B' series engine. In 'as built' condition with a small yellow warning panel No. D5381 is seen at Kentish Town in March 1962.

B.L. Jackson

Locomotives Nos D5379–D5415 were allocated from new to the London Midland Region, where they were deployed on St Pancras area local duties. The first of the LMR allocated fleet is seen at Turvey during driver training and proving operations.

Alec Swain

When constructed the first 22 locomotives were allocated new to Scotland, the other 'English' machines being allocated to Scotland in 1967–8. On 27th May 1965 No. 5356 skirts the shores of Loch Leven near Ballachulish Ferry with the 12.08pm Ballachulish–Oban freight.

Noel A. Machell

Locomotives allocated from new to Scotland were given space for token exchange apparatus under the driver's cab side windows, but this was seldom used. No. D5367 is seen on the Oban line at Crianlarich Junction on 5th May 1971.

The late Derek Cross

The most significant Class 27 development came in 1970, when it was decided to use two locomotives one either end of a rake of six Mk II coaches on the 'new' high-speed Edinburgh–Glasgow service. Locomotives for this duty were rebuilt with remote control apparatus and reclassified 27/1 and 27/2. Class 27/2 No. 27203 leads a push-pull service for Glasgow past Cadder Yard on 5th April 1976.

Tom Noble

Like the Class 26 locomotives the front end communicating doors saw little use on this fleet, and were dispensed with during the late 1960s. Following the elimination of train reporting numbers the route indicator boxes were blanked off to show just two white lights through a black background. No. 27046 is seen at Glasgow Queen Street on 15th November 1984 with empty stock for Cowlairs.

Colin J. Marsden

The demise of the Class 27 fleet came between 1985 and 1987, when the entire fleet was withdrawn as surplus to requirements. Some locomotives have thankfully been saved in preservation. No. D5410, later renumbered 27123, 27205 and finally 27059, is now restored to working order on the Severn Valley Railway and painted in 1960s green livery. The locomotive is seen on 8th May 1992 arriving at Bewdley with the 11.55 Bridgnorth-Kidderminster.

Colin J. Marsden

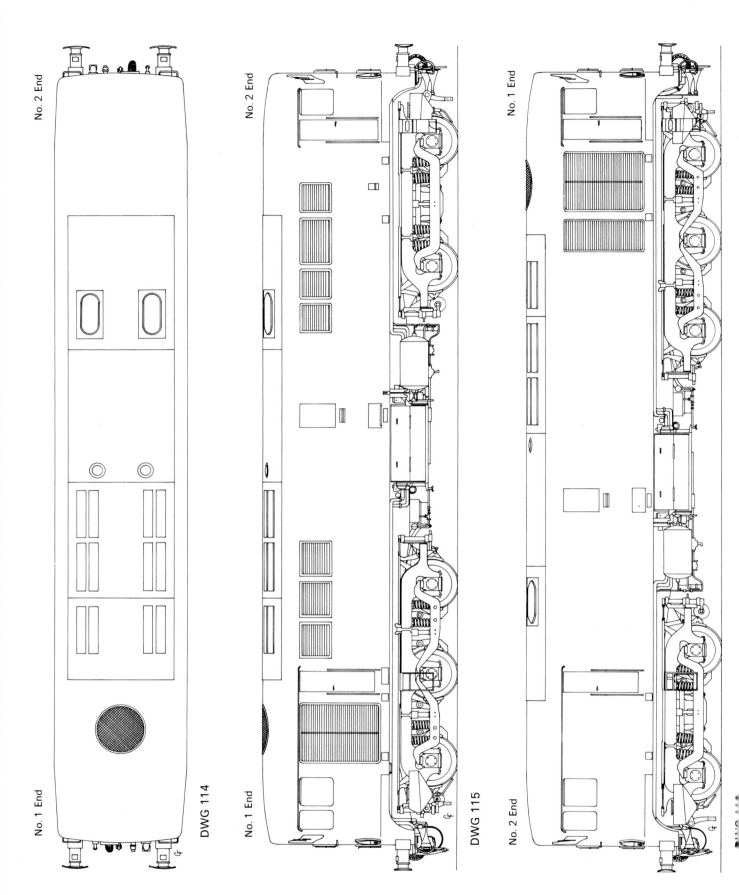

No. 2 End

No. 1 End

DWG 114

No. 2 End

No. 1 End

DWG 115

No. 1 End

No. 2 End

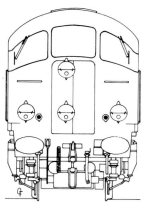

DWG 117

DWG 114
Class 28 roof detail.

DWG 115
Class 28 side elevation showing side 'A' with the No. 1 end to the left (original window layout shown).

DWG 116
Class 28 side elevation showing side 'B' with the No. 1 end to the right (original window layout shown).

DWG 117
Class 28 front end layout (original window layout shown).

Class 28 (D5700–D5719)

Class	28	Heating Type	Steam – Spanner
Former Class Codes	D12/1, later 12/5		Mk 1
Number Range	D5700–D5719	Multiple Coupling Restriction	Red Circle
Built by	Metropolitan	Brake Force	35 tonnes
	Vickers	Engine Type	Crossley HSTV 8
Introduced	1958–59	Engine Horsepower	1,200hp
Wheel Arrangement	Co-Bo	Power at Rail	hp
Weight (operational)	97 tonnes	Tractive Effort	50,000lb
Height	12ft 8³/₈in	Cylinder Bore	10¹/₂in
Width	9ft 2¹/₂in	Cylinder Stroke	13¹/₂in
Length	56ft 7¹/₂in	Main Generator Type	Met Vic TG4204
Min Curve negotiable	3¹/₂ chains	Aux Generator Type	Met Vic TAG
Maximum Speed	75mph	Number of Traction Motors	5
Wheelbase	42ft 7in	Traction Motor Type	Met Vic 137 BZ
Bogie Wheelbase	8ft 6in/12ft 2¹/₂in	Gear Ratio	15:67
Bogie Pivot Centres	32ft 4in	Fuel Tank Capacity	510gal
Wheel Diameter	3ft 3¹/₂in	Cooling Water Capacity	gal
Brake Type	Vacuum	Lub Oil Capacity	gal
Sanding Equipment	Pneumatic	Boiler Water Capacity	600gal
Route Availability	8		

The most unusual locomotive design to come from the pilot orders of the modernisation scheme was for 20 Type 2 locomotives constructed by Metropolitan Vickers and mounted on a 4-wheel bogie at one end and a 6-wheel bogie at the other (Co-Bo). The number range allocated was D5700–D5719.

The BTC order to Metropolitan Vickers was made in 1956, with construction of the locomotives commencing at the Company's Bowsfield Works in Stockton-on-Tees in 1957, the first completed locomotive being ready for delivery in July 1958. After active testing the locomotive was allocated to Derby along with the remainder of the fleet and commenced operation of Midland main-line services,

the complete fleet coming into service by October 1959. The power-unit incorporated was a Crossley HSTV8 which was a 2-stroke machine and caused the BTC enormous headaches. Such were the problems that the entire fleet was stored at various locations from early 1961 until the manufacturers could carry out remedial work. This was effected during late 1961 but the availability of the fleet was far from good.

Once sufficient diesel locomotives were in service again, this problem fleet was sent north to the Barrow area from where they were deployed on local passenger and freight duties. One service that was a regular Co-Bo duty was the "Condor" block freight train which operated daily between

Hendon and Glasgow, a distance of 404 miles for which ten hours were allotted. This duty was usually performed by a pair of Co-Bo locomotives and carried a distinctive headboard.

Some interesting features were fitted to the locomotives including wrap round driver's windows, which caused problems and were later replaced by the flat type, front communicating doors, which were never used and the cause of cab drafts, red circle (electro-magnetic) multiple control system, which was non standard, and the provision for buck-eye couplers, which were never installed.

Due to the many serious problems that befell this fleet it was decided to withdraw them from 1967, with the last locomotive being taken out of stock in December 1968. After withdrawal one locomotive, No. D5705 was taken over by the Research Division at Derby from where it was used on a number of test trains. After replacement in this field the locomotive was then used for carriage pre-heating purposes and later purchased by enthusiasts and is now under restoration to as near as possible original condition.

When constructed the locomotives were in all over green livery with silver bogies and a broad duck-egg blue band just above sole bar height, yellow warning panels being added later. One locomotive, No. D5701 was outshopped by Crewe works in standard blue livery during early 1968.

Without doubt the most unusual locomotive design to appear under the Modernisation Plan was this fleet of 20 Co-Bo locomotives, built by Metropolitan Vickers. Locomotive No. D5716 is illustrated from its No. 1 (Co) end.

GEC Traction

One service that will always be associated with the Co-Bo fleet is the "Condor" containerised freight train which the locomotives operated from its inception in the late 1950s. Locomotives Nos D5701 and D5703 are seen with a rake of 'Conflat' containers and a dynamometer car during pre service trials.

Author's Collection

Following their initial introduction and allocation to Derby the locomotives were used on many Midland line services, usually single headed where performance was satisfactory for the Type 2 output. On 21st April 1960 No. D5719 passes Chinley with the 4.00pm Derby–Manchester Central.

Alec Swain

After the Co-Bo fleet were modified by Metropolitan Vickers in 1961 to improve their technical performance, one structural amendment was made, the removal of the curved driver's front windows, which were replaced by a standard corner post and flat glass. This modification is clearly visible if this view of No. D5716 at Crewe Works in 1964 is compared with the previous illustrations.

Alec Swain

Class 31 (D5500–D5699/D5800–D5862)
31001–31469

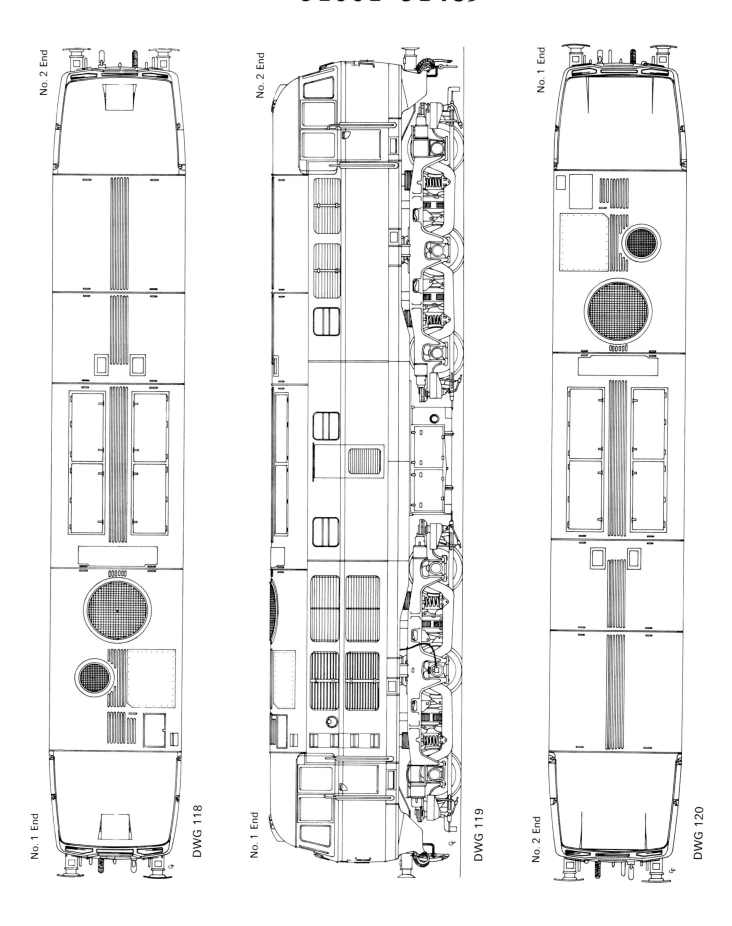

No. 2 End

No. 1 End

DWG 118

No. 2 End

No. 1 End

DWG 119

No. 1 End

No. 2 End

DWG 120

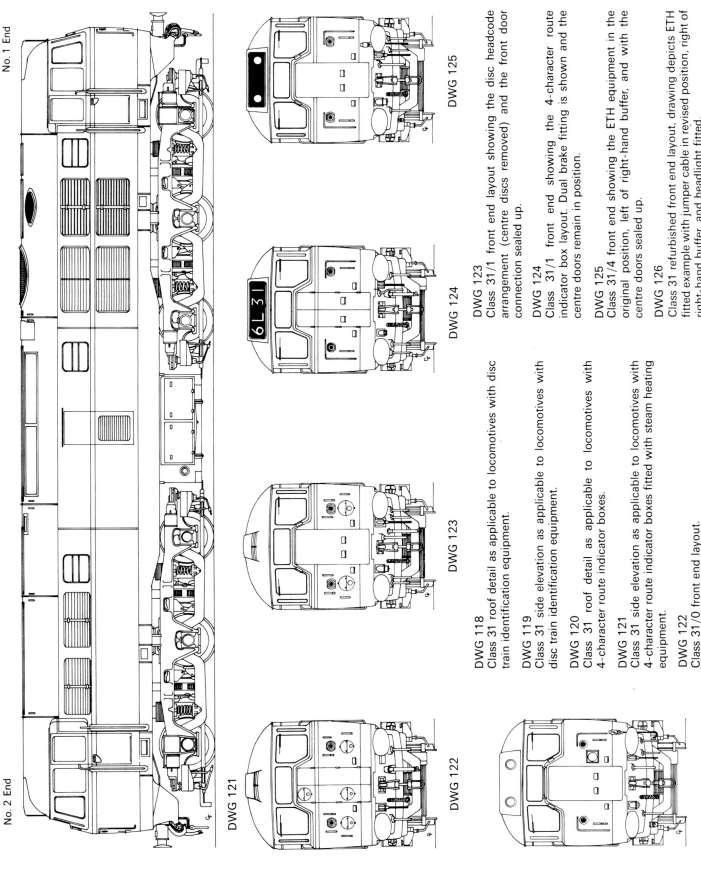

No. 1 End

No. 2 End

DWG 121

DWG 122

DWG 123

DWG 124

DWG 125

DWG 126

DWG 118
Class 31 roof detail as applicable to locomotives with disc train identification equipment.

DWG 119
Class 31 side elevation as applicable to locomotives with disc train identification equipment.

DWG 120
Class 31 roof detail as applicable to locomotives with 4-character route indicator boxes.

DWG 121
Class 31 side elevation as applicable to locomotives with 4-character route indicator boxes fitted with steam heating equipment.

DWG 122
Class 31/0 front end layout.

DWG 123
Class 31/1 front end layout showing the disc headcode arrangement (centre discs removed) and the front door connection sealed up.

DWG 124
Class 31/1 front end showing the 4-character route indicator box layout. Dual brake fitting is shown and the centre doors remain in position.

DWG 125
Class 31/4 front end showing the ETH equipment in the original position, left of right-hand buffer, and with the centre doors sealed up.

DWG 126
Class 31 refurbished front end layout, drawing depicts ETH fitted example with jumper cable in revised position, right of right-hand buffer, and headlight fitted.

	31/0	31/1	31/4	31/5	31/6
Class					
Former Class Codes (As built)	D12/2, later 12/2	D14/2, later 14/2	-	-	-
(Rebuilt)	D14/2	-	-	-	-
(TOPS)	30	-	-	-	-
Number Range TOPS	31001-31019	31101-31327, 31970	31401-31469	31507-31569	31601-31602
Former Number Range	D5500-D5519	D5518-D5862	31/1 series	31/4 series	31/1 series
Built by	Brush Ltd	Brush Ltd	Brush Ltd	Brush Ltd	Brush Ltd
Introduced	1957-58	1958-62	1972-87	1990-91	1999
Wheel Arrangement	A1A-A1A	A1A-A1A	A1A-A1A	A1A-A1A	A1A-A1A
Weight (operational)	107 tonnes	108-110 tonnes	110-113 tonnes	110-113 tonnes	109 tonnes
Height	12ft 7in	12ft 7in	12ft 7in	12ft 7in	12ft 7in
Width	8ft 9in	8ft 9in	8ft 9in	8ft 9in	8ft 9in
Length	56ft 9in	56ft 9in	56ft 9in	56ft 9in	56ft 9in
Min Curve negotiable	4½ chains	4½ chains	4½ chains	4½ chains	4½ chains
Maximum Speed	75mph	31101-116 - 80mph 31117-327 - 90mph	90mph	90mph	90mph
Wheel base	42ft 10in	42ft 10in	42ft 10in	42ft 10in	42ft 10in
Bogie Wheelbase	14ft 0in	14ft 0in	14ft 0in	14ft 0in	14ft 0in
Bogie Pivot Centres	28ft 10in	28ft 10in	28ft 10in	28ft 10in	28ft 10in
Wheel Diameter (Driving)	3ft 7in	3ft 7in	3ft 7in	3ft 7in	3ft 7in
(Unpowered)	3ft 1½in	3ft 1½in	3ft 1½in	3ft 1½in	3ft 1½in
Brake Type	Vacuum	Dual (Note: 3)	Dual	Dual	Dual
Sanding Equipment	Pneumatic	Pneumatic	Pneumatic	Pneumatic	Pneumatic
Route Availability	5	5	6	6	5
Heating Type (If fitted)	Steam Spanner Mk 1	Steam Spanner Mk 1	Steam Spanner Mk1 / Electric - index 66 (Note: 1)	Electric (isolated)	Through wired
Multiple Coupling Restriction	Red Circle	Blue Star	Blue Star	Blue Star	Blue Star
Brake Force	49 tonnes	49 tonnes	49 tonnes	49 tonnes	49 tonnes
Engine Type (As built)	Mirrlees JVS12T	Mirrlees JVS12T	EE12SVT	EE12SVT	EE12SVT
(Rebuilt)	EE12SVT	EE12SVT			
ETS Alternator					
Engine Horsepower (As built)	1,250hp	1,365hp	1,470hp	1,470hp	1,470hp
(Rebuilt)	1,470hp	1,470hp			
Power at Rail (As built)	1,050hp	1,076hp	1,170hp	1,170hp	1,170hp
(Rebuilt)	1,170hp	1,170hp			
Tractive Effort	42,000lb	31101-116 - 42,800lb 31117-327 - 39,500lb	39,500lb	39,500lb	39,500lb
Cylinder Bore (As built)	9 3/4in	9¾in			
(Rebuilt)	10in	10in	10in	10in	10in
Cylinder Stroke (As built)	10½in	10½in			
(Rebuilt)	12in	12in	12in	12in	12in
Main Generator Type	Brush TG160-48	Brush TG160-48	Brush TG160-48	Brush TG160-48	Brush TG160-48
Aux Generator Type	Brush TG69-42	Brush TG69-42	Brush TG69-42	Brush TG69-42	Brush TG69-42
ETS Alternator			Brush EL100-30	Brush EL100-30	
Number of Traction Motors	4	4	4	4	4
Traction Motor Type	Brush TM73-68	Brush TM73-68	Brush TM73-68	Brush TM73-68	Brush TM73-68
Gear Ratio	64:17	31101-116 - 64:15 31117-327 - 60:19	64:15	64:15	64:15
Fuel Tank Capacity	650gal	530gal (Note: 2)	530gal	530gal	530gal
Cooling Water Capacity	156gal	156gal	156gal	156gal	156gal
Lub Oil Capacity	110gal	110gal	110gal	110gal	110gal
Boiler Water Capacity	600gal	600gal	600gal		
Boiler Fuel Capacity	100gal	100gal	100gal		

Class 31 (D5500-D5699, D5800-D5862) 31001-31970

The first 20 locomotives of this fleet were ordered under the Modernisation Plan from Brush Traction of Loughborough. Several repeat orders for like locomotives with minor equipment differences followed until a fleet of 263 locomotives was in service, the number range used being the D55xx series which later extended into the D56xx and D58xx ranges. Under the numerical classification system the fleet became Class 30 and 31.

The original order for 20 locomotives was placed in 1955; traction was to be provided by a Mirrlees JVS12T engine developing 1,250hp, and the locomotives mounted on an A1A-A1A bogie configuration. Construction of the first locomotive commenced in February 1957 and was completed for main-line testing by September. Initial proving runs were carried out over the Peak Forest route, and on 31st October 1957 a special ceremony was held at Loughborough to hand over the locomotive to the BTC. After acceptance the locomotive was based at Stratford in East London. All 20 of the initial order were delivered in around ten months and performed totally satisfactorily. The BTC was very pleased with its new purchases and placed several repeat orders, but it was decided to alter the specification on the subsequent locomotives to incorporate the more conventional electro-pneumatic control equipment rather than the electro-magnetic system used on the first 20.

The production locomotives commenced delivery in early 1959, again being allocated to the Eastern Region, incorporating the same power unit as those ordered under the pilot scheme, but set to develop 1,365hp. During the course of building the production fleet, BR deemed the disc train identification system obsolete and four-character alpha/numeric displays were progressively fitted to the series Nos D5531-D5560, and to all locomotives after D5561.

The repeat orders for the Brush Type 2s provided a constant production run at the Brush Falcon Works until October 1962 when locomotive No. D5862 emerged. During 1963, in the quest to provide a higher output, No. D5835 was fitted with a Mirrlees JVS12 engine set to produce 2,000hp. Following installation the locomotive operated on many ER Type 4 schedules but the experimental fitting was not adopted as the norm.

In 1964 when some of the Mirrlees JVS12T engines were given classified attention, major problems were identified, mainly involving fatigue. Following some deliberation it was decided that repair work would be a time-consuming and costly undertaking and that re-engining would be the best answer. Therefore a batch of English Electric 12SVT units with an output of 1,470hp was ordered and progressively fitted under a three-year modernisation programme.

Under the BR numerical classification system, locomotives fitted with the original power units were classified 30, while those re-engined became Class 31. This class was in turn broken up into three sub classifications: 31/0 for pilot scheme locomotives; 31/1 standard re-engined examples and 31/4 for locomotives later fitted with electric train supply equipment, which was fitted to a total of 69 locomotives between 1972 and 1987. Two further sub-classifications have been introduced in more recent times — 31/5 for 31/4s with electric train supply equipment isolated and 31/6 for privately owned Fragonset Railway locomotives fitted with through ETS control equipment.

When introduced the entire class was intended for Eastern Region operation; however, following the withdrawal of diesel-hydraulic traction on the Western Region, some machines were transferred to this area, while in the 1980s the London Midland Region became associated with the class.

Under the rationalisation of BR traction in the late 1970s the first 20 (pilot scheme) locomotives which were non-standard in a number of ways were phased out. Major refurbishing was carried out on most 31/1s and 31/4s to extend their life until the mid-1990s, when major withdrawals took place. By the end of 1999 just a handful of locomotives remain operated by EWS, while a small number are in the hands of Fragonset Railways, a private traction supplier.

When constructed all locomotives emerged in Brunswick green livery, yellow panels being applied in the early 1960s. Two locomotives of special note were Nos D5578 and D5579, which emerged from Brush painted in light blue and golden ochre liveries respectively. After a short period both were repainted green. After blue was adopted as standard, all locomotives were painted in this scheme. Following sectorisation, with a considerable number of the fleet being operated under the Railfreight banner, the grey and yellow livery scheme was applied to a large proportion of the class. A further change came in the early 1990s when a small number of 31/4s used on passenger services were repainted in Regional Railways colours to match rolling stock, and many were painted in all over general grey or engineers' 'Dutch' colours. A further major livery variant came in the late 1990s when Fragonset Railways was launched, its all over black livery offset by a maroon band being applied and looking very smart.

1. Steam heat equipment was progressively removed.

2. The standard fuel tank capacity for a Class 31 was 530gal; however No. 31178 had extended capacity to hold 1,230gal.

3. When built all locomotives had vacuum brakes only, dual air/vacuum brakes being fitted subsequently.

Main body differences
Locomotives Nos. 31101-112 and certain locomotives up to No. 31143 were built with the disc style of train identification; however, selectively from No. 31113, and on all locomotives after No. 31143, a four position roof mounted headcode box was fitted.

Sub Class differences
31/1 Standard locomotive — originally steam heat fitted.
31/4 Electric Train Supply fitted locomotive.
31/5 Electric Train Supply locomotives with equipment isolated.
31/6 Standard 31/1s fitted with through ETS control cables.

The pilot order for Brush Type 2 locomotives was placed in 1955, with the first complete locomotive entering service in October 1957. The 'prototype', No. D5500 is seen in workshop primer at the Brush works in September whilst static testing was being carried out.

Brush Ltd

After release to traffic, the 20 pilot order locomotives were shedded at Stratford in East London. Displaying the original livery style of all over Brunswick green and grey roof, black underframe and two white body bands No. D5504 is seen at Stratford in January 1962. In later years the bodyside footholes were plated over.

Alec Swain

Subsequent to the pilot order, the BTC eventually placed contracts for another 242 similar machines with, when built, a slightly more powerful engine. 4-character route indicator fitted No. D5623 passes Hitchin on 18th August 1965 with an up coal duty.

John Faulkner

Cab side detail of No. 1 end of production locomotive. Note the footholes are still in situ, giving access to the boiler water filler. The livery shown on this example is green with yellow ends.

BR

When introduced the main beneficiary of the Brush Type 2 build was the Eastern Region who, by the early 1960s were deploying the class on an ever increasing number of passenger and freight turns on a wide variety of routes. In Summer 1961 No. D5802 leaves Cambridge on a diverted Liverpool St.–King's Lynn service.

Colin Boocock

After the mid 1960s engine problems, and the subsequent re-engining with English Electric units, the locomotives, now classified Class 31, had performed to a high standard to virtually all corners of the rail network. On 20th May 1982, No. 31324 approaches Monkwearmouth with a Newcastle–Sunderland parcels.

Colin J. Marsden

With the reorganisation of motive power following the elimination of the WR diesel-hydraulics the WR became owners of a small fleet of Class 31s. On a beautiful morning No. 31165 passes Langstone Rock between Dawlish and Dawlish Warren with the empty newspaper train from Plymouth to Old Oak Common.

Colin J. Marsden

The production locomotives that were built with disc train identification equipment have received some minor alterations in more recent years, namely the removal of some or all discs and replacement by marker lights. Minus its two centre discs No. 31121 approaches Teesside Airport on 21st May 1982 with a Tees Yard–Darlington freight.

Colin J. Marsden

With the constant introduction of Electric Train Heated (ETH) fitted coaching stock, a fleet of Class 31 locomotives were adapted to supply ETH between 1972–87. Locomotives so fitted are recognisable by the additional ETH jumper and socket on the buffer beam. ETH fitted No. 31438 approaches Finsbury Park on 19th October 1984 with a King's Cross–York 'Motorail' service.

Colin J. Marsden

A total of 69 locomotives were modified to provide electric train supply, but today this is not needed as the class do not operate passenger services. During the brief existence of Mainline Freight No. 31407 was repainted by Toton depot in the distinctive aircraft blue and silver colours, and is seen outside the depot on 27th February 1996.
Colin J. Marsden

Front end layout of dual (steam and electric) heat Class 31/4, with the ETS jumper cable in the original position. This was later housed on the right of the buffer. The front end communicating doors can be seen to have been plated over.
Colin J. Marsden

For many years rail blue was the standard livery for the Class 31s; however, after introduction of the various operating sectors a number appeared in Railfreight grey with wrap-round yellow ends. Railfreight liveried No. 31209 passes Stenson Junction on 10th July 1986 with a Willesden-York empty stock train.

Colin J. Marsden

Following the privatisation of our national rail network, a number of new private operators emerged to provide spot hire of main line diesel traction. One such company was Fragonset Railways based at Tyseley, which now offers a range of Class 31s and 47s to mainstream passenger and freight operators. The Fragonset fleet is maintained to national Group Standards and is in the most painted in black livery with a wide body band of maroon. No. 31452 is seen at Lidlington on the Bletchley-Bedford route on 9th October 1998.

Colin J. Marsden

Class 33 (D6500–D6597)
33001–33212

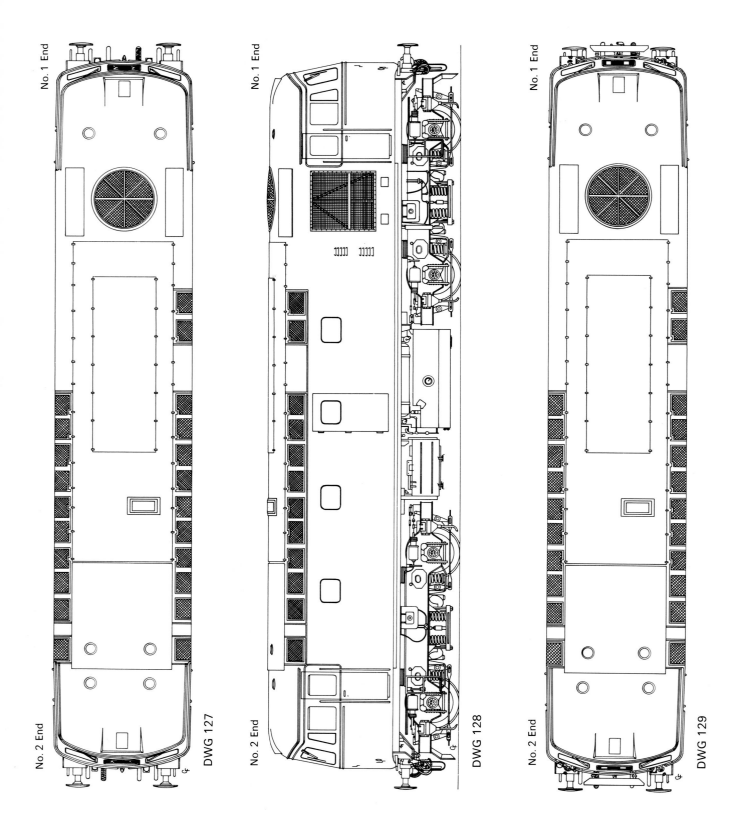

No. 1 End

No. 2 End

DWG 127

No. 1 End

No. 2 End

DWG 128

No. 1 End

No. 2 End

DWG 129

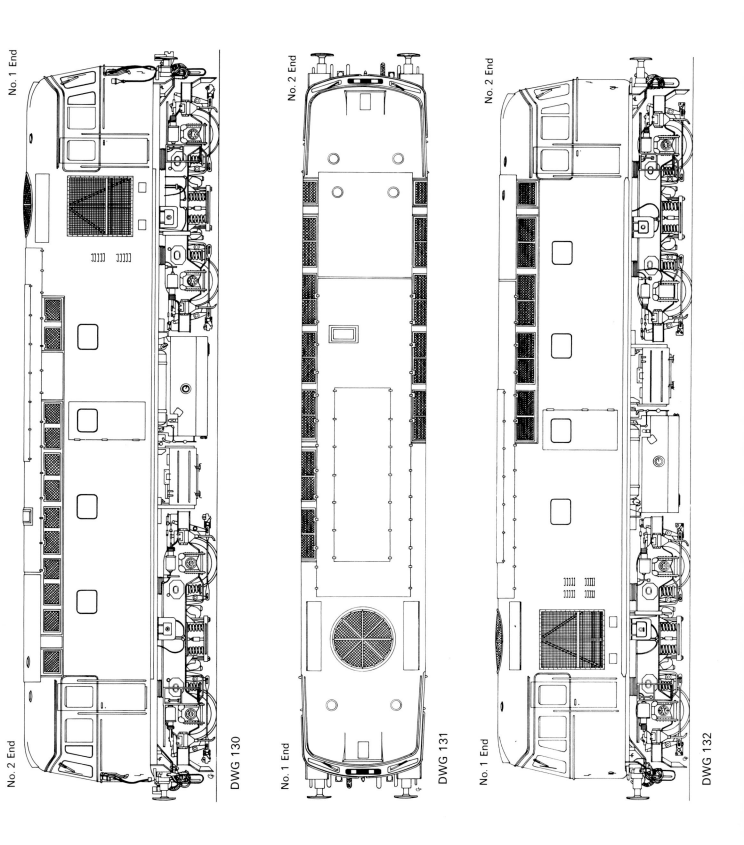

No. 1 End

No. 2 End

DWG 130

No. 2 End

No. 1 End

DWG 131

No. 2 End

No. 1 End

DWG 132

133

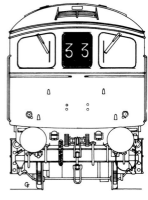

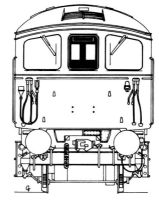

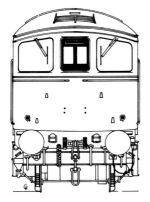

| DWG 133 | DWG 134 | DWG 135 |

DWG 127
Class 33/0 roof detail.

DWG 128
Class 33/0 side elevation, the No. 1 end being to the right.

DWG 129
Class 33/1 roof detail.

DWG 130
Class 33/1 side elevation, the No. 1 end being to the right.

DWG 131
Class 33/2 roof detail.

DWG 132
Class 33/2 side elevation, No. 1 end being to the left.

DWG 133
Class 33/0 front end layout.

DWG 134
Class 33/1 front end layout.

DWG 135
Class 33/2 front end layout.

Class 33 (D6500–D6597)
33001–33212

Class	33/0	33/1	33/2
Former Class Codes	D15/1, later 15/6	–	D15/2, later 15/6A
Number Range TOPS	33001–33065	33101–33119	33201–33212
Former Number Range	D6500–D6585	Random from 33/0 fleet	D6586–D6597
Built by	Birmingham R.C. & W. Ltd	Birmingham R.C. & W. Ltd	Birmingham R.C. & W. Ltd
Introduced	1960–62	1965–67	1962
Wheel Arrangement	Bo–Bo	Bo–Bo	Bo–Bo
Weight (operational)	77 tonnes	78 tonnes	77 tonnes
Height	12ft 8in	12ft 8in	12ft 8in
Width	9ft 3in	9ft 3in	8ft 8in
Length	50ft 9in	50ft 9in	50ft 9in
Min Curve negotiable	4 chains	4 chains	4 chains
Maximum Speed	85mph	85mph	85mph
Wheelbase	39ft	39ft	39ft
Bogie Wheelbase	10ft	10ft	10ft
Bogie Pivot Centres	29ft	29ft	29ft
Wheel Diameter	3ft 7in	3ft 7in	3ft 7in
Brake Type	Dual	Dual	Dual
Sanding Equipment	Pneumatic	Pneumatic	Pneumatic
Route Availability	6	6	6
Heating Type	Electric – Index 48 (Note: 1)	Electric – Index 48 (Note: 1)	Electric – Index 48 (Note: 1)
Multiple Coupling Restriction	Blue Star	Blue Star	Blue Star
Brake Force	35 tonnes	35 tonnes	35 tonnes
Engine Type	Sulzer 8LDA28B	Sulzer 8LDA28B	Sulzer 8LDA28B
Engine Horsepower	1,550hp	1,550hp	1,550hp
Power at Rail	1,215hp	1,215hp	1,215hp
Tractive Effort	45,000lb	45,000lb	45,000lb
Cylinder Bore	11in	11in	11in
Cylinder Stroke	14in	14in	14in
Main Generator Type	Crompton CG391–A1	Crompton CG391–A1	Crompton CG391–A1
Aux Generator Type	Crompton CAG193–A1	Crompton CAG193–A1	Crompton CAG193–A1
ETS Generator Type	Crompton CAG392–A1	Crompton CAG392–A1	Crompton CAG392–A1
Number of Traction Motors	4	4	4
Traction Motor Type	Crompton C171–C2	Crompton C171–C2	Crompton C171–C2
Gear Ratio	62:17	62:17	62:17
Fuel Tank Capacity	750gal	750gal	750gal
Cooling Water Capacity	230gal	230gal	230gal
Lub Oil Capacity	108gal	108gal	108gal

1. The Electric Train Supply fitted to the Class 33s is designed for operation with SR allocated 750v DC heated stock.

All locomotives are fitted with snowplough brackets, and a number of machines are kept fitted with ploughs throughout the year.

Main differences between sub-classes

Class 33/0: Standard locomotives
Class 33/1: Modified locomotives, fitted with buck-eye couplers, waist height air connections, and multiple unit compatible jumpers. Locomotives can operate in multiple with all post 1951 SR emu stock, fitted with conventional draw-gear.
Class 33/2: Narrow profile locomotives, these locomotives were built to operate on the Hastings line, where limited clearances prevented standard width traction.

Designed expressly for Southern Region operation, this fleet of 98 Type 3s was ordered from the Birmingham Railway Carriage & Wagon Co. (BRCW) in 1957. Construction was effected at the company's Smethwick works and the number range allocated was D6500-D6597.

The first locomotive was constructed during 1958-59, being handed over to the BTC on 4th December 1959 and allocated to Hither Green depot in South East London. The BRCW Type 3s contained a number of unique features amongst traction of the day, the most significant being the installation of Electric Train Supply (ETS) equipment. SR multiple unit style two-character train reporting boxes were also fitted between the two cab windows. By the summer of 1960 20 locomotives were available, being deployed on many Charing Cross-Dover and other South Eastern section main-line duties. At the onset of winter a major problem faced the Southern operators when there was a dire shortage of electrically heated vehicles to work with the new locomotives. The answer was found in coupling a steam heat fitted Type 2 between the BRCW and train to provide heat! The ETS fitment to an entire class of locomotives was something new, and many tests were carried out to decide whether this system would be developed any further. In February 1961 No. D6504 was loaned to the technical services section at Derby and used on numerous specials, taking the machine to a number of 'foreign' parts, including the Peak Forest route and Edinburgh.

When the order was placed for the final twelve locomotives these were to be constructed to the narrower 'Hastings' profile. BRCW were keen to supply the locomotives and readily agreed to this size reduction. However, when the work was in hand the cost of the operation was excessive, and probably hastened the decline of the BRCW company. The final narrow bodied locomotive was delivered in June 1962. Between 1962 and the summer of 1963 the entire fleet was allocated to the South Eastern section and operated on both passenger and freight duties, the South Western section

receiving its first BRCW Type 3s at the end of 1963 to operate Waterloo-Bournemouth/Weymouth line services. By the beginning of 1965 all three SR operating sections were regularly using the fleet, which was returning an availability of around 85%.

In the summer of 1965 No. D6580 was fitted with an experimental push-pull system whereby it could be controlled from a remote trailer control cab. The system was highly successful and in conjunction with the Waterloo-Bournemouth electrification scheme 19 locomotives were fitted with a like push-pull control system. Locomotives so fitted differed considerably from standard machines in having drop head buck-eye couplers, retractable buffers and waist-height air and control connections.

Under the BR numerical classification system the BRCW Type 3s became Class 33, with three sub-classes formed: 33/0 for standard locomotives, 33/1 for push-pull fitted locomotives and 33/2 for narrow 'Hastings' profile locomotives.

For their entire lives under the British Rail banner the fleet remained allocated to the SR, but their duties took them to many faraway places with regular diagrams (at various times) to West Wales and Devon.

When introduced the locomotives were all painted in Brunswick green livery with a mid-height narrow grey band and white window surrounds. Yellow warning panels were later added and full yellow ends applied from the mid 1960s. After 1967 all locomotives were outshopped in BR blue with full yellow ends. In mid-1988 some examples were outshopped in the new sub-sector double grey livery. Further livery changes came when some examples were painted in engineers 'Dutch' colours and a couple in Network SouthEast livery. Under privatisation one locomotive also emerged in full EWS maroon and gold livery.

Withdrawal of life-expired and collision-damaged locomotives commenced in the mid 1980s and the entire fleet was withdrawn by early 1999. A large number of machines have entered the world of preservation and some are now authorised to operate on the main line once again.

Following privatisation of the UK rail network, the remaining Class 33s passed to EWS, and after the entire fleet was withdrawn several locomotives were placed in 'store'; two have now been returned to the main line for use by EWS on trip and freight pilot work in the Aberdeen area, the two machines, Nos 33025/030, working north to their new home in Aberdeen in early December 1999.

One of the most successful classes ordered from a private company was the BRCW Type 3 fleet, now Class 33, which are allocated to the SR. Sporting the originally applied green livery without any yellow warning ends. No. D6521 passes Farnborough with an up vans train on 20th August 1964.
Alec Swain

The BRCW Type 3s or 'Cromptons' as they have more usually been known were the first production type to be equipped with electric train heating from new. Slowing for the speed restriction at Woking Junction No. D6525 heads a Portsmouth–London Midland Region troop special on 14th August 1966.

Martin Welch

Although when first introduced all 'Cromptons' were allocated to the South Eastern Division at Hither Green, it was not long before all three SR divisions saw the machines at work. On 6th November 1962 No. D6506 is seen departing from Guildford with the Nine Elms breakdown crane.

John Faulkner

During the mid 1960s when the BTC deemed that all locomotives must carry a yellow warning panel, the BRCW Type 3s were so modified, and perhaps this scheme looked the most impressive ever applied to the class. No. D6530 passes Deepcut on 8th July 1967 wth a Southampton Docks–Waterloo train.

John Faulkner

Towards the latter part of the 1960s the full yellow warning end was announced as standard, and the Class 33s were soon to be seen appearing in this scheme. Painted in green livery, but with a full yellow end, No D6553 takes the Eastleigh road at Romsey on 2nd February 1969 with a Salisbury–Redbridge engineers special.

Geoff Gillham

In conjunction with the electrification of the Bournemouth line a fleet of 19 Class 33s were modified for push-pull operation. This alteration included the installation of waist height air pipes and control jumpers. Push-pull locomotives were later re-classified 33/1. No. 33113 is seen at Manchester Victoria on 13th March 1984 with a 'Gatwick Express' exhibition special.

Colin J. Marsden

The final twelve locomotives of the fleet were built to the narrower 'Hastings' profile, due to limited clearances on certain tunnels on the Hastings line, narrow bodied locomotives later being classified 33/2. No. 33212 is seen near Guildford on 13th October 1981 whilst working the 13.48 Woking–Hoo Junction engineers train.

Andrew French

"Slim Jim" 'Crompton' No. 33211 passes Archcliff Junction, Dover on 4th September 1987 with a Paddock Wood–Dover Western Docks 'Speedlink' duty. From the outside the narrow bodied locomotives are immediately recognisable as the body side continues onto the frame member straight, unlike the standard width members.

Michael J. Collins

With the majority of the SR now electrified and inter-regional services in the hands of other regions' motive power the Class 33s do not see a lot of main line passenger work. Push-pull No. 33113 approaches Northam Junction on 12th April 1984 with the 06.00 Derby–Poole working.

Colin J. Marsden

Throughout the early 1980s the Class 33s were regularly diagrammed for WR duties, on West of England local services, West Wales operations, and on the Crewe-Cardiff line. Departing from Newton Abbot and heading for Aller Junction No. 33005 heads the Exeter-Paignton train on 6th July 1984.

Colin J. Marsden

In June 1986 No. 33008 was repainted by Eastleigh into Brunswick green livery, initially with full yellow ends, but in more recent times a 1965 'authentic' scheme with small yellow panels has been adopted. In green and with full yellow ends No. 33008 *Eastleigh* passes Wimbledon on 26th July 1986 with the 10.35 Waterloo-Bournemouth "Bournemouth Belle" VSOE special.
Colin J. Marsden

A pair of Class 33s, led by 33/0 No. 33065 with 'Hastings' Class 33/2 No. 33208 trailing, pass Fairwood Junction, Westbury with a Meldon Quarry-Woking ballast train on 17th September 1991. Both these locomotives are painted in the 'Dutch' livery and are seen with their No. 2 ends leading.

Colin J. Marsden

Although looking very smart, the application of NSE blue, white, red and grey livery to a Class 33 was little welcomed by most class followers. No. 33114, one of the Bournemouth-Weymouth push-pull locos, was repainted by Selhurst into the livery for its naming as *Ashford 150* on 30th May 1992 The machine is seen at Ashford depot in immaculate condition.

Colin J. Marsden

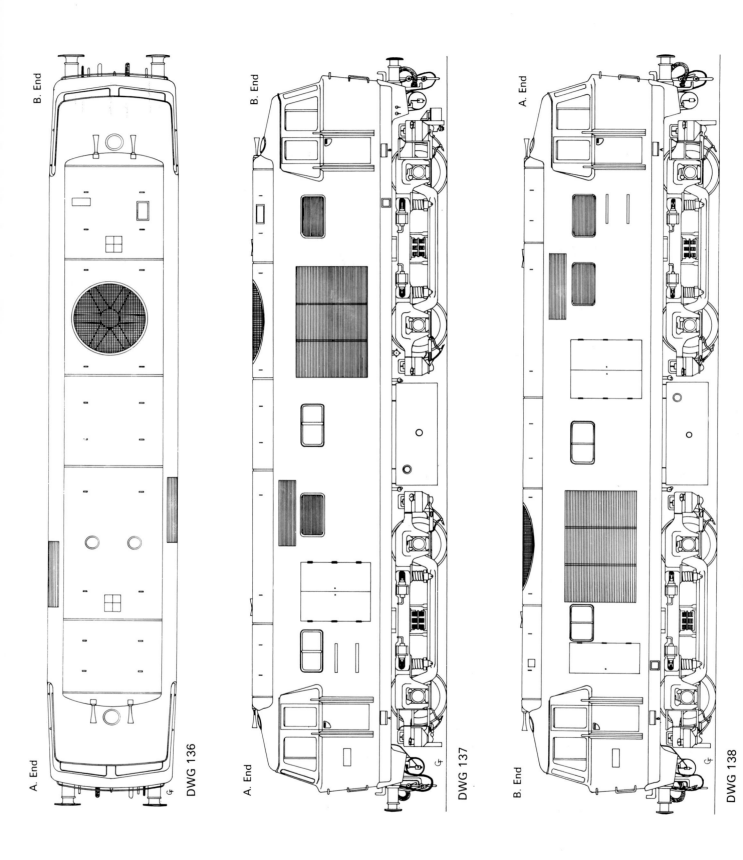

A. End   B. End

DWG 136

A. End   B. End

DWG 137

B. End   A. End

DWG 138

DWG 139

DWG 136
Class 35 roof detail.

DWG 137
Class 35 side elevation, showing side 'A'. The 'A' end is to the left.

DWG 138
Class 35 side elevation, showing side 'B'. The 'A' end is to the right.

DWG 139
Class 35 front end layout.

Class 35 (D7000–D7100)

Class	35	Heating Type (D7000–D7044)	Steam – Stone OK 4616
Former Class Codes	D17/2, later 17/7	(D7045–D7100)	Steam – Spanner Mk 3
Number Range	D7000–D7100	Multiple Coupling Restriction	Yellow Triangle
Built by	Beyer Peacock	Brake Force	33 tonnes
Introduced	1961–65	Engine Type	Maybach MD870
Wheel Arrangement	B–B	Engine Horsepower	1,740hp
Weight (operational)	74 tonnes	Power at Rail	hp
Height	12ft 10^9/$_{16}$in	Tractive Effort	46,600lb
Width	8ft 8^1/$_2$in	Cylinder Bore	7.3in
Length	51ft 8^1/$_2$in	Cylinder Stroke	7.9in
Min curve negotiable	4 chains	Transmission Type	Mekydro K184U
Maximum Speed	90mph	Fuel Tank Capacity	800gal
Wheelbase	36ft	Cooling Water Capacity	gal
Bogie Wheelbase	10ft 6in	Lub Oil Capacity	gal
Bogie Pivot Centres	25ft 6in	Boiler Water Capacity	800gal
Wheel Diameter	3ft 9in	Boiler Fuel Supply	From main tank
Brake Type	Vacuum		
Sanding Equipment	Pneumatic		
Route Availability	6		

The 1955 Modernisation Plan did not cater for the construction of locomotives in the Type 3 (1,500–1,999hp) power classification, so this situation was remedied when the second generation orders were placed. For the Western Region, who had adopted a diesel-hydraulic fleet, the Type 3 power group was filled by a fleet of 101 B-B 'Hymek' locomotives constructed by Beyer Peacock of Manchester.

The power unit used was a single Maybach 16-cylinder air cooled unit of type MD870, which was set to deliver 1,700hp. The transmission attached was a Mekydro K184.

The original order for 'Hymek' Type 3s, allocated numbers in the D70xx range, was for 45 locomotives. Whilst these were in the course of production repeat orders for 46 locomotives led to an eventual production run of 101 locomotives. Construction of the first example was effected in BP's Gorton Works during 1960 and completed in April 1961. In common with all locomotives of the build, after completion, testing was carried out in the Manchester-

Derby area. After its acceptance onto BR tracks No. D7000 was handed over to the BTC in a ceremony at Paddington on 16th May 1961. Although 'handed-over' the locomotive was still the subject of extensive testing which was carried out from Swindon.

Once allocated to the traffic fleet its home was Bristol Bath Road from where it was deployed along with other deliveries on Paddington, Cardiff and Weymouth duties. The delivery of locomotives was at the rate of about one per month with the repeat orders dove-tailing with the original. Although basically identical some technical differences existed with the second series, namely the fitting of Westinghouse brake equipment in place of Laycock Knorr, and Spanner boilers in place of Stones equipment. However the physical appearance of locomotives remained the same. By February 1964 all 101 locomotives were in traffic, replacing many steam classes from the West and South Wales. By the mid 1960s the machines had taken over the famous Lickey banking duties, and could be found operating to virtually all corners of the Western Region, although their duties in Cornwall were very few.

Under the rationalisation of traction and the BRB's intention to standardise its motive power as much as possible, the diesel-hydraulic fleets were all doomed, and after only five years in traffic it was rumoured that the entire fleet was to be withdrawn, even in the light of excellent performance. Towards the end of the 1960s it was announced that all hydraulic classes would be eliminated by September 1973, but as time proved this was not the case. For the 'Hymek' fleet withdrawals began in January 1971, with the final locomotives being withdrawn in March 1975. Under the numerical classification system the

'Hymek' fleet became Class 35, but none were renumbered into the 5-figure TOPS scheme. Several 'Hymek' locomotives have been saved by the diesel preservation movement enabling enthusiasts to hear the deep Maybach growl for many years to come.

When built the locomotives were finished in all over Brunswick green livery with white window surrounds and a light green solebar band. During the mid 1960s yellow warning ends were applied, which after several years gave way to the full yellow end. After BR blue was adopted this livery was applied to all locomotives, however some early blue examples did emerge with a small yellow warning panel, a scheme in which the locomotives perhaps looked their best.

Broadside elevation of 'Hymek' Type 3 No. D7000, the 'A' end being on the left. The design of this fleet was probably the most pleasing aesthetically of all the WR hydraulic types. The livery illustrated is Brunswick green, with a light green base band and white cab window surrounds, with a grey roof.

BR

After the original and subsequent orders for 'Hymek' locomotives were in service the fleet numbered 101, and were deployed throughout the Western Region on secondary passenger and freight operations, as well as making occasional outings on the main line. In June 1962, No. D7027 crosses Frampton Mansell Viaduct wth a Swindon bound local.

R.C. Riley

Small yellow panels were later added to the Brunswick green livery, and on some locomotives this gave way to a full yellow end. No. D7067 is seen approaching West Ealing on 18th April 1964 with an up parcels train bound for Paddington.

John Faulkner

After the introduction of blue livery the 'Hymek' fleet was outshopped in this scheme, firstly with small yellow panels and latterly wth full yellow ends. No. D7042 is seen in sidings at Somerton on 20th June 1971 on a ballast train.

Geoff Lendon

Class 37 (D6600–D6608/D6700–D6999) 37001–37906

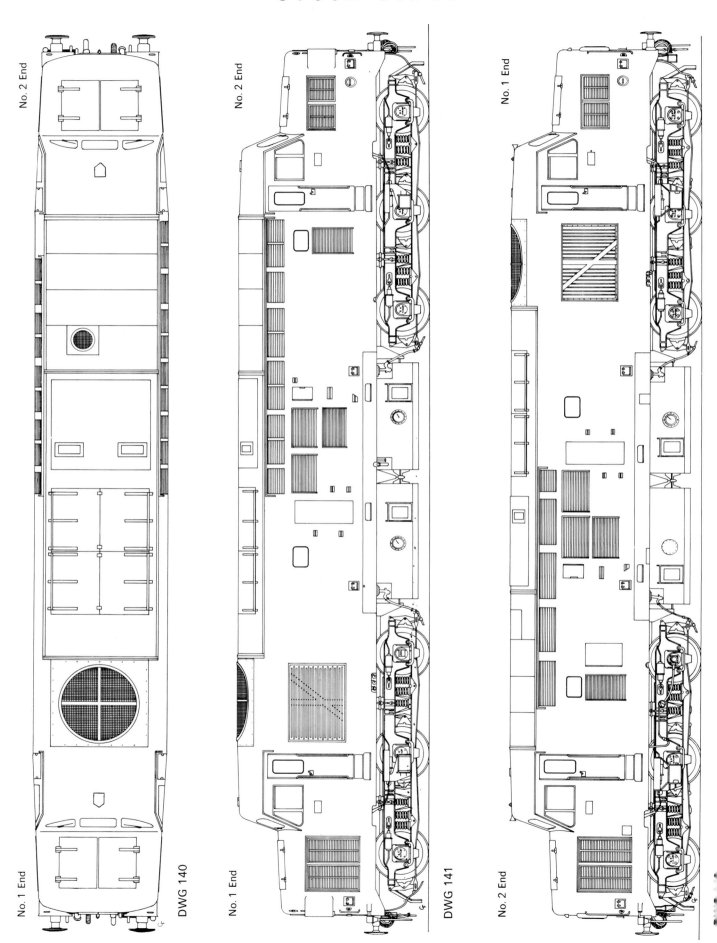

No. 2 End

No. 1 End

DWG 140

No. 2 End

No. 1 End

DWG 141

No. 1 End

No. 2 End

No. 2 End

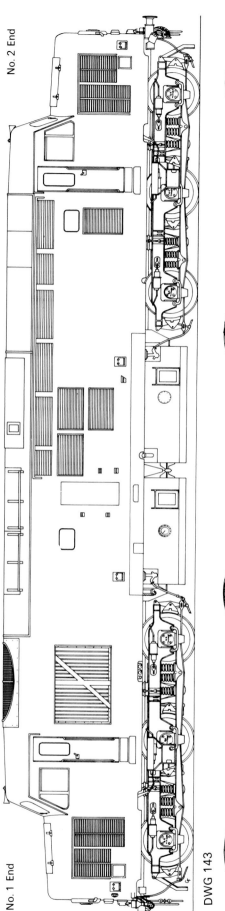

No. 1 End

DWG 143

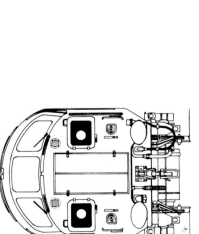

DWG 145

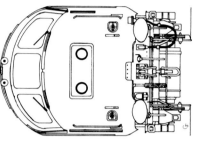

DWG 144

DWG 147

DWG 146

DWG 140
Class 37 roof layout, showing the split-box front end as fitted to locomotives Nos D6700–D6818 (37001–118).

DWG 141
Class 37 side elevation showing side 'A', with the No. 1 end to the left, and the split-box front, as fitted to locomotives Nos D6700–D6818 (37001–118).

DWG 142
Class 37 side elevation showing side 'B', with the No. 1 end to the right, and the solid central headcode box as fitted to locomotives Nos D6819–D6999/D6600–D6608 (37119–308).

DWG 143
Class 37 side elevation showing refurbished locomotive from the original batch D6819–D6999/D6600–D6608 the No. 1 end being to the left. Applicable to 37/4–37/9.

DWG 144
Class 37 front end showing original split headcode boxes (sporting white dots) central communicating doors, the original skirt valance, vacuum brakes, steam heating and oval buffers.

DWG 145
Class 37 front end showing solid central route indicator box, dual brakes, no steam heat pipe. The original skirt valance is retained and round buffers fitted.

DWG 146
Class 37 front end showing solid central route indicator box, carrying sealed beam marker lights. Dual brakes are shown as well as a modified skirt valance and oval buffers.

DWG 147
Class 37 front end showing refurbished central route indicator box type.

147

	37/0	37/3	37/4	37/5 (Note:1)	37/6	37/7 (Note: 4)	37/9
Class							
Former Class Codes	D17/1, later 17/3	-	-	-	-	-	-
Number Range TOPS	37001-37326	37330-37384	37401-37431	37501-37521 37667-37699	37601-37612	37701-37719 37796-37803 37883-37899	37901-37906
Former Number Range	D6600-D6999	From 37/0 fleet	From 37/0 fleet	From 37/0 fleet	From 37/0 fleet	From 37/0 fleet	From 37/0 fleet
Built by	EE & RSH Ltd	EE & RSH Ltd	EE & RSH Ltd	EE & RSH Ltd	EE & RSH Ltd	EE & RSH Ltd	EE & RSH Ltd
Introduced	1960-65	1988	1985-86	1986-88	1994-96	1986-88	1986-87
Wheel Arrangement	Co-Co	Co-Co	Co-Co	Co-Co	Co-Co	Co-Co	Co-Co
Weight (operational)	102-108 tonnes	106 tonnes	107 tonnes	107 tonnes	106 tonnes	120 tonnes	120 tonnes
Height	12ft 9 1/16in	12ft 9 1/16in	12ft 9 1/16in	12ft 9 1/16in	12ft 9 1/16in	12ft 9 1/16in	12ft 9 1/16in
Width	8ft 10 3/8in	8ft 10 3/8in	8ft 10 3/8in	8ft 10 3/8in	8ft 10 3/8in	8ft 10 3/8in	8ft 10 3/8in
Length	61ft 6in	61ft 6in	61ft 6in	61ft 6in	61ft 6in	61ft 6in	61ft 6in
Min Curve negotiable	4 chains	4 chains	4 chains	4 chains	4 chains	4 chains	4 chains
Maximum Speed (Note: 6)	80mph	80mph	80mph	80mph	90mph	80mph	80mph
Wheelbase	50ft 8in	50ft 8in	50ft 8in	50ft 8in	50ft 8in	50ft 8in	50ft 8in
Bogie Wheelbase	13ft 6in	13ft 6in	13ft 6in	13ft 6in	13ft 6in	13ft 6in	13ft 6in
Bogie Pivot Centres	37ft 2in	37ft 2in	37ft 2in	37ft 2in	37ft 2in	37ft 2in	37ft 2in
Wheel Diameter- Driving	3ft 9in	3ft 9in	3ft 9in	3ft 9in	3ft 9in	3ft 9in	3ft 9in
Brake Type	Dual (Note: 7)	Dual	Dual	Dual	Air	Dual	Dual
Sanding Equipment	Pneumatic	Pneumatic	Pneumatic	Pneumatic	Pneumatic	Pneumatic	Pneumatic
Heating Type	Steam (Note: 2)	Not fitted	Electric - index 38	Not fitted	Through wired	Not fitted	Not fitted
Train Heat Alternator	Not fitted	Not fitted	Brush BAH701	Not fitted	Not fitted	Not fitted	Not fitted
Route Availability	5	5	5	5	5	7	7
Coupling Restriction	Blue Star	Blue Star	Blue Star	Blue Star	Blue Star/Special	Blue Star	Blue Star
Brake Force	50 tonnes	50 tonnes	50 tonnes	50 tonnes	50 tonnes	60 tonnes	60 tonnes
Engine Type	EE 12CSVT	EE 12CSVT	EE 12CSVT	EE 12CSVT	EE 12CSVT	EE 12CSVT	Mirrlees MB275T (37901-37904) Ruston RX270T (37905-37906)
Engine Horsepower	1,750hp	1,750hp	1,750hp	1,750hp	1,750hp	1,750hp	1,800hp
Power at Rail	1,250hp	1,250hp	1,254hp	1,250hp	1,250hp	1,250hp	1,300hp
Tractive Effort	55,500lb	56,180lb	57,440lb	55,590lb	55,500lb	61,910lb	62,680lb
Cylinder Bore	10in	10in	10in	10in	10in	10in	10¼in
Cylinder Stroke	12in	12in	12in	12in	12in	12in	12¼in
Main Generator Type	EE822/10G	EE822/10G	Not fitted	Not fitted	Not fitted	Not fitted	Not fitted
Traction Alternator Type	Not fitted	Not fitted	Brush BA100SA	Brush BA100SA	Brush BA100SA	Brush BA100SA (37701-719/883-899) GEC G564 (37796-803)	Brush BA100SA (37901-904) GEC G564 (37905-906)
Aux Generator Type	EE 911/5C	EE 911/5C	Not fitted	Not fitted	Not fitted	Not fitted	Not fitted
Traction Alternator Type	Not fitted	Not fitted	Brush BA606A	Brush BA606A	Brush BA606A	Brush BA606A (37701-719/883-899) GEC G658 or G659 (37796-803)	Brush BA606A (37901-904) GEC G658 or G659 (37905-906)
Number of Traction Motors	6	6	6	6	6	6	6
Traction Motor Type	EE 538/1A	EE 538/5A	EE 538/5A	EE 538/5A	EE 538/5A	EE 538/5A	EE 538/5A
Gear Ratio	53:18	59:16	59:16	59:16	59:16	59:16	59:16
Fuel Tank Capacity (Note: 3)	1,690gal	1,690gal	1,690gal	1,690gal	1,690gal	1,690gal	1,690gal
Cooling Water Capacity	160gal	160gal	160gal	160gal	160gal	160gal	160gal
Boiler Water Capacity	800gal (Note:2)	Not fitted	Not fitted	Not fitted	Not fitted	Not fitted	Not fitted
Lub Oil Capacity	120gal	120gal	120gal	120gal	120gal	120gal	120gal
Boiler Fuel Capacity	From main supply	Not fitted	Not fitted	Not fitted	Not fitted	Not fitted	Not fitted

1. Locomotives renumbered 37501-37521 are refurbished phase 1 locomotives from the original number range 37001-37119, and are fitted with Brush BA100SA alternators.

Locomotives renumbered 37667-37699 are refurbished phase 2 locomotives from the original series 37120-37308, and are fitted with Brush BA100SA alternators.

2. Steam heating is now a thing of the past. Most locomotives were originally boiler fitted.

3. As locomotives were refurbished, the existing boiler water tanks were converted into additional fuel tanks, doubling the locomotives' operating range.

4. Locomotives renumbered in the series 37701-37719 are refurbished phase 1 locomotives from the original batch 37001-37119, and fitted with Brush BA100SA alternators. Locomotives renumbered 37796-37799 are from the same series but fitted with GEC G564 alternators. Locomotives numbered 37800-37803 are refurbished phase 2 locomotives from the original batch 37120-37308, fitted with GEC G564 alternators. Locomotives numbered 37883-37899 are the same but fitted with Brush BA100SA alternators.

5. Various locomotives are fitted with slow speed control equipment.

6. When built the maximum speed was 90mph, this being reduced in 1985-86 to the present level.

7. When built locomotives were fitted with vacuum train brakes only, dual equipment being fitted in the 1970-80s.

Main detail differences

37/0 Standard locomotive.

37/3 Unrefurbished locomotives, fitted with CP7 bogies.

37/4 Electric Train Supply (ETS) modified locomotives.

37/5 Refurbished locomotives with route availability of 5. Some are fitted with slow speed control.

37/6 Rebuilt Class 37/5s for use on Eurostar UK 'Nightstar' services between Swansea/Plymouth and Waterloo. Service abandoned and six locomotives then sold to DRS.

37/7 Refurbished locomotives with route availability of 7. Some fitted with slow speed control. All have ballast weights.

37/9 Refurbished locomotives fitted with experimental power units.

Body differences

Under the original number system, phase 1 locomotives 37001-119 were built with split route indicator box front ends, ie two characters either side of a central gangway door. Phase 2 locomotives 37120-308 were built with a four-character central headcode box.

Under the refurbishing scheme locomotives with split headcode boxes had them removed and marker lights installed in their place, while locomotives with a central headcode box retained the fitment but had it plated over and two marker lights fitted centrally.

The largest fleet of Type 3s ordered by the BTC were the English Electric built 1,750hp locomotives ordered in 1959 and delivered in the early 1960s. The external appearance was very similar to the EE 2,000hp (Type 4) machines previously built (Class 40).

The first order for what was to become BR's standard Type 3 locomotive was for just 42 machines; however, due to many subsequent orders being placed the production run eventually extended to 309, being delivered over a five-year period. After English Electric received the order for the first batch, construction was sub-contracted to the Vulcan Foundry in Newton-le-Willows, which eventually produced the majority of locomotives. During the early 1960s when construction space at Vulcan was at a premium, Robert Stephenson & Hawthorns assisted.

The first completed locomotive, carrying the number D6700, was released from Vulcan Foundry in November 1960 and after inspection at Doncaster Works was sent to its new home at Stratford in East London, where the first 30 locomotives were shedded. By mid-1961 several members of the fleet were available and operating ER(GE) services, where their performance was excellent. However a bogie fracture problem was discovered in March 1961 which led to all locomotives being returned to the builders for attention.

After the delivery of No. D6729 the next twelve locomotives were allocated to the North Eastern, primarily for freight operation. Throughout 1962 locomotives were delivered to the Eastern Region, and were by now operating a considerable number of passenger and freight duties. In March 1963 the Western Region received its first locomotive, allocated to Cardiff Canton, for operation on South Wales and Valley Line freight services. The final locomotive of the build was delivered to the WR in November 1965.

The power unit installed in this fleet was the English Electric 12CSVT developing 1,750hp, with electrical equipment also being supplied by English Electric. During the production of this sizeable fleet, BR deemed the central nose-end gangway no longer required, enabling English Electric to redesign the front end to incorporate a solid 4-character route indicator box. Details of the frontal designs are tabulated under the technical data. Between 1965 and 1983 the Class 37s, as the class became known under the numerical classification system, operated on all regions of BR and gave one of the highest availability figures of any locomotive type.

When it became obvious that finance was not available to replace many hundreds of locomotives during the mid 1980s, a major refurbishing scheme of some existing classes was authorised, the Class 37s being one of the selected fleets. This major operation was undertaken by BREL Crewe Works and included the virtual rebuilding of the locomotives from the frames upwards; all electrical equipment was replaced, the engines refurbished, and several alterations made to the auxiliary equipment. A fleet of 31 locomotives was equipped with Electric Train Supply (ETS) equipment, while others had slow speed control, and additional ballast weight added to improve adhesion. Details of the major differences are given in the technical section. Six locomotives, reclassified as 37/9, were fitted with two types of experimental power unit supplied by Mirrlees and Ruston to evaluate their possible future applications. The refurbishment programme, although curtailed in 1988, meant that the class remained active until well into 2000.

When constructed the locomotives were painted in Brunswick green livery, yellow panels and full yellow ends being applied during the 1960s. From 1967 BR blue livery was applied, with full yellow ends. Following refurbishment many machines received the 'more yellow' livery style with large BR logo and numbers. After adoption of the Railfreight grey livery in 1985 the majority of locomotives emerged in this colour. From 1987 when dedicated sector liveries were launched Class 37s have been repainted in these colours.

A major development within the Class 37 fleet came in 1994 when European Passenger Services (EPS) obtained 12 locomotives for conversion to power the non-electrified legs of 'Nightstar' services between Plymouth/Swansea and London. These locomotives, reclassified 37/6, were rebuilt with revised front end connections at Doncaster Works; following the abolition of the 'Nightstar' services, six of the fleet were sold to private operator DRS and are now in DRS blue livery and allocated to Carlisle.

Major inroads have been made to the Class 37s in the late 1990s, with the vast majority of the fleet under the ownership of EWS — as this company is investing heavily in new traction the long term future of the fleet looks bleak. In 1999 40 members entered a hire contract to operate in France on the construction of a new high speed line.

Several Class 37s have been saved from scrap by the preservation movement and a handful are now authorised for main line operation.

was authorised, the Class 37s being one of the selected fleets. The major operation was undertaken by BREL Crewe Works and included the virtual rebuilding of the locomotives from the frame upwards, all electrical equipment being replaced, the engines refurbished, and several alterations made to the auxiliary equipment. A fleet of 31 locomotives was equipped with Electric Train Supply (ETS) equipment, while others had slow speed control, and additional weight added to improve adhesion. Details of the major differences are given in the technical section. Six locomotives of the fleet, reclassified as 37/9 were fitted with two types of experimental power unit supplied by Mirrlees and Ruston to evaluate their possible future applications.

The refurbishing which was completed as far as present budgets permitted in 1988, has meant that representatives of this class will be seen in traffic well into the next century.

When constructed the locomotives were painted in Brunswick green livery, yellow panels, full yellow ends being applied during the 1960s. From 1967 BR blue livery was applied, with full yellow ends. After the adoption of the 'Railfreight' livery of grey during 1985 several locomotives emerged in this colour. From 1987 when dedicated sector liveries were launched Class 37s have been repainted in these colours.

The first of what was to become the standard BR Type 3, later Class 37, emerged at the end of 1960, being delivered to Stratford in January 1961, when this official front 3/4 view was taken. The locomotive is viewed from the No. 2 end.

BR

By the summer of 1960 the ER (GE) allocation of Type 3 locomotives had grown to 20, with locomotives being deployed on a number of express passenger services. No. D6707 is seen at speed in the East Anglian countryside in August 1960.

Author's Collection

The first 119 locomotives were constructed with nose end gangway doors, with one 2-digit route indicator box being positioned either side. From locomotive No. D6819 a solid 4-position headcode box was installed, shown here on locomotive No. D6829. By the time this locomotive was released to traffic in April 1963, the small yellow warning panel had been applied as standard.

GEC Traction

When Type 3 No. D6999 was released to traffic it was the 300th standard Type 3 locomotive built by EE for BR. To mark this major achievement a special 'painted' headboard was carried on the yellow end. The locomotive is seen near Radyr with a coal train for Spencer Steelworks at Llanwern.

Author's Collection

In the mid/late 1960s the entire EE Type 3 fleet, now Class 37, was repainted into standard blue livery with full yellow ends. Sporting plated route indicator boxes Nos 37049 and 37173 pass Stratford with a 'Freightliner' bound for the nearby London International Freight Terminal.

Colin J. Marsden

It was not until the early 1980s that the Class 37s began to work in Scotland, taking over from Class 26 and 27 locomotives. No. 37090, still retaining its nose end doors stands in Glasgow Queen Street on 15th November 1984 with the 16.50 service for Fort William.

Colin J. Marsden

The Class 37s, often described as BR's most successful mixed traffic locomotive, have always been at their best with a heavy load in tow, and for their Type 3 power output have returned some outstanding performances. Nos 37010 and 37054 are seen lifting an empty MGR train out of Healey Mills Yard on 11th September 1981. Both locomotives would be under the control of one driver via the blue star multiple control equipment.

Colin J. Marsden

Today the Class 37s are almost extinct from passenger operations, except on the North Wales Coast and in the Cardiff Valleys — the majority of work is freight under the EWS banner. On 10th February 1987 No. 37248 approaches West Ealing with the 14.30 Chessington-Didcot empty household coal working.

Colin J. Marsden

Pairs of Class 37s were regularly deployed on heavy Peak District aggregate duties for many years, where the excellent tractive effort characteristics of the type could be exploited to the full. On 11th July 1986, Nos 37126 and 37130 slowly depart from Peak Forest with the 14.23 'Peakstone' train to Hope Street.

Colin J. Marsden

During the mid 1980s a major refurbishment programme was authorised for a number of class members, thus extending their projected lifespan into the third millennium. This major rebuilding, carried out at BREL Crewe, led to the formation of several new sub-classes; here Class 37/5 No. 37694 approaches Acton with a 'Speedlink' coal train on 18th February 1987.

Colin J. Marsden

The Class 37 refurbishment programme also covered six locomotives re-engined with Ruston or Mirrlees units — externally the locomotives were the same as conventional machines. No. 37906 (fitted with a Ruston RK270T engine) emerges from Hillfield Tunnel, Newport on 26th March 1987, with a rake of steel carrying wagons.

Colin J. Marsden

The refurbishing of the earlier split box Class 37s led to a completely new front end layout being developed, as shown here on No. 37504, which was previosly No. 37039. The livery shown is Railfreight grey with wrap-round yellow ends and large BR logo. Some examples were also given a red sole bar band.

Colin J. Marsden

By 1987 the Class 37 fleet was allocated to all regions except the Southern, but could be found operating on all regions. Two of the Thornaby allocated, steel sub-sector operated locomotives Nos 37502 and 37501 are seen at Derby with just a single steel wagon, en route from Burton-upon-Trent wagon depot to Toton Yard on 16th September 1987.

Colin J. Marsden

With the 1987 dedication of motive power to individual sub-sectors, selected batches of locomotives were allocated to a specific depot for certain duties. Class 37/5s Nos 37676-688 were for example allocated to Tinsley for use on Peak area stone duties. Nos 37678 and 37677 pass Chinley on 17th September 1987 with the 12.42 Tunstead-Collyhurst.

Colin J. Marsden

Displaying European Passenger Services (EPS) triple grey livery with Channel Tunnel segment logos on the side, a pair of Class 37/6s with number 37605 nearest the camera stand at Doncaster works with a generator van on 25th October 1995. Note the additional front end jumper cables and connections.

Colin J. Marsden

Following the sale of the freight operations in the UK to American owned Wisconsin Central and the formation of English Welsh & Scottish Railway, a number of Class 37s emerged in the distinctive maroon and gold EWS colours. No. 37670 is seen piloting 'Dutch' liveried Class 31 No. 31466 at Goodrington on 23rd May 1998 with the 14.40 Paignton-Kingswear.

Colin J. Marsden

Class 40 (D200–D399) 40001–40199

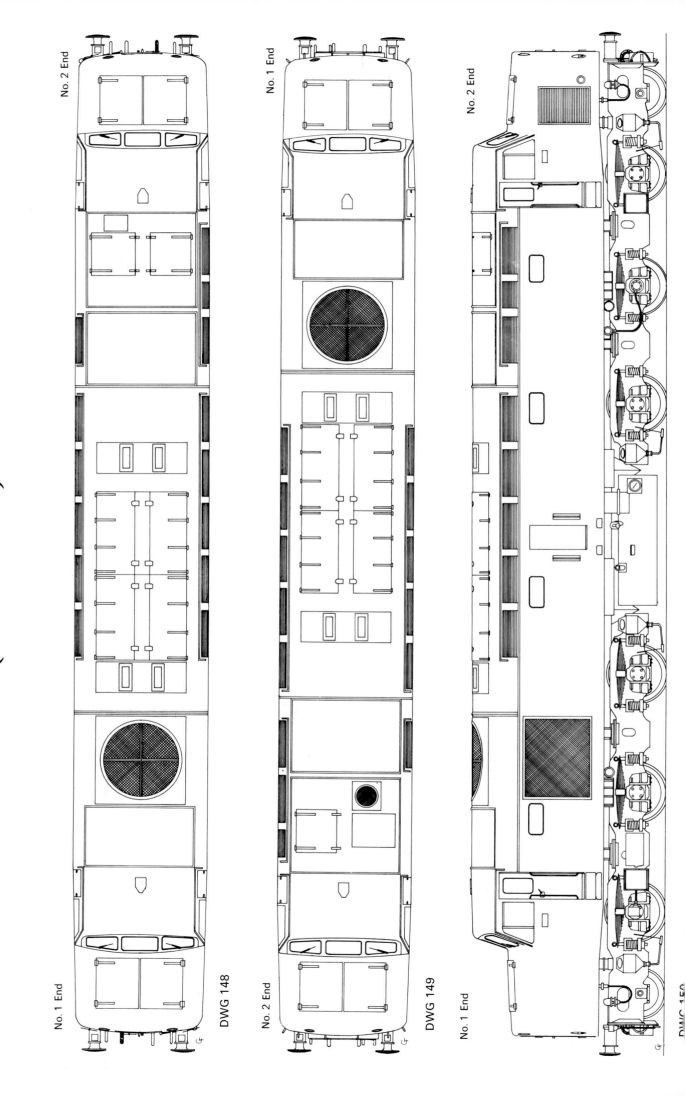

No. 2 End

No. 1 End

DWG 148

No. 1 End

No. 2 End

DWG 149

No. 2 End

No. 1 End

No. 1 End

No. 2 End

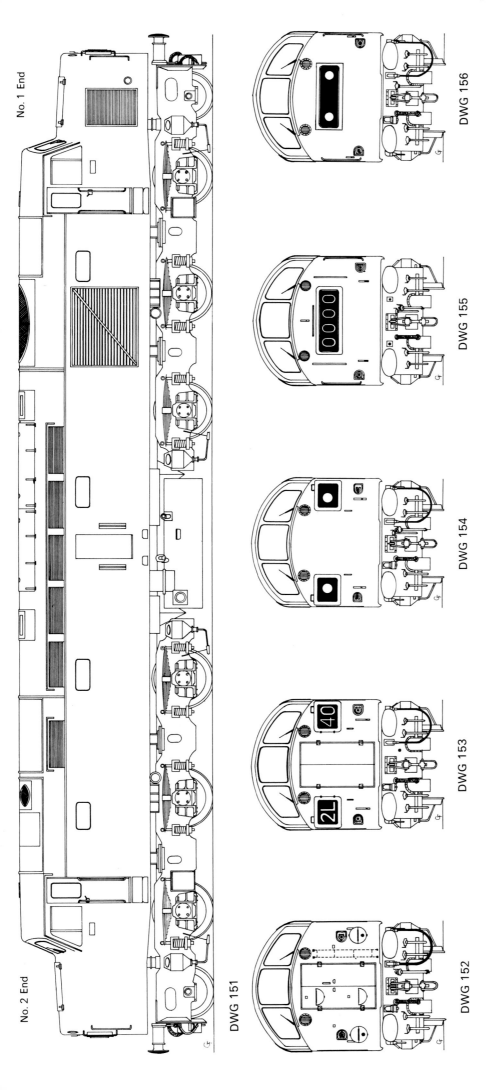

DWG 151

DWG 152

DWG 153

DWG 154

DWG 155

DWG 156

DWG 148
Class 40 roof detail, as applicable to locomotives sporting the disc train reporting system, Nos D200–D323 (40001–123). Modification to boiler exhaust could be found on some examples.

DWG 149
Class 40 roof detail, as applicable to locomotives fitted with the solid centre route indicator box, Nos D346–D399 (40146–199). Modification to boiler exhaust could be found on some examples.

DWG 150
Class 40 side elevation showing side 'A', the No. 1 end is on the left. Layout applicable to disc fitted locomotives, Nos D200–D323 (40001–123).

DWG 151
Class 40 side elevation showing side 'B', the No. 1 end is on the right. Layout applicable to solid centre headcode fitted locomotives, Nos D346–D399 (40146–199).

DWG 152
Class 40 front end layout, showing original style with train identification discs, vacuum braking, steam heating. MU fitment and central doors. The ladder position is also marked.

DWG 153
Class 40 front end layout, showing the split 4-character route indicator box as fitted to locomotives Nos D324–D345 (40124–145). The communicating doors and MU fitment are shown, but the steam heat pipe is omitted.

DWG 154
Class 40 front end layout, again showing the split 4-character route indicator, but this time the central door is sealed and dual brakes fitted.

DWG 155
Class 40 front end layout, showing the solid centre headcode as fitted to locomotives Nos D346–D399 (40146–199). The headcode is showing the mid-1970s '0000', the MU equipment has been removed, and dual brakes fitted.

DWG 156
Class 40 front end layout, again showing the solid 4-character route indicator box, as modified from disc fitment in 1965 by Scottish Region, D260–D266 (40060–40066). Handrails and lower body in front.

Class 40 (D200–D399)
40001–40199

Class	40	Multiple Coupling Restriction	Blue Star
Former Class Codes	D20/1, later 20/3	Brake Force	51 tonnes
Number Range TOPS	40001–40199	Engine Type	English Electric
Former Number Range	D200–D399		16SVT Mk 11
Built by	EE & RSH Ltd	Engine Horsepower	2,000hp
Introduced	1958–62	Power at Rail	1,550hp
Wheel Arrangement	1Co-Co1	Tractive Effort	52,000lb
Weight (operational)	136 tonnes	Cylinder Bore	10in
Height	12ft 10in	Cylinder Stroke	12in
Width	9ft	Main Generator Type	EE822
Length	69ft 6in	Aux Generator Type	EE911–2B
Min Curve negotiable	4$^1/_2$ chains	Number of Traction Motors	6
Maximum Speed	90mph	Traction Motor Type	EE526–5D
Wheelbase	61ft 3in	Gear Ratio	61:19
Bogie Wheelbase	21ft 6in	Fuel Tank Capacity	710gal
Bogie Pivot Centres	34ft 4in	Cooling Water Capacity	200gal
Wheel Diameter (Driving)	3ft 9in	Boiler Water Capacity	800gal
(Pony)	3ft	Lub Oil Capacity	140gal
Brake Type	Dual (Note: 1)	Boiler Fuel Capacity	200gal
Sanding Equipment	Penumatic		
Heating Type	Steam–Stones OK		
	4625		
Route Availability	6		

1. When built locomotives were fitted with vacuum train brakes, dual brake equipment being fitted in the 1970s.

To operate main-line passenger services the BTC ordered a fleet of ten 2,000hp express locomotives under the pilot scheme of the Modernisation Plan. The locomotives were very successful and several subsequent orders were placed which eventually led to a production run of 200 locomotives. The number range allocated being D200–D399.

The order for the main-line power went to English Electric, who sub-contracted the assembly work to Vulcan Foundry. The prime mover used was of established English Electric origin and previously used in both the LMS and SR main-line prototypes. In the form used now it was classified as 16SVT and set to deliver 2,000hp. Electric equipment was provided by English Electric. The sizeable locomotive was mounted on a 1Co-Co1 wheel configuration and had a length of 69ft 6in. Construction of the first machine commenced in 1956 and the finished product was unveiled for the first time in March 1958. After the locomotive's initial testing around its manufacturer's works it was brought to London and allocated to Stratford depot. The locomotives first outing being 18th March when it powered a special from Liverpool Street to Norwich and back.

By September 1958 the ten locomotives of the original order were in service and by this time the BTC had placed several follow-on orders. During the summer of 1959 the operational area of the locomotives was increased when ER (GN) services became diesel powered. By May 1959 the first of the follow-on orders were coming on stream, being allocated to the London Midland Region. Between May 1959 and September 1962 the locomotives were delivered at a rate of more than one per month, all except the batch D305–D324 being constructed by Vulcan Foundry. Locomotives D305–D324 were constructed by Robert Stephen-

son & Hawthorn of Darlington. Allocation was divided between the Eastern, London Midland and Scottish Regions.

When built locomotives Nos D200–D323 were fitted with the steam style disc train identification system. By the time locomotives D324–D345 were constructed this had been superseded by the 4-character alpha/numeric reporting system, two characters being fitted either side of the central gangway connection. By early 1961 when the nose end doors were decreed obsolete, locomotives Nos D346–D399 were built with a solid 4-character route box on the front.

Train heating on the fleet was provided by a steam heating boiler, however when No. D255 was constructed an early form of Electric Train Supply (ETS) was fitted. Due to the general lack of suitable stock the equipment was only used on a handful of occasions and removed in the mid 1960s.

The locomotives were identified as Class 40 under the numerical classification system and remained in general service until 1985 when the class was deemed obsolete. One locomotive, the pioneer No. D200 was retained by BR and used for numerous enthusiasts' specials and was withdrawn in May 1988. Several of the fleet have been saved from the cutters' torch by enthusiast groups who have managed to restore them to full operational condition.

When constructed the locomotives were all outshopped in BR Brunswick green livery, yellow warning panels being added in the mid 1960s. From 1967 locomotives were repainted in BR blue as they passed through works for classified attention, however one, No. D306 (40106) was retained in green with yellow warning ends.

The first of the BTC English Electric Type 4 locomotives No. D200 was delivered to Stratford in March 1958 and operated its first passenger train to Norwich on the 18th of the month. No. D200, resplendent in Brunswick green livery is seen at Witham on its inaugural run.

Author's Collection

In the summer of 1959 the EE Type 4 operating area was considerably enlarged, with locomotives going to the ER(GN) section powering services such as the "Master Cutler" and "Tees-Tyne Pullman." No. D201 obviously specially prepared for its duty is seen powering six Pullman vehicles on the inaugural diesel-hauled "Master Cutler".

Author's Collection

With locomotives of the post pilot scheme Type 4 orders coming on stream from May 1959, it was not long before the locomotives found their way onto the London Midland Region, replacing steam traction on many express passenger duties. One of the later built locomotives incorporating a solid central route indicator, No. D382 departs from Euston with the "Ulster Express".

Colin J. Marsden

Soon after construction a batch of 25 locomotives were given cast nameplates of famous ocean liners, to symbolise the ties between the London Midland Region and the port of Liverpool via the Euston–Liverpool service. The nameplate *Empress of Britain* as carried by No. D210 is shown.

Colin J. Marsden

One unusual feature of this EE type, was the buffers and draw gear being attached to the bogie frame and not the locomotive bodywork as in normal practice. This gave some rather peculiar appearances if a view of the front end was seen with the locomotive on tight curvature track, as portrayed here with an illustration of the front end of split routebox No. 40129.

Colin J. Marsden

As detailed in the introductory text and drawings, three different front end designs were installed on the Class 40 fleet, the most common type using the disc identification system. Showing the express passenger code No. 40033 descends Shap incline at Greenholme on 4th June 1979 with the 11.15 Glasgow – Nottingham service diverted via the WCML.

Colin J. Marsden

The split 4-character route indicator box was fitted to locomotives Nos D324-D345 (40124-145). In common with earlier locomotives these incorporated nose communicating doors, which were plated over in later years, in an attempt to reduce cab draughts. No. 40144 passes Foxlow Junction with a ballast train bound for Sheffield on 30th January 1980.

Colin J. Marsden

The most aesthetically pleasing front end layout on the Class 40 fleet was the solid 4-character centrally mounted route box, but alas only the final 54 members were so treated. On a bitterly cold February morning in 1983, No. 40152 poses in the stone sidings at Ribblehead whilst loading takes place.

Colin J. Marsden

The general 'run-down' of the Class 40 fleet commenced during the early 1980s, with the final general service locomotive being withdrawn in 1985 and the final example, No. 40122 being withdrawn in May 1988. During their last few years the fleet were deployed on many secondary and non-passenger duties, such as this working on 31st August 1982 when No.40013 was captured on film departing from Doncaster with empty vans for Manchester.

Colin J. Marsden

The 'prototype' locomotive of the Class No. D200 (40122) was, after initial withdrawal, reinstated to traffic and repainted into green livery, being used for revenue earning and enthusiasts' specials. No. 40122 is seen near Crosby Garrett on the Settle & Carlisle line with a Leeds – Carlisle working.

Colin J. Marsden

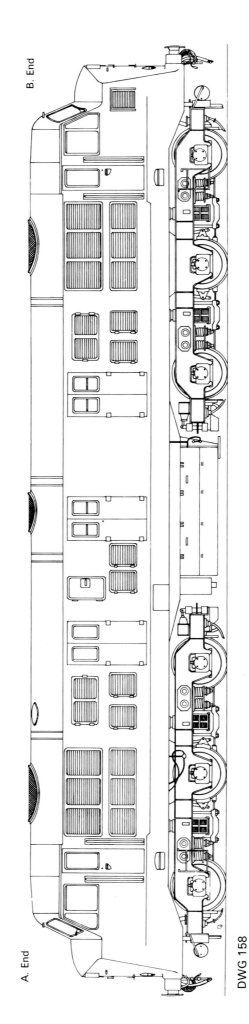

B. End

A. End

DWG 157

B. End

A. End

DWG 158

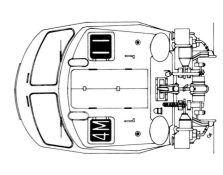

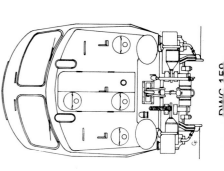

DWG 157
Class 41 roof detail.

DWG 158
Class 41 side elevation.

DWG 159
Class 41 original front end layout.

DWG 160
Class 41 modified front end layout incorporating split route indicator boxes.

164

Class 41 (D600–D604)

Class	41	Multiple Coupling Restriction	Orange Square
Former Class Codes	D20/2, later 20/4		(Note: 1)
Number Range	D600–D604	Brake Force	88 tonnes
Built by	NBL Ltd	Engine Type	2 x NBL L12V
Introduced	1958–59		18/21A
Wheel Arrangement	A1A-A1A	Total Horsepower	2,000hp
Weight (operational)	118 tonnes	Power at Rail	hp
Height	12ft 10in	Tractive Effort	50,000lb
Width	8ft 8in	Cylinder Bore	7.1in
Length	65ft	Cylinder Stroke	8.3in
Min Curve negotiable	4^1/2 chains	Transmission Type	Voith L306r
Maximum Speed	90mph	Fuel Tank Capacity	800gal
Wheelbase	50ft	Cooling Water Capacity	gal
Bogie Wheelbase	15ft	Lub Oil Capacity	gal
Bogie Pivot Centres	35ft	Boiler Water Capacity	1,000gal
Wheel Diameter (Driving)	3ft 7in	Boiler Fuel Capacity	From main tank
(Carrier)	3ft 3^1/2in		
Brake Type	Vacuum		
Sanding Equipment	Pneumatic		
Route Availability	5		
Heating Type	Steam–Spanner		
	Mk 1		

1. The Orange Square code of this class must not be confused with the code applied to the Class 50s in the 1960s. The Orange Square code applied to the Class 41s permitted multiple operation with the first six Class 22s only.

The first major step made by the BTC to replace steam traction on the Western Region came in 1955 when an order for five diesel-hydraulic locomotives was placed with the North British Locomotive Co. of Glasgow. The number range allocated being D600–D604.

After the order was placed and works tooling carried out production of the first locomotive commenced at the end of 1956. Construction took almost a year and the locomotive appeared for the first time in November 1957 when it was engaged on test running in Scotland. The locomotive was handed over to the BTC on 4th December 1957, and took up testing from Swindon. In January 1958 the locomotive carrying the number D600 commenced driver training in the Bristol area and operated its first train on 17th February between Paddington and Bristol. The second of the order was delivered during March 1958 and after acceptance tests joined No. D600 on West of England duties. No D601 hit the headlines on 16th June 1958 when it powered the Westbound "Cornish Riviera Express" non-stop from Paddington to Plymouth and managed the assault on Hemerdon Bank without assistance. All five locomotives were in service by January 1959 and performed very well,

giving around 71% availability, which at that time was quite acceptable.

The prime mover installed in this fleet was a pair of NBL/MAN L12V 18/21S engines, each set to develop 1,000hp, the transmissions being Voith L306r units.

Throughout the early 1960s the D600 or 'Warship' class as they became because of their names, operated on the Paddington–Bristol–Plymouth–Penzance route, being joined from the end of 1958 by the Swindon and later North British 'production' locomotives of the D800 series. When introduced the D600s were painted in all over green livery and sported disc train identification equipment. During the early 1960s small yellow warning ends were applied, as were split box 4-character alpha/numeric route indicators. Two locomotives were later repainted in standard BR blue (D600/D602).

After the Railways' decision to standardise on diesel-electric traction, and the policy to withdraw diesel-hydraulic fleets, this series of locomotives had no future at all. Withdrawal of the entire fleet being made on 30th December 1967 with all locomotives subsequently sold for scrap.

The Western Region's first diesel-hydraulic locomotives were ordered in 1955 from the NBL Company of Glasgow, who in 1956-57 constructed five machines at their Springburn works. After their construction testing took place in Scotland, before the locomotives were sent south. No. D600 Active is seen on trial during November 1957.

NBL Ltd

Once on the WR the first diesel-hydraulic 'Warship' locomotive was engaged on much testing, working its first passenger service on 17th February 1958 between Paddington and Bristol, seen here on its return to the Capital near Twyford.

BR

After the D600 class 'Warships' were delivered to Swindon, painted in Brunswick green with a thin off-white band at the base of the body, a thorough inspection and test running programme was carried out. On 26th April 1958 No. D601 *Ark Royal* is seen passing Chipping Sodbury with a test special returning to Swindon.

Ivo Peters

For their entire, rather short lives the D600 class locomotives were always given classified attention by Swindon Works, however daily service checks and intermediate examinations were carried out by various running depots. No. D600 is seen awaiting works attention in Swindon on 24th October 1962.

L. Price

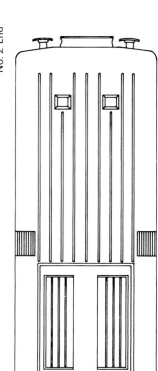

No. 2 End

No. 1 End

DWG 161

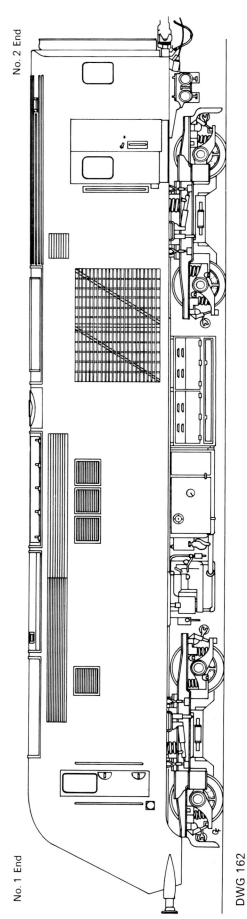

No. 2 End

No. 1 End

DWG 162

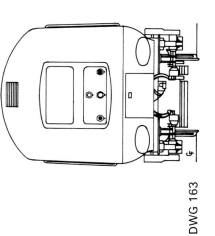

DWG 163

DWG 161
Prototype HST roof detail.

DWG 162
Prototype HST side elevation.

DWG 163
Prototype HST front end (nose) layout.

Class 41 (252) (41001–41002) 43000–43001

Class		41 (IC125 Power Cars)	Sanding Equipment	Not fitted
Set Classification		252	Heating Type	Electric
Number Range	(Original)	41001–41002	Route Availability	6
	(Revised)	43000–43001	Multiple Coupling Restriction	Not fitted
Built by		BREL Crewe	Brake Force	tonnes
Introduced		1972	Engine Type	Paxman Valenta 12RP200L
Wheel Arrangement		Bo-Bo		
Weight (operational)		66 tonnes	Horsepower	2,250hp
Height		12ft 10in	Power at Rail	1,770hp
Width		9ft	Tractive Effort	17,980lb
Length		56ft 3in	Cylinder Bore	$7^{3}/4$in
Min Curve negotiable		4 chains	Cylinder Stroke	$8^{1}/2$in
Maximum Speed		125mph	Main Alternator Type	Brush BA1001B
Wheelbase		42ft 3in	Number of Traction Motors	4
Bogie Wheelbase		8ft 6in	Traction Motor Type	Brush TMH68–46
Bogie Pivot Centres		33ft 9in	Gear Ratio	
Wheel Diameter		3ft 4in	Fuel Tank Capacity	1,000gal
Brake Type		Air	Cooling Water Capacity	gal
			Lub Oil Capacity	gal

In the early 1970s the BRB were faced with a position that within around ten years the majority of their main-line diesel traction would need replacement. Financial limitations were tight and the possibility of mass electrification was not possible, therefore a new generation of high-speed diesel train had to be developed. This culminated in the production of a 'Prototype' high-speed set originally classified as locomotive and stock. The locomotives or power cars were Class 41, (later 252). After seeing the advantages of this design, production orders were placed for like trains for operation on the Western, Eastern, Scottish and London Midland Regions.

The prototype set was developed at the Railway Technical Centre, Derby, with the power cars being constructed by BREL Crewe Works in 1972. The passenger cars (which are not dealt with in this book) being constructed at BREL at Derby Litchurch Works. The power cars or locomotives as they were initially known had a main driver's position at one end which was aerodynamically shaped, the other, flat end, having an auxiliary driving position for shunting purposes. The two power cars which were of light-weight construction were assembled in early 1972, emerging in June and August. As soon as suitable stock was available trial running commenced, first on the

Eastern Region and latterly on the Western.

The power-unit used in these power cars was a Paxman 'Valenta' 12RP200L developing 2,500hp, electrical equipment was supplied by Brush.

Upon introduction the two power cars were numbered 41001 and 41002. After a short period the entire 'set' including the passenger coaches became unit Class 252, at the same time the power cars were renumbered 43000-9 and 43001. After operating its initial proving trials on the Eastern Region the prototype High Speed Twin (HST) was transferred to the Western Region where it was deployed on Paddington–Bristol/Weston-super-Mare services. Following the introduction of production HST sets the prototype unit was withdrawn, the power cars passing to the Research Division at Derby, being used to power various high speed development trains.

In more recent times one of the power cars has become a resident in the National Railway Museum (NRM) at York, while the other lies dumped at Derby. Most of the prototype passenger coaches were later converted into production HST cars, but some have seen further departmental use.

The prototype HST was painted in grey livery with a broad blue band on the upper part of the body and full yellow ends were applied.

The semi-streamlined 'prototype' High Speed Train (HST) power cars were constructed by BREL Crewe in 1972. Vaguely resembling the "Blue Pullman" driving cars, the HST motors were classified as 'locomotives' carrying numbers 41001-2. Locomotive No. 41001 is illustrated when new.

Colin J. Marsden

After a fleet of 'prototype' high speed trailer vehicles had been constructed, and the whole set tested, the new generation train operated on the Eastern and London Midland Regions on proving runs. The new and old orders of InterCity are seen side by side in this view.

BR

Throughout 1973 the prototype 'set' was operated on the Eastern Region, usually being maintained by Leeds Neville Hill depot. During the course of its Eastern operating several high-speed performance tests were carried out on the section north of York. The set is seen in this illustration carrying out one of its ECML runs.

BR

After working on the Eastern Region the set, now reclassified as a DMU (Class 252) was transferred to the Western Region, where after initial testing, it was deployed on the Paddington–Bristol route. On 20th May 1975 the set is seen near Corsham with the 13.45 Bristol–Paddington.

John Cooper-Smith

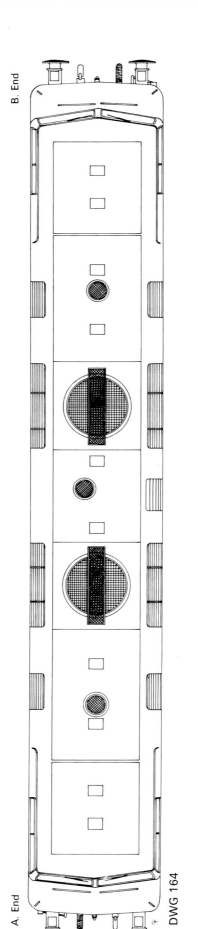

B. End

A. End

DWG 164

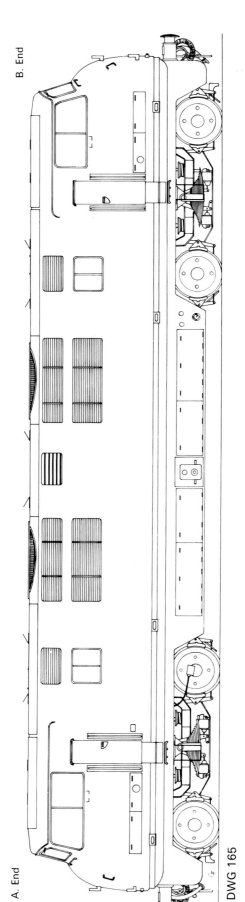

B. End

A. End

DWG 165

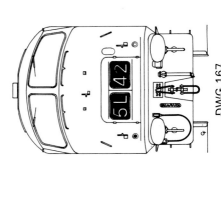

DWG 167

DWG 164
Class 42 roof detail, as for Nos D813–D829/D831–D832.

DWG 165
Class 42 side elevation.

DWG 166
Class 42 original front end layout as fitted to locomotives
Nos D803–D812 when built.

DWG 167
Class 42 front end layout incorporating 4-character route
indicator box, MU equipment is removed.

DWG 166

Class 42 (D800–D832/ D866–D870)

Class	42	(D818)	Steam – Spanner Mk 3
Former Class Codes (D800–D802)	D22/1, later 22/1	Multiple Coupling Restriction	
(D803–D832/D866–D870)	D20/1, later 20/1	D800–02)	Not fitted)
Number Range	D800–D832,	D803–70)	White Diamond)
	D866–D870	Brake Force	35 tonnes
Built by	BR Swindon	Engine Type (D800–29/31–32/	
Introduced	1958–61	66–70)	2x Maybach
Wheel Arrangement	B–B		MD650
Weight (operational)	79 tonnes	(D830)	2x Paxman 12YJXL
Height	12ft 9^1/$_2$in	Total Horsepower	
Width	8ft 8^1/$_2$in	(D800–03)	2,000hp
Length	60ft	(D804–29/31–70)	2,200hp
Min Curve negotiable	4^1/$_2$ chains	D830)	2,400hp
Maximum Speed	90mph	Power at Rail	hp
Wheelbase	48ft 3in	Tractive Effort	52,400lb
Bogie Wheelbase	10ft 6in	Cylinder Bore	7^3/$_4$in
Bogie Pivot Centres	37ft 9in	Cylinder Stroke	8^1/$_4$in
Wheel Diameter	3ft 3^1/$_2$in	Transmission Type	Mekydro K104
Brake Type	Vacuum	Fuel Tank Capacity	270gal
Sanding Equipment	Pneumatic	Cooling Water Capacity	270gal
Route Availability	6	Lub Oil Capacity	80gal
Heating Type (D800–12/66–70)	Steam – Spanner Mk 1	Boiler Water Capacity	940gal
(D813–17/19–65)	Steam – Stones 4616	Boiler Fuel Supply	From main tank

The Western Region's first production order for diesel-hydraulic locomotives was made in 1956 for the WR's own workshops at Swindon to produce a fleet of Type 4 locomotives. The original order for three and subsequent follow-on orders lead to a production run of 38 locomotives.

The design of these locomotives was based on the highly successful German V200 class, but due to BR's smaller loading restriction a considerable amount of scaling down had to be done. The power units for these locomotives were two Maybach MD650 engines each producing 1,000hp (1,100hp on later locomotives). Transmission being by two Mekydro K104 units. The original order was for just three locomotives, the first of which was constructed in 1957–58 and which was completed and handed over to the BTC on 3rd June 1958. The locomotive numbered D800 and named *Sir Brian Robertson,* was put to work on Paddington–Bristol/West of England line services, after testing. It was soon joined by the other two locomotives of the original order.

During the course of production of the first three, subsequent orders were placed with both BR and the private sector to produce a further 68 locomotives of like design. The Swindon contract was for 35 examples, for which construction started in mid 1958 and deliveries resumed in March 1959, the final locomotive being released to traffic in October 1961. Once in service the locomotives were deployed on many Paddington–West of England line

services, as well as selected inter-regional duties. In later years the fleet was used on the Waterloo–Exeter route. The overall performance of the fleet was good, with few complete failures ever being reported, the presence of two power units usually enabled the locomotives to hobble home! When the first 13 locomotives were built three digit 'stencil' route indicator frames were fitted, however after the construction of No. D812 the standard 4-character alpha/numeric boxes were fitted, early examples being modified when passing through works.

One locomotive of special note is No. D830 which, when built, was fitted with two Paxman 'Ventura' power units each developing 1,200hp the drive being via the standard Mekydro K104 transmission. Performance of this locomotive was satisfactory, but not on a par with the MD650 powered machines. Under the numeric classification of locomotives these Swindon 'Warships' became Class 42, but none were renumbered into the five digit TOPS series.

When constructed all locomotives were finished in Brunswick green livery. During the mid 1960s the majority were repainted into WR style maroon, before being repainted into the corporate BR blue scheme.

Like other diesel-hydraulic classes this fleet was deemed as non-standard and withdrawals commenced in 1968 with the final locomotive being deleted from stock in 1972. Two members of the fleet, Nos D821 and D832 have been preserved and are now restored to full working condition.

The first Swindon 'Warship' was built in 1957-8, with the production run eventually extending to 35 members. No. D803 *Albion* is illustrated showing the stencil type route indicator system and disc reporting codes fitted to the first 13 locomotives.

BR

Commencing with the construction of No. D813 4-character route indicator boxes were installed, enabling the ends to be slightly restyled. The front end layout of No. D813 *Diadem* is illustrated. Draw gear equipment is of the standard style with coupling, vacuum pipe, steam heat pipe, and multiple control connections being present.

BR

After their introduction the initial batch of Swindon built 'Warship' locomotives were allocated to Laira depot, from where they were deployed on Penzance, London, and selected inter-regional duties. Outside the old Laira steam depot 'Warship' No. D819 *Goliath* shares depot space with NBL Type 2s and another 'Warship'.

Colin Boocock

During the 1960s the majority of 'Warship' locomotives were repainted into maroon livery, before being re-painted into corporate blue. Now identified as Class 42, No. D827 *Kelly* departs from Gillingham with the 08.50 Exeter–Waterloo service on 29th August 1970.

Hugh Ballantyne

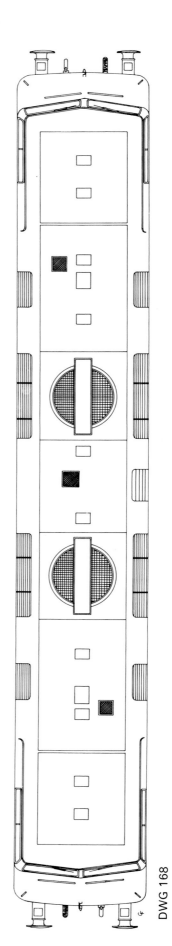

DWG 168

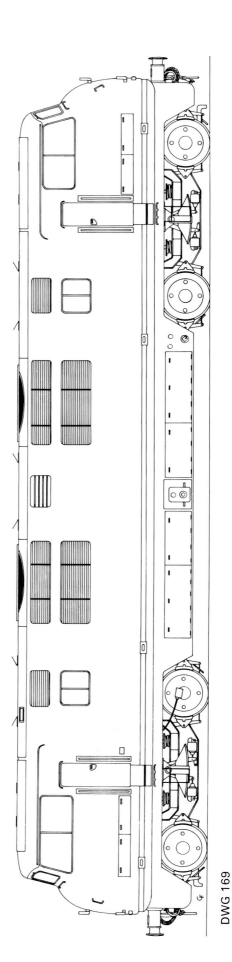

DWG 169

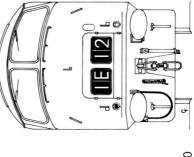

DWG 170

DWG 168
Class 43 roof detail.

DWG 169
Class 43 side elevation.

DWG 170
Class 43 front end layout showing MU equipment in position.

Class 43 (D833–D865)

Class	43	Route Availability	6
Former Class Codes	D22/2, later 22/2, 22/4	Heating Type	Steam – Stones OK 4616
Number Range	D833–D865	Multiple Coupling Restriction	White Diamond
Built by	NBL Ltd	Brake Force	35 tonnes
Introduced	1960–62	Engine Type	2 x NBL/MAN L12V18/21
Wheel Arrangement	B–B		
Weight (operational)	79 tonnes	Total Horsepower	2,200hp
Height	12ft 9$\frac{1}{2}$in	Power at Rail	hp
Width	8ft 8$\frac{1}{2}$in	Tractive Effort	49,030lb
Length	60ft	Cylinder Bore	7.1in
Min Curve negotiable	4$\frac{1}{2}$ chains	Cylinder Stroke	8.3in
Maximum Speed	90mph	Transmission Type	Voith LT306r
Wheelbase	48ft 3in	Fuel Tank Capacity	800gal
Bogie Wheelbase	10ft 6in	Cooling Water Capacity	270gal
Bogie Pivot Centres	37ft 9in	Lub Oil Capacity	76gal
Wheel Diameter	3ft 3$\frac{1}{2}$in	Boiler Water Capacity	940gal
Brake Type	Vacuum	Boiler Fuel Capacity	From main tank
Sanding Equipment	Pneumatic		

When the BTC placed the production orders for the 'Warship' locomotives, the North British Locomotive Co. of Glasgow was awarded a contract to construct a batch of 33 locomotives, which later became Class 43.

The NBL locomotives were ordered during 1958, with construction of the first locomotive being carried out in 1959–60. The power units and transmission fitted to the NBL built locomotives were different from the Swindon product. The engines being two NBL/MAN L12V18/21B units set to develop 1,100hp each, while the transmissions were Voith LT306r units. NBL completed their first locomotive during May 1960, and after trial running in Scotland it was delivered to Swindon Works in June, being taken into WR capital stock on 6th July 1960. The NBL production line produced around two locomotives per month, with the final locomotive of the contract arriving on the WR in June 1962.

External appearance of the NBL examples was almost identical to the Swindon products, except for minor detail differences mainly on the front ends.

This fleet while returning a satisfactory reliability figure was never quite as good as their Swindon brothers with problems affecting power units and transmission being not uncommon. When constructed the locomotives were painted in BR Brunswick green livery, which was changed to WR maroon during the mid 1960s. BR blue was applied from 1967 with of course full yellow warning ends.

The NBL 'Warships' shared allocation space with the Swindon locomotives but were usually operated only on WR internal services and North–South inter-regional diagrams, the Waterloo–Exeter route seldom seeing these machines. This segregation was due to drivers on the Southern not being trained on the North British equipment.

Again due to their non standard equipment and BR's decision to withdraw hydraulic classes the Class 43s began to disappear from stock in 1969, with the final example being withdrawn in 1971. Unfortunately none of this class were preserved.

The NBL 'Warships' of almost identical appearance to the Swindon product, started to appear during the summer of 1960. Painted in all over Brunswick green livery No. D844 *Spartan* departs from Bath with a Taunton–Paddington working on 12th August 1961.

The late Derek Cross

The entire fleet of both BR and NBL built 'Warships' were given names associated with the Royal Navy. Naming was done in strict alphabetical order with the NBL locomotives using the letters P to Z. *Sharpshooter* No. D843 passes Bathampton in September 1961 with the down ''Bristolian''.

The late Derek Cross

When introduced the entire fleet of NBL 'Warships' was allocated to Laira, but subsequently a number were re-allocated to Newton Abbot and Old Oak Common depots. Soon after its re-allocation to Newton Abbot No. D839 *Relentless* is seen on 23rd June 1962 at Exeter with the 12.20 Penzance–Kensington milk train.

R.C. Riley

After repainting into blue livery No. D859 *Vanquisher* is seen departing from Torquay with the 10.45 Paignton–Paddington. By the time this illustration was taken the locomotives had been deemed as Class 43, but thankfully none were to be renumbered into the five figure scheme.

L. Riley

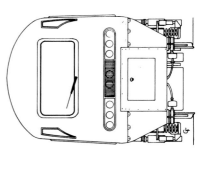

DWG 174

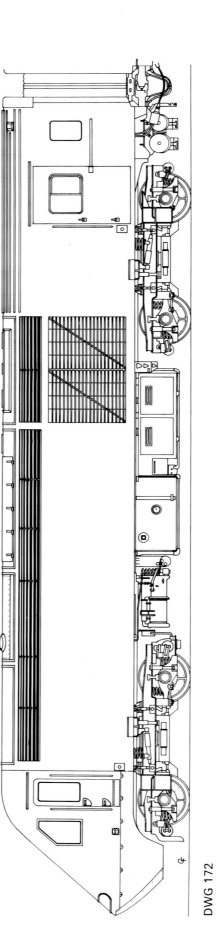

DWG 171

DWG 172

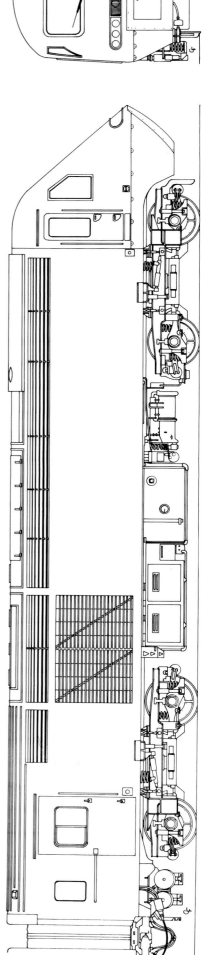

DWG 173

DWG 171
Production HST roof detail.

DWG 172
Production HST side elevation showing side 'A' in original condition. Drawing applicable to vehicles Nos 43002–151.

DWG 173
Production HST side elevation showing side 'B' with modified exhaust cowling. Drawing applicable to vehicles Nos 43002–151.

DWG 174
Production HST front end (nose) detail.

Class 43 (253/254) 43002–43198

Class	43 (IC125 Power Cars)	Horsepower	
Set Classification	253, 254	(43002–166/171–198)	2,250hp
Number Range	43002–43198	(43167–170)	2,400hp
Built by	BREL Crewe	Power at Rail	
Introduced	1976–82	(43002–166/171–198)	1,770hp
Wheel Arrangement	Bo-Bo	(43167–170)	1,940hp
Weight (operational)	70 tonnes	Tractive Effort	17,980lb
Height	12ft 9in	Cylinder Bore	
Width	8ft 11in	(43002–166/171–198)	$7^3/_4$in
Length	58ft 5in	(43167–170)	in
Min Curve negotiable	4 chains	Cylinder Stroke	
Maximum Speed	125mph	(43002–166/171–198)	$8^1/_2$in
Wheelbase	42ft 3in	(43167–170)	in
Bogie Wheelbase	8ft 6in	Main Alternator Type	Brush BA1001B
Bogie Pivot Centres	33ft 9in	Number of Traction Motors	4
Wheel Diameter	3ft 4in	Traction Motor Type	
Brake Type	Air	(43002–123/153–198)	Brush TMH68-46
Sanding Equipment	Not fitted	(43124–152)	GEC G417AZ
Heating Type	Electric	Gear Ratio	
Route Availability	6	Fuel Tank Capacity	1,000gal
Multiple Coupling Restriction	Not fitted	Cooling Water Capacity	gal
Brake Force	tonnes	Lub Oil Capacity	gal
Engine Type			
(43002–166/171–198)	Paxman Valenta 12RP200L		
(43167–170)	Mirrlees Blackstone MB190		

Car Nos 43002–43152 were built with full guards facilities, and classified DMB; cars 43153–43198 were built without this facility and classified DM. DMB cars have an additional window to the rear of the luggage door and are progressively being rebuilt to DM standards.

Following the success of the trials undertaken with the prototype High Speed Train, a production order was placed during 1973 for a total of 196 power cars and a suitable number of passenger trailers. The power car design only differing slightly from the prototype style. The number range allocated being 43002–198.

BREL Crewe Works was awarded the construction contract, where work commenced during late 1974, the first finished product emerging in late 1975 and entering capital stock in February 1976. Production at Crewe then continued with around twelve vehicles usually under construction at the same time until the last car, No. 43198 was completed in August 1982. Simultaneous with power car construction the intermediate coaching vehicles were assembled at BREL Derby Litchurch Lane.

The external appearance of the power cars differed slightly from the prototype, the most noticeable[1] change being the omission of external drawgear, and the inner end driving position was also dispensed with. The prime mover installed was again a Paxman 12RP200L, but the output was set at 2,250hp.

Production HST sets classified 253 emerged in early 1976 being allocated to the Western Region, where from the October timetable 125mph operations commenced on the Paddington–Bristol route, their operating range being progressively increased as more sets came on stream. After the WR had taken delivery of 27 sets the Eastern and Scottish Regions began receiving an allocation for ECML services. Whilst these power cars were identical to earlier built WR members their classification was 254. As time progressed and more power cars were delivered, virtually the entire WR InterCity network was transferred to their operation, as did the East Coast route and later the Midland line from St Pancras to Sheffield and Nottingham. From 1982 sufficient sets were available for the North East–South West services to be introduced to the IC125 network.

After 121 production cars had been delivered the Brush traction electrical equipment was replaced by similar equipment supplied by GEC. This continued for just 30 vehicles when the installation of Brush equipment resumed. Over the subsequent years the GEC equipment has been operationally inferior to the Brush, and the cause of many problems.

During the course of the build it was decided to move the guard's compartment out of the power car, therefore after the building of vehicle No. 43152 minor alterations were incorporated in the power car including the removal of the former guard's window.

When new the first two power cars were painted black and yellow, but the livery was soon changed to blue and yellow, a scheme in which the entire fleet entered service. Following the introduction of various InterCity liveries these have been progressively applied to power cars and trailer stock.

In 1986 it was decided to re-engine four power cars (Nos 43167-170) with Mirrlees MB190 engines. Further re-engining took place in the 1990s with nine vehicles fitted with state-of-the-art Paxman VP185 engines.

To provide 'surrogate' driving vehicles for early East Coast Main Line Mk4 push-pull trains, a batch of eight power cars was modified by the Engineering Development Unit at Derby and Stratford Works for this use. Modified vehicles were fitted with conventional draw gear on their nose end and a TDM remote control feature. Once their use on the East Coast had ceased the cars were transferred to InterCity CrossCountry use and today operate as part of the Virgin Trains fleet.

With the privatisation of the UK railways the IC125 fleet is now operated on First Great Western, Midland Mainline, Virgin Trains and Great North Eastern Railway services; each operator has now repainted its fleet in a distinctive livery, and interiors have generally been redesigned to be more 'user-friendly'. It seems likely that the class will continue to operate for many years as, at the beginning of 2000, very few new main-line passenger train designs were on the drawing board.

Soon after the prototype HST entered service, orders were placed for a production batch, which eventually stretched to 196 power-cars, and several hundred trailer vehicles. Construction of power-cars which were different from the prototype vehicles, was carried out by BREL Crewe. Power-car No. 43057 for set No. 254 001 (the first ER allocated set) is seen just after completion.

BR

The first production HST sets or "InterCity 125s" were delivered to the WR at the beginning of 1976, taking up regular high-speed operation from the following October. On 5th January 1980 set No. 253 004 passes Challow with the 11.45 Paddington–Bristol service.

Colin J. Marsden

Probably the most distinctive of the new liveries to be seen under privatisation is the red of Virgin Trains. A full IC125 rake in VT colours led by power car No. 43155 *City of Aberdeen* passes Langstone Rock, Dawlish, on 28th August 1999 with the 06.05 Summer Saturday Leeds-Newquay express.

Colin J. Marsden

Two liveries for Great Western have been carried since privatisation; at first, a white and green scheme with a Merlin logo was adopted but, following full absorption within FirstGroup, a revision was made with a gold base band and green shading bands to break up the while band effect on the lower body. The two Great Western livery variants are seen here, with the train in the original version and the leading power car No. 43198 in the FirstGroup derivative. The train is seen passing Cockwood Harbour in south Devon.

Colin J. Marsden

Midland Mainline IC125s carry a turquoise, orange and grey livery which looks very impressive when seen in action. A full rake of MML stock led by power car No. 43074 approaches Derby on 22nd May 1997 with the 12.24 Sheffield-St Pancras.

Colin J. Marsden

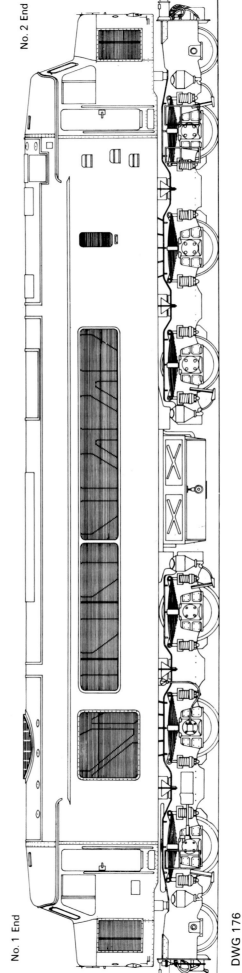

No. 2 End

No. 1 End

DWG 175

No. 2 End

No. 1 End

DWG 176

DWG 175
Class 44 roof detail.

DWG 176
Class 44 side elevation. No. 1 end is at the left.

DWG 177
Class 44 front end layout showing original condition with
steam heat pipe and MU jumpers.

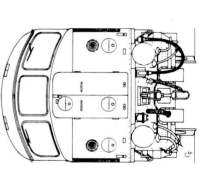

DWG 177

Class 44 (D1–D10) 44001–44010

Class	44	Engine Horsepower	2,300hp
Former Class Codes	D23/1. later 23/1	Power at Rail	1,800hp
Number Range TOPS	44001–44010	Tractive Effort	70,000lb
Former Number Range	D1–D10	Cylinder Bore	11.02in
Built by	BR Derby	Cylinder Stroke	14.17in
Introduced	1959–60	Main Generator Type	Crompton
Wheel Arrangement	1Co-Co1		CG462A1
Weight (As built)	138 tonnes	Aux Generator Type	Crompton
(Modified)	133 tonnes		CAG252A1
Height	12ft 10^1/$_8$in	Number of Traction Motors	6
Width	8ft 10^5/$_8$in	Traction Motor Type	Crompton C171B1
Length	67ft 11in	Gear Ratio	62:17
Min Curve negotiable	5 chains (Note: 1)	Fuel Tank Capacity	840gal
Maximum Speed	90mph	Cooling Water Capacity	346gal
Wheelbase	59ft 8in	Lub Oil Capacity	190gal
Bogie Wheelbase	21ft 6in	Boiler Water Capacity	1,340gal (Note: 2)
Bogie Pivot Centres	32ft 8in	Boiler Fuel Capacity	From main supply
Wheel Diameter (Driving)	3ft 9in		(Note: 2)
(Pony)	3ft		
Brake Type	Vacuum		
Sanding Equipment	Pneumatic		
Heating Type	Steam – Stones OK		
	4625 (Note: 2)		
Route Availability	7		
Multiple Coupling Restriction	Note: 3		
Brake Force	63 tonnes		
Engine Type	Sulzer 12LDA28A		

1. The Minimum Curve figure was reduced to 3^1/$_2$ chains from 1971 following bogie modifications.

2. Steam heat equipment was installed when built, but removed during the early 1960s.

3. When introduced multiple control (blue star) equipment was fitted.

Part of the British Transport Commission's (BTC) home-placed orders for Type 4 main-line traction under the pilot scheme was for these ten machines. Later to become known as the 'Peak' class, subsequent orders for similar locomotives followed to the same body design, but with technical differences.

The pilot scheme order was placed in December 1955 with Derby workshops, planning and tooling being effected over the following two years and construction commencing in mid 1958. Building work of the first locomotive took just under a year, when No. D1 named *Scafell Pike* emerged in April 1959. On works and local testing followed and on 21st April No. D1 was sent to St Pancras for inspection by the BTC and official handing over. For most of the 1959 summer the machine was the subject of extensive road testing, on various parts of the London Midland Region. Progressive delivery of the ten locomotives was completed by February 1960 from when all were allocated at Camden depot in London and deployed on Euston main-line services. Their passenger duties did not last long, as following deliveries of other main-line traction, particularly the subsequent 'Peak' builds, this fleet became displaced

onto freight duties in the Nottinghamshire area, being allocated to Toton, where they remained until their final withdrawal.

The power unit used in this fleet was the Sulzer 12LDA28A, set to produce 2,300hp, the drive from which powered Crompton Parkinson electrical equipment. When constructed electro-pneumatic multiple control equipment was installed, this being subsequently removed after the machines were transferred to freight operation.

When constructed all locomotives were finished in Brunswick green, with a light grey sole-bar band between the cabs. Yellow warning ends were progressively applied during the early 1960s. As locomotives passed through works after mid-1967 BR standard blue livery was applied with full yellow ends.

When the rationalisation of BR's traction fleet took place in the 1970s this fleet's days were numbered, with withdrawals commencing in 1976 and the final locomotive being taken out of service in 1980. The modern traction preservationists managed to save two examples of this pioneering fleet, which are now restored to operational condition.

BR Derby Works produced ten 1Co-Co1 locomotives under the pilot scheme of the Modernisation Plan. These were usually known as the 'Peak' class, as all were named after famous mountain and hill peaks. The livery applied to all ten was Brunswick green with a mid-grey band between the cabs at the base of the body. No. D7 *Ingleborough* being illustrated, the No.1 end is on the left.

BR

In common with other pilot scheme types, the 'Peaks' incorporated a disc train identification system, and the nose ends contained corridor connections. This view clearly shows the front end and buffer beam layout of No. D1 *Scafell Pike*. Note the multiple control equipment was later removed.

Author's Collection

When introduced the ten pilot 'Peak' locomotives were deployed on main line passenger services, but following the introduction of subsequent types, the class was relegated to freight duties. Sporting a yellow panel to its green livery No. D1 *Scafell Pike* is seen on the Midland main line near Leicester.

Author's Collection

After their demise from passenger diagrams the pilot locomotives were reallocated to Toton depot, where all maintenance except major overhauls was undertaken. Sporting its TOPS five figure number No. 44008, *Penyghent* is seen outside Toton depot on 9th June 1979.

Peter Gater

No. 2 End

No. 1 End

DWG 178

No. 2 End

No. 1 End

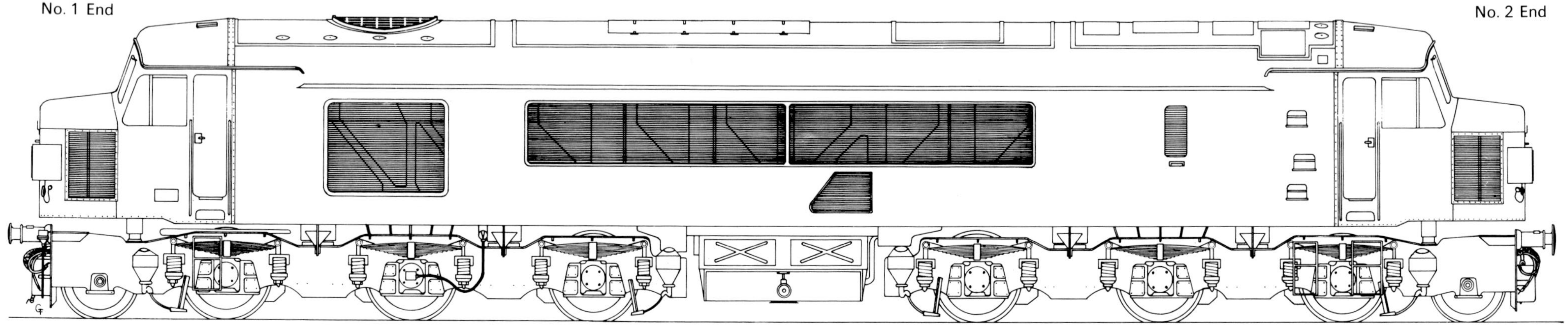

DWG 179

No. 1 End

No. 2 End

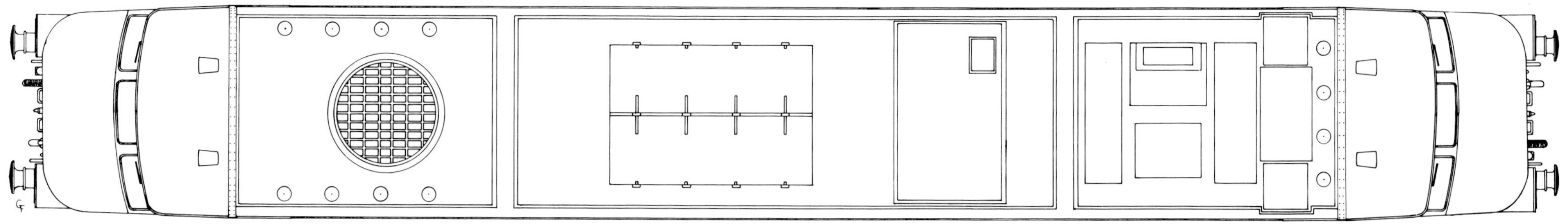

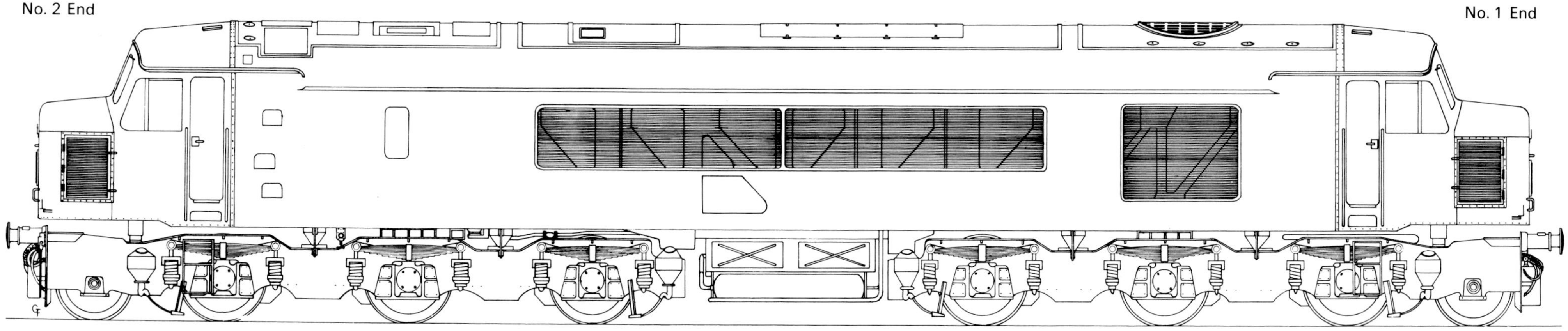

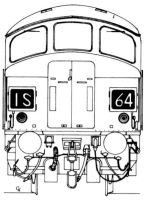
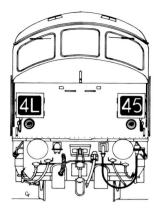
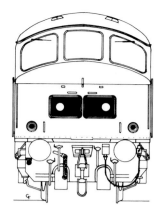

DWG 181

DWG 182

DWG 183

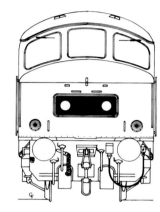
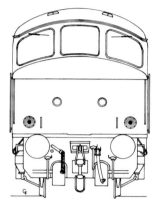

DWG 184

DWG 185

Class 45 (D11–D137) 45001–077/45101–150

DWG 178
Class 45 roof detail as applicable to locomotives Nos D11–D31/D68–D107.

DWG 179
Class 45 side elevation, No. 1 end is at the left showing the split box layout and MU jumpers fitted.

DWG 180
Class 45 side elevation, No. 1 end is at the right, showing the central headcode box as fitted to Nos D32–D67/D108–D137. This drawing shows the ETH equipment.

DWG 181
Class 45 front end showing split route indicator boxes as fitted to Nos D11–D31/D68–D107. The central doors are shown intact as well as the MU jumpers and steam pipes.

DWG 182
Class 45 front end again showing the split box configuration but this time with the central doors sealed.

DWG 183
Class 45 front end showing the centre split box as fitted to Nos D32–D67/D108–D137. Dual braking is depicted as well as the ETH fitment.

DWG 184
Class 45 front end showing the mid-1960s applied solid central 4-character route indicator box, as well as ETH and dual brake fitments.

DWG 185
Class 45 front end layout showing the sealed beam marker lights as installed to all locomotives during the 1980s. This drawing depicts the steam heat fitted type.

Class 45 (D11–D137)
45001–077/45101–150

	45/0	45/1
Class		
Former Class Codes	D25/1, later 25/1	D25/1, later 25/1
Number Range TOPS	45001–45077 (Note: 1)	45101–45150 (Note: 1)
Former Number Range	D11–D137	D11–D137
Built by	BR Derby and Crewe	BR Derby & Crewe
Introduced	1960–62	1973–75
Wheel Arrangement	1Co-Co1	1Co-Co1
Weight (operational)	138 tonnes	135 tonnes
Height	12ft 10^1/8in	12ft 10^1/8in
Width	8ft 10^5/8in	8ft 10^5/8in
Length	67ft 11in	67ft 11in
Min Curve negotiable	5 chains (Note: 4)	5 chains (Note: 4)
Maximum Speed	90mph	90mph
Wheelbase	59ft 8in	59ft 8in
Bogie Wheelbase	21ft 6in	21ft 6in
Bogie Pivot Centres	32ft 8in	32ft 8in
Wheel Diameter (Driving)	3ft 9in	3ft 9in
(Pony)	3ft	3ft
Brake Type	Dual	Dual
Sanding Equipment	Pneumatic	Pneumatic
Heating Type	Steam – Stones OK 4625 (Note: 2)	Electric – Index 66
Route Availability	7	6
Multiple Coupling Restriction	Not multiple fitted (Note: 3)	Not multiple fitted (Note: 3)
Brake Force	63 tonnes	63 tonnes
Engine Type	Sulzer 12LDA28B	Sulzer 12LDA28B
Engine Horsepower	2,500hp	2,500hp
Power at Rail	2,000hp	2,000hp
Tractive Effort	55,000lb	55,000lb
Cylinder Bore	11in	11in
Cylinder Stroke	14in	14in
Main Generator Type	Crompton CG426A1	Crompton CG426A1
Aux Generator Type	Crompton CAG252A1	Crompton CAG252A1
ETS Alternator	Not fitted	Brush BL 100-30 Mk II
Number of Traction Motors	6	6
Traction Motor Type	Crompton C172A1	Crompton C172A1
Gear Ratio	62:17	62:17
Fuel Tank Capacity	840gal	840gal
Cooling Water Capacity	346gal	346gal
Lub Oil Capacity	190gal	190gal
Boiler Water Capacity	1,040gal	Not fitted
Boiler Fuel Capacity	From main supply	Not fitted

1. The renumbering of the Class 45s was carried out as locomotives passed through works for overhaul and does not reflect their original numbers in any way.

2. Steam heat is now extinct, and most members of the fleet had the equipment either removed or isolated in later years.

3. When introduced multiple control equipment was fitted.

4. The minimum curve figure was reduced to 3^1/2 chains from 1971 following bogie manufacturers.

Main detail differences

45/0 Basic locomotive, fitted with steam heat equipment. Route availability 6.

45/1 Electric Train Supply (ETS) fitted locomotive. Route availability 7.

Front end differences

When constructed locomotives Nos D11–D31 and D68–D107 were fitted with a split route indicator box, two digits either side of the central gangway. When locomotives Nos D32–D67 and D108–D137 were built the central gangway was removed and a central route indicator formed of two sections was fitted. Over the years a number of solid central route indicator boxes were fitted, when the locomotives were receiving work's attention.

In more recent years all route indicator boxes have given way to sealed beam headlights.

In 1957 when orders for post pilot scheme locomotives were being placed, the BTC decided to order a batch of 127 similar locomotives to Nos D1–D10 ('Peak') class, but desired a slightly more powerful 'B' series engine able to deliver 2,500hp.

After the order was placed in Spring 1957 Derby Works was awarded the constructional contract for the first 39 examples (Nos D11–D49) while Crewe Works was given the job of building the remainder (Nos D50–D137). Construction commenced at Derby in early 1960, with their first machine being wheeled out on 7th October. Crewe's construction was about on par, their first example emerging on 14th October. Construction from both works continuing at a steady pace until the final locomotive was delivered in July 1963. The external differences from this batch to the pilot order were minimal, the most noticeable being the provision of 4-character route indicator boxes in place of the disc identification system. The alpha/numeric boxes being originally fitted with 2-digits either side of the central nose end door, but after this device was dispensed with a solid central mounted box was fitted. Details of which locomotives had the different front designs can be found below the technical details. When delivered the locomotives were allocated to both the London Midland and Eastern Regions, where operation proved very successful.

In the early 1970s when the majority of new coaching stock was to be heated by the electric system it was decided to install a batch with an electric train heat generator. Conversion work was undertaken by BREL Derby Works from where a total of 50 locomotives were dealt with between 1973 and 1975. At about the same time the numerical classification of locomotives came about which led to steam heat fitted machines being classified as 45/0, and those fitted for electric train heating 45/1.

Until displaced by IC125s the main stamping ground for the fleet was the Midland main line, as well as some North East–South West inter-regional services. After displacement from the Midland the locomotives found use on the Trans-Pennine routes until their gradual decline during the mid 1980s, the final members of the fleet being withdrawn in 1988.

When introduced the locomotives were painted in Brunswick green, again with the grey band at the base of the body between the cabs, yellow warning ends being applied as time progressed. Standard blue livery was applied from 1967.

During the early 1980s the majority of locomotives had their 4-character route indicator boxes removed in favour of sealed beam marker lights, headlights also being fitted from 1985.

Subsequent to the order for the ten Pilot 'Peak' locomotives came a production order for 127 similar locomotives, incorporating a slightly more powerful engine. Looking almost identical to the broad side of No. D7 on page 186, this view shows No. D34, the No. 1 end being on left. Note the minor bodyside louvre alterations between the two types.

Author's Collection

With the introduction of the production locomotives came the fitting of 4-character route indicator boxes, initially fitted both sides of the nose doors, and latterly as a central unit. Sporting green livery with a small yellow warning panel, split centre box No. D54 *The Royal Pioneer Corps* is seen at St Pancras.

Author's Collection

The initial allocation of production BR 'Peak' locomotives was to the London Midland Region, but their subsequent operations have taken them to virtually all corners of the network. No. 45058 departs from Eastleigh yard with a freight bound for Severn Tunnel Junction on 15th April 1985.

Colin J. Marsden

To cater for the increased number of electrically heated vehicles, a batch of Peak (Class 45) locomotives were converted by Derby Works to provide an electric train supply. Split headcode box No. 45127 takes the Plymouth line at Aller Junction on 21st August 1980 with a Leeds – Plymouth working.

Colin J. Marsden

Following the demise of the 4-character reporting number system, BREL Derby, during the course of classified overhauls, removed the route boxes completely and fitted sealed beam marker lights to the nose ends, as shown here on No. 45001 shunting at Loughborough on 18th February 1985.

Colin J. Marsden

With the introduction of high-intensity headlights in the mid 1980s, the majority of Class 45s were so fitted, the light being centrally positioned between the two marker lights. On 14th July 1986 No. 45126 passes Marsden with the 12.03 Liverpool Lime Street – Scarborough.

Colin J. Marsden

On 11th June 1985, Class 45/1 No. 45143 operated the 05.43 Exeter St Davids – Waterloo service, this being the first ever recorded 'Peak' over the LSWR route. The purpose of this unusual occurrence was to re-twin the locomotive with the *5th Royal Inniskilling Dragoon Guards* and unveil an additional line to the nameplate – *1685-1985,* which was carried out at Waterloo prior to departure of the 13.10 service to Exeter. This view shows the up train passing Surbiton.

Colin J. Marsden

The remaining 'Peak' locomotives were withdrawn in 1989, but thankfully a number have been preserved. Class 45/0 No. 45044 is seen powering a rake of vacuum brake fitted ICI wagons at Chinley on 22nd February 1985.

Colin J. Marsden

In 1986 a token ban was imposed on 'Peak' locomotives operating West of Bristol. Whilst this certainly reduced the number of machines visiting the West, sightings of the Class as far west as Devon still occurred in late 1987. In days when 'Peaks' were permitted in the West, on 15th September 1983 No. 45027 traverses the sea wall near Dawlish with an Exeter–Plymouth freight.

Colin J. Marsden

No. 2 End

No. 1 End

DWG 186

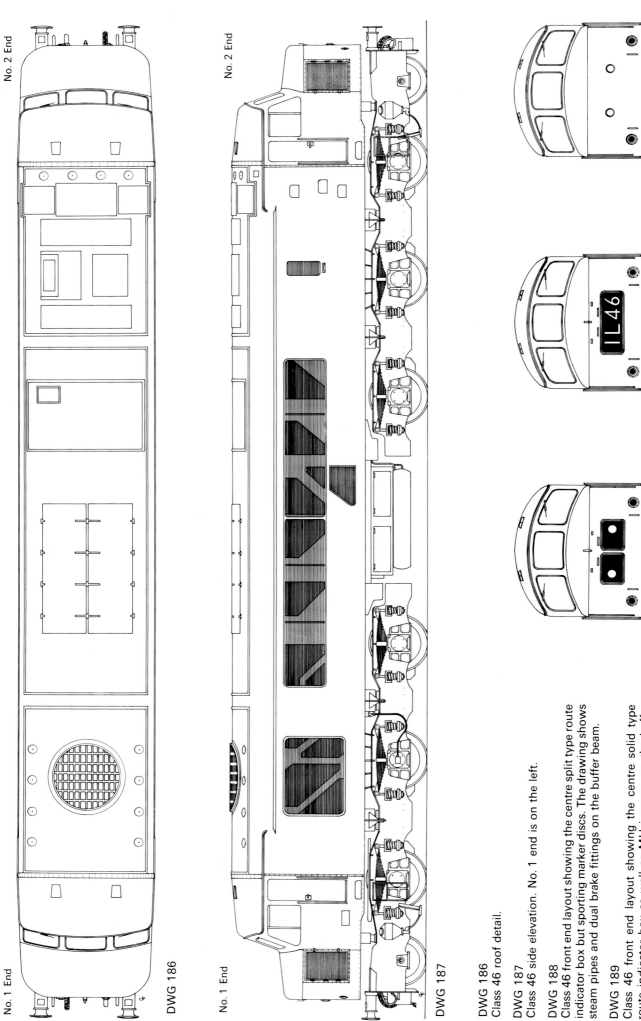

No. 2 End

No. 1 End

DWG 187

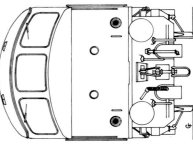

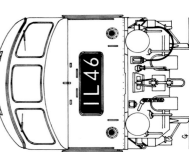

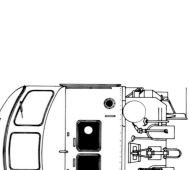
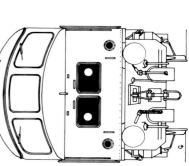

DWG 186
Class 46 roof detail.

DWG 187
Class 46 side elevation. No. 1 end is on the left.

DWG 188
Class 46 front end layout showing the centre split type route indicator box but sporting marker discs. The drawing shows steam pipes and dual brake fittings on the buffer beam.

DWG 189
Class 46 front end layout showing the centre solid type route indicator box as well as MU jumpers on the buffer beam and steam heat pipes.

DWG 190
Class 46 front end layout showing the later fitted marker light frontal indicators.

Class 46 (D138–D193)
46001–46056

Class	46
Former Class Code	25/1A
Number Range TOPS	46001–46056
Former Number Range	D138–D193
Built by	BR Derby
Introduced	1961-63
Wheel Arrangement	1Co-Co1
Weight (operational)	138 tonnes
Height	12ft 10^1/8in
Width	8ft 10^5/8in
Length	67ft 11in
Min Curve negotiable	5 chains (Note: 1)
Maximum Speed	90mph
Wheelbase	59ft 8in
Bogie Wheelbase	21ft 6in
Bogie Pivot Centres	32ft 8in
Wheel Diameter (Driving)	33ft 9in
(Pony)	3 ft
Brake Type	Dual
Sanding Equipment	Pneumatic
Heating Type (D138–D165)	Steam – Stones OK 4625
(D166–D193)	Steam – Spanner Mk 111
Route Availability	7

Multiple Coupling Restriction	Not multiple fitted (Note: 2)
Brake Force	63 tonnes
Engine Type	Sulzer 12LDA28B
Engine Horsepower	2,500hp
Power at Rail	2,000hp
Tractive Effort	55,000lb
Cylinder Bore	11.02in
Cylinder Stroke	14.17in
Main Generator Type	Brush TG 160–60
Aux Generator Type	Brush TAG 69–28
Number of Traction Motors	6
Traction Motor Type	Brush TM 73–68
Gear Ratio	62:19
Fuel Tank Capacity	840gal
Cooling Water Capacity	346gal
Lub Oil Capacity	190gal
Boiler Water Capacity	1,350gal
Boiler Fuel Capacity	From main supply

1. The Minimum Curve figure was reduced to 3^1/2 chains from 1971 following bogie modifications.

2. When built multiple control equipment (blue star) was fitted, but later removed.

In 1959 a further order for 'Peak' locomotives was placed when the BTC ordered 76 locomotives from BR Derby Works, with electrical equipment supplied from Brush. However as time passed only 56 locomotives of the design were constructed, the balance of ordered electrical equipment going into the first 20 Brush type 4 locomotives. Under the numerical classification system this fleet of 'Peaks' became Class 46.

Construction of the first of this class commenced at Derby Works in January 1961, and emerged the following October, being allocated to Derby shed. The external appearance of this fleet was almost identical to the final members of the earlier order (Class 45) except for minor grille and battery box ribbing detail. The delivery of the fleet lasted for 15 months until the last locomotive, No.D193 was introduced. On being released to traffic the first 28 examples were shedded on the Midland at Derby, while the remainder were allocated to the North Eastern at Gateshead, being deployed on both passenger and freight operations. After the withdrawal of diesel-hydraulic traction from the WR, a batch of Class 46s went to the WR, both at Bristol and Laira depots from where they operated very successfully on the abundance of North East – South West inter-regional duties, until displaced by IC125 traction in the early 1980s.

For a number of reasons mainly involving life expired technical equipment and a certain amount of 'non-standard' fittings, the Class 46 fleet was deemed for early withdrawal. The first members being deleted from stock in 1977 and the last member withdrawn in 1984. After withdrawal four locomotives became the property of the Research Division at Derby, No. 46035 became No. 97403 *Ixion* and is still used for test purposes. No. 46045 was retained as spares for *Ixion.* The others, Nos 46009/023 were sent to the division as traction for the British Nuclear Fuels flask collision demonstration at Old Dalby, No. 46009 being used in the collision and No. 46023 being held as spare.

Like the Class 45s, when introduced this fleet was painted in green livery, yellow ends being applied soon after delivery. Blue livery was progressively applied to all examples from late 1967. No. 97403 at Derby is now painted in Research red and blue livery, and should remain in traffic for several years as it is currently involved in experiments relating to adhesion.

The third order for 'Peak' locomotives, constructed by Derby Works, with Brush equipment, started to emerge at the end of 1960. Showing its small yellow warning panel located under the split centre position route indicator box, No. D152 stands at Carlisle with the up "Thames-Clyde Express" on 22nd August 1962.

John Faulkner

With its former route indicator box painted black, and two white cut-outs acting as marker lights, blue liveried No. 46020 reaches the summit of Hemerdon Bank with the 11.14 Plymouth–Manchester service on 26th June 1980. The North East–South West route was synonymous with this class for many years, with members being allocated to both Laira and Gateshead depots.

Colin J. Marsden

In common with their Class 45 sisters the Class 46 'Peaks' all had their route indicator boxes replaced with sealed beam marker lights in the early 1980s, but none however survived to receive high-intensity headlights. On 9th September 1981 No. 46014 passes Dringhouses near York with an additional Birmingham–Newcastle service.

Colin J. Marsden

Only one locomotive of the Class 46 fleet was named. No. D163 (46026) *Leicestershire & Derbyshire Yeomanry,* the plates being fitted immediately after construction in April 1962. This locomotive, which was one of the last to remain in service, was often requested for enthusiasts' specials. Here, on 17th June 1984 the locomotive is seen passing Wimbledon on the SR with the 'Class 46 Tribute' tour.

Colin J. Marsden

Class 47 (D1100–D1999) 47001–47901

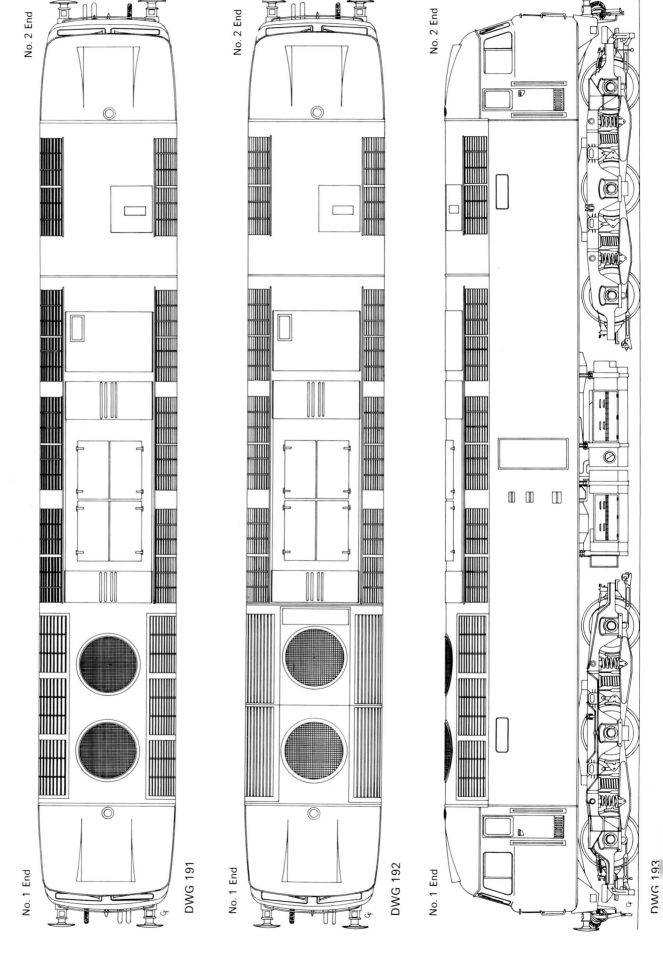

No. 2 End

No. 2 End

No. 2 End

No. 1 End

No. 1 End

No. 1 End

DWG 191

DWG 192

DWG 193

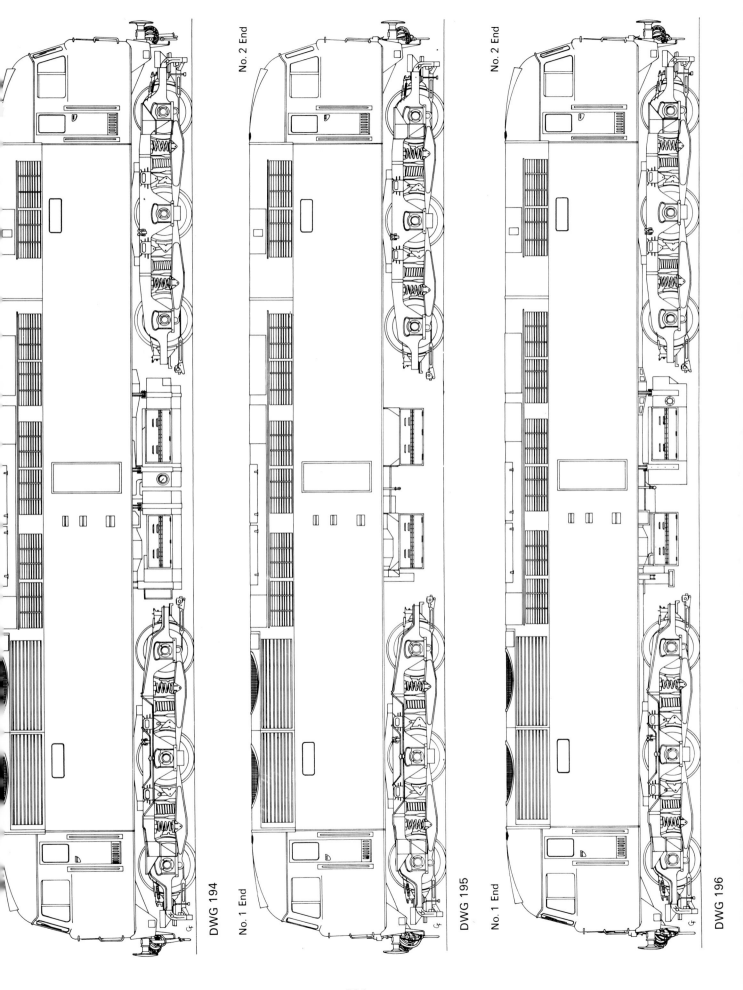

No. 2 End

DWG 194

No. 1 End

No. 2 End

DWG 195

No. 1 End

No. 2 End

DWG 196

No. 2 End

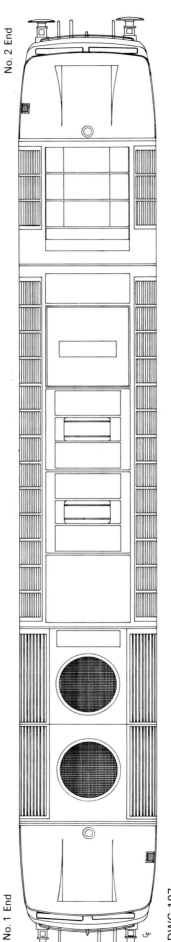

No. 1 End

DWG 197

No. 2 End

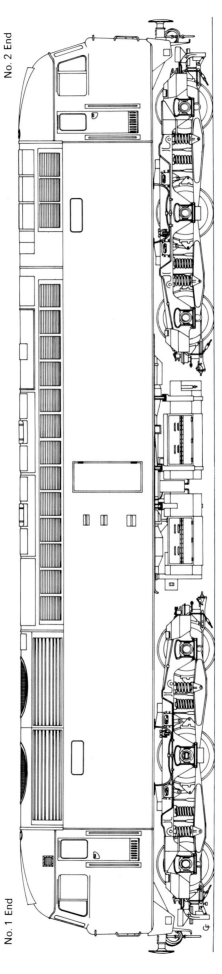

No. 1 End

DWG 198

DWG 199

DWG 191
Class 47 roof details – original type.

DWG 192
Class 47 roof details – standard type.

DWG 193
Class 47 side elevation with original type roof, as applied to early Brush built D15xx examples.

DWG 194
Class 47 side elevation showing standard roof layout, complete with all between-bogie tanks and steam heat equipment.

DWG 195
Class 47 side elevation showing locomotive without boiler water tanks and fitted with electric train heating.

DWG 196
Class 47/7 side elevation.

DWG 197
Class 47/9 roof detail.

DWG 198
Class 47/9 side elevation, showing the No. 1 end at the left.

DWG 199
Class 47/9 front end layout.

DWG 200

DWG 201

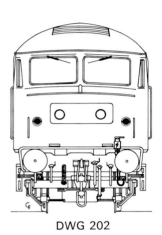

DWG 202

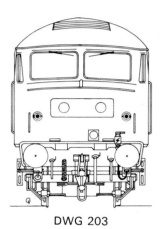

DWG 203

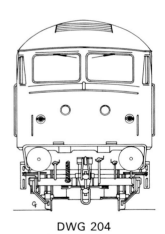

DWG 204

DWG 205

DWG 200
Class 47 front end layout showing original steam heat and dual brake buffer beam configuration.

DWG 201
Class 47/4 front end detail showing the ETH jumper to the right of the right hand buffer, as fitted to the original 20 ETH examples and the majority of 1985/6 rebuilds.

DWG 202
Class 47/4 front end detail showing the ETH jumper to the left of the right hand buffer, as well as steam heat pipe on the buffer beam.

DWG 203
Class 47/4 front end layout showing the headlight position. (The headlight position is standard for all Class 47 types).

DWG 204
Class 47/0 or 47/3 front end layout, without any provision for train heating. The route indicator box shows the 'filled-in' style incorporating sealed beam marker lights.

DWG 205
Class 47/7 front end layout showing additional 'push-pull' (RCH) jumpers on the body end and the original style 'spot' headlight.

Class 47 (D1100-D1111, D1500-D1999) 47001-47981

Class	47/0*	47/3*	47/4	47/6	47/7	47/7	47/9
Former Class Codes	27/2	27/2	27/2				
Number Range TOPS	47001-47299	47301-47381, 47981	47401-47854, 47971-47976, 47798-47799	47671-47677	47701-47717	47721-47793	47901
Former Number Range	D1521-D1998 (Note: 1)	D1782-D1900	Note: 2	47/0 series	Note: 3	47/4 series	D1628, 47601
Built by	BR Crewe & Brush Ltd	BR Crewe & Brush Ltd	BR Crewe & Brush Ltd	BR Crewe & Brush Ltd	BR Crewe & Brush Ltd	BR Crewe & Brush Ltd	BR Crewe
Introduced	1962-67	1964-65	Note: 4	1991	1979-84	1993-95	1979
Wheel Arrangement	Co-Co	Co-Co	Co-Co	Co-Co	Co-Co	Co-Co	Co-Co
Weight (operational)	111-121 tonnes	114 tonnes	120-125 tonnes	122 tonnes	119 tonnes	118 tonnes	117 tonnes
Height	12ft 9⅜in	12ft 9⅜in	12ft 9⅜in	12ft 9⅜in	12ft 9⅜in	12ft 9⅜in	12ft 9⅜in
Width	9ft 2in	9ft 2in	9ft 2in	9ft 2in	9ft 2in	9ft 2in	9ft 2in
Length	63ft 6in	63ft 6in	63ft 6in	63ft 6in	63ft 6in	63ft 6in	63ft 6in
Min Curve negotiable	4 chains	4 chains	4 chains	4 chains	4 chains	4 chains	4 chains
Maximum Speed	75mph (Note: 11)	75mph (Note: 11)	95mph	95mph	95mph	95mph	75mph
Wheelbase	51ft 6in	51ft 6in	51ft 6in	51ft 6in	51ft 6in	51ft 6in	51ft 6in
Bogie Wheelbase	14ft 6in	14ft 6in	14ft 6in	14ft 6in	14ft 6in	14ft 6in	14ft 6in
Bogie Pivot Centres	37ft	37ft	37ft	37ft	37ft	37ft	37ft
Wheel Diameter	3ft 9in	3ft 9in	3ft 9in	3ft 9in	3ft 9in	3ft 9in	3ft 9in
Brake Type	Dual (Note: 8)	Dual (Note: 8)	Dual	Dual	Dual	Dual	Air
Sanding Equipment	Not fitted	Not fitted	Not fitted	Not fitted	Not fitted	Not fitted	Pneumatic
Heating Type	Steam (Note: 5)	Not fitted	Dual or electric - index 66	Electric - index 75	Electric - index 66	Electric - index 66	Not fitted
Route Availability	6	6	6	6	7	6	6
Coupling Restriction	Not applicable*	Not applicable*	Not applicable§	Not applicable	RCH fitted	RCH fitted	Not applicable
Brake Force	60 tonnes	60 tonnes	60 tonnes	60 tonnes	60 tonnes	60 tonnes	60 tonnes
Engine Type	Sulzer 12LDA28C	Sulzer 12LDA28C	Sulzer 12LDA28C	Sulzer 12LDA28C	Sulzer 12LDA28C	Sulzer 12LDA28C	Paxman 12RK3CT
Engine Horsepower	2,580hp (Note 12)	2,580hp (Note 12)	2,580hp (Note 12)	2,580hp (Note 12)	2,580hp (Note 12)	2,580hp (Note 12)	3,300hp
Power at Rail	2,080hp	2,080hp	2,080hp	2,080hp	2,080hp	2,080hp	2,808hp
Tractive Effort	60,000lb	60,000lb	60,000lb	60,000lb	60,000lb	60,000lb	57,325lb
Cylinder Bore	11in	11in	11in	11in	11in	11in	10in
Cylinder Stroke	14in	14in	14in	14in	14in	14in	12in
Main Generator Type	Brush TG160-60 or Brush TG172-50	Brush TG160-60 or Brush TG172-50	Brush TG160-60 or Brush TG172-50	Brush TG160-60 or Brush TG172-50	Brush TG160-60 or Brush TG172-50	Brush TG160-60 or Brush TG172-50	Not fitted
Main Alternator Type	Not fitted	Not fitted	Not fitted	Not fitted	Not fitted	Not fitted	Brush BA1101A
Aux Generator Type	Brush TG69-20 or Brush TG69-28	Brush TG69-20 or Brush TG69-28	Brush TG69-20 or Brush TG69-28	Brush TG69-20 or Brush TG69-28	Brush TG69-20 or Brush TG69-28	Brush TG69-20 or Brush TG69-28	Not fitted
Aux Alternator Type	Not fitted	Not fitted	Not fitted	Not fitted	Not fitted	Not fitted	Brush BAA602A
ETS Generator	Not fitted	Not fitted	Note: 6	Not fitted	Not fitted	Not fitted	Not fitted
ETS Alternator	Not fitted	Not fitted	Note: 7	Not fitted	Brush BL100-30	Brush BL100-30	Not fitted
Number of Traction Motors	6	6	6	6	6	6	6
Traction Motor Type	Brush TM64-68	Brush TM64-68	Brush TM64-68	Brush TM64-68	Brush TM64-68	Brush TM64-68	Brush TM64-68+
Gear Ratio	66:17	66:17	66:17	66:17	66:17	66:17	66:17
Fuel Tank Capacity	720, 970 or 1,221gal	720, 970 or 1,221gal	720 or 1,295gal	720 or 1,295gal	1,295gal	1,295gal	765gal
Cooling Water Capacity	300gal	300gal	300gal	300gal	300gal	300gal	300gal
Boiler Water Capacity	1,250gal	Not fitted	1,250gal if fitted	Not fitted	Not fitted	Not fitted	Not fitted
Lub Oil Capacity	190gal	190gal	190gal	190gal	190gal	190gal	190gal
Boiler Fuel Capacity	From main supply	Not applicable	From main supply	Not applicable	Not applicable	Not applicable	Not applicable

Class 48 (D1702-D1706)

As Class 47/0 except:

Class	48	Built By	Brush Ltd	Power at Rail:	2,090hp
Former Class Code:	26/2	Introduced:	1965	Tractive Effort:	62,000lb
Number Range:	D1702-D1706	Engine Type	Sulzer 12LVA24	Cylinder Bore:	9.44in
		Engine Horsepower:	2,650hp	Cylinder Stroke:	11.02in

* Some locomotives reclassified at Class 47/2 and fitted with green spot multiple control equipment.
§ Some locomotives fitted with RCH jumpers
+ Modified design

1. The Class 47/0 fleet was renumbered from the fleet D1521-D1998 in order at the time of TOPS renumbering in 1974. Since then a number of locomotives have been converted to Electric Train Supply (ETS) and reclassified as Class 47/4.

2. The Class 47/4 fleet of ETS fitted locomotives was renumbered in sequence at the time of TOPS renumbering in 1974, but since then a considerable number of further ETS conversions took place, which has meant that the present numbers do not follow the sequence of the original range.

3. The Class 47/7s were renumbered from Class 47/4s upon conversion.

4. The first purpose built ETS Class 47/4s emerged in 1962. In more recent years conversions of steam heat Class 47/0s have taken place, continuing until 1987.

5. The majority of Class 47/0 members were originally fitted with steam heat, using the Stones OK4610 or Spanner Mk 111 steam generator. All had been removed or isolated by the late 1980s.

6. Brush TH160-16 ETS generators were fitted to numbers 47401-420.

7. Brush BL100-30 ETS alternators were fitted to numbers 47421-665.

8. Some locomotives now have vacuum brakes isolated.

9. Some members of Class 47/4 were fitted with dual steam and electric heat equipment; the steam facility had been removed by the late 1980s.

10. Locomotives Nos 47401-420 have a tractive effort of 55,0001b.

11. The maximum speed of Class 47/0 and 47/3 locomotives was originally 95mph, reduced to 75mph from mid-1987 to increase overhaul periods.

12. When built the available horsepower was 2,750hp, reduced soon after introduction.

Type differences

Class 47/0: This classification includes locomotives numbered in the 471xx and 472xx series, and covers locomotives built with steam heat equipment, although this is now isolated.

Class 47/2: Modified Class 47/0 and 47/3 locomotives fitted with green spot multiple control equipment.

Class 47/3: Locomotives built with no provision for train heating, primarily for freight train operation.

Class 47/4: This classification now includes locomotives in the number ranges 475xx, 476xx and 478xx series which are fitted with electric train supply; some were fitted with dual heat but all steam equipment is now removed.

Class 47/6: Not an official classification — Class 47/4 fitted with phosphorous brake blocks and higher ETS output.

Class 47/7 47701-47717: Class 47/7s were similar to Class 47/4s but were fitted with remote control equipment permitting operation at the remote ends of trains formed with a DBSO coach leading.

Class 47/7 47721-47793: These locomotives are modified Class 47/4s used by RES (now EWS) and fitted with RCH end jumpers and PCV control cab equipment.

Class 47/8: Not an official classification — Class 47/4s fitted with long-range fuel tanks

Class 47/9: The 47/9 classification was held by just one locomotive, which was converted as an active testbed for new equipment used in the Class 58 build; it was previously the sole official member of Class 47/6 as No. 47601, used as a development tool for Class 56 power equipment.

By the late 1950s the British Transport Commission (BTC) was seeking designs for second generation main-line diesel traction in the Type 4 power range. Several prototypes were put forward by various manufacturers but the design eventually adopted came from Brush, and thus the Brush Type 4, which became BR's standard Type 4 diesel, was born.

During February 1961 the BTC placed a contract with Brush to produce 20 Type 4 locomotives. The power unit was to be the Sulzer 12LDA28C developing 2,750hp; electrical equipment was to be provided by Brush and consisted of the over-ordered equipment for the 20 cancelled 'Peak' locomotives. Construction of the first machine commenced at Brush's Loughborough works in January 1962, the finished product emerging in late September. After being handed over to the BTC in a special ceremony, the locomotive, carrying the number D1500, commenced test running on the London Midland and Western Regions. Prior to delivery of the first locomotive, Brush was awarded an order for a further 30. Over the ensuing years many repeat orders were placed for this design of locomotive, the majority being constructed by Brush, but when workshop space was full at Loughborough, the BR works at Crewe assisted, all technical components then being supplied by Brush with only the body and assembly work being undertaken by BR. Construction of the fleet continued uninterrupted until early 1967. In total, 512 locomotives were built, thus forming the largest single class of main-line diesel locomotives in the country.

During the course of the build a number of minor alterations were incorporated. This included the first 20 being fitted from new with dual-heat steam/electric equipment, a batch of 81 given no provision for train heating, and five (Nos D1702-6) built with experimental Sulzer 12LVA24 engines which were later replaced with standard power units.

After several years of satisfactory operation it was decided to derate the Sulzer power units from 2,750hp to 2,580hp, thus improving reliability and extending maintenance schedules, whilst not significantly altering the locomotives' overall performance.

As will be seen from the accompanying drawings and illustrations, a number of different front end styles have been carried on this fleet. When introduced 4-character alpha/numeric panels were installed; this later gave way to a black panel with white cut-outs, which was in turn superseded by fixed beam marker lights of varying styles.

Under the numerical classification scheme this large fleet became Class 47 (the 12LVA24 engined examples being Class 48 until re-engined). Various sub-classes were formed: 47/0 for standard locomotives, 47/2 for green spot multiple control machines, 47/3 for locomotives without provision for train heating and 47/4 for electric or dual heat fitted locomotives — this sub-class has considerably grown in recent years with steam to electric conversions continuing until 1986. The 47/7 classification was devised in 1979 when a batch of electric heat locomotives was converted for push-pull operation on the Edinburgh-Glasgow route; this sub-class increased in the 1990s with conversion of RCH fitted locomotives for Rail Express Systems. The sole official Class 47/6 was a standard locomotive rebuilt in the early 1970s a testbed for projected Class 56 equipment and renumbered 47601; when later rebuilt with Class 58 equipment it was reclassified as Class 47/9 and renumbered 47901.

Today, in much depleted form, the Class 47 fleet still operates throughout the country at the head of both passenger and freight duties, but their once superb reliability has declined with age. During the early 1980s most locomotives passed through BREL Crewe Works and received heavy general overhauls. Withdrawals of life-expired or collision-damaged locomotives commenced in the mid-1980s, and by the end of the 1990s less than half the original build still survive.

Following privatisation of the UK rail industry, Class 47s passed to both major players in the freight business — EWS and Freightliner — as well as the passenger lease companies. In terms of passenger traffic, First Great Western and Virgin Trains are the main users at the end of 1999, with Anglia Railways having just one locomotive on its books.

A number of Class 47s have passed into preservation and private ownership, and several are now authorised for operation on Railtrack metals by one of the growing number of private traction providers.

When built some of the Western allocated locomotives were given cast GWR style nameplates. Naming was resumed in the late 1970s with some 40% of the fleet eventually being given names. After being introduced in two-tone green livery with small yellow panels and subsequently emerging in corporate blue from the late 1960s, a vast number of new liveries have been carried by this class, ranging from 'mock' GWR green to the gaudy Network SouthEast blue, red white and grey. Following BR's sectorisation and eventual privatisation the Class 47 fleet has seen a further diversity of liveries.

The largest fleet of like design diesel locomotives to be constructed was the Brush Type 4, with a total of 512 locomotives being built by Brush of Loughborough and BR Crewe. This general view of the Brush erecting shop shows three locomotives of the original batch under construction.
Brush Ltd

During the course of building, design consultants Wilks & Ashmore devised a revised BR green livery for this fleet, utilising the Brunswick green at top and base of the body separated by a wide band of a lighter green colour. The cab side of No. D1504 is illustrated, clearly showing the livery division. The buffer beam was painted signal red.
Author's Collection

The green livery with small yellow warning panel soon gave way to the full yellow end, shown here on No. D1907, a locomotive introduced in September 1965. In this view we see the machine heading a Gulf oil train from Milford Haven near Caerleon in South Wales on 25th September 1968.

BR

In 1964 when BR were developing their new corporate image, and considering further modernisation, Brush Type 4 No. D1733 was outshopped in 'prototype' blue livery, with small yellow warning panels, on the cab sides was a red panel with the 'new' double arrow logo in white. After introduction the locomotive was used on numerous advertising runs usually hauling the equally new XP64 coaching stock.

Author's Collection

Today the Class 47s are formed into five sub-classes, and operated on all regions of the railway system, at the head of virtually all train consists. Blue liveried No. 47363 pulls away from Acton on 18th February 1987 with the 08.00 Southampton–Ripple Lane freightliner.

Colin J. Marsden

Since the demise of 4-character route indicators this equipment has been plated over on most locomotives with just two white glasses set into the former box to provide marker lights. In recent years high-intensity headlights have also been fitted to all surviving examples, slightly off-set to the driver's side. On 16th November 1984 No. 47108 departs from Nairn with the 12.35 Inverness–Aberdeen.

Colin J. Marsden

The Class 47/3 sub class are locomotives that were constructed without any provision for train heating, and were thus in the winter months confined to freight operation. Sporting its number on the cab roof No. 47374 approaches Peterborough on 12th October 1984 with a southbound freightliner.

Colin J. Marsden

Apart from the handful of dual-heat locomotives, when built the majority of Brush Type 4, later Class 47, locomotives were steam heat fitted. With the gradual increase in electric heat rolling stock, nearly 150 locomotives were adapted to provide an electric train supply. ETH fitted No. 47501 approaches Totnes on 27th June 1980 with the 15.07 Plymouth–Manchester.

Colin J. Marsden

After BR's traction fleet being in something of the doldrums as far as liveries were concerned for many years, the 1980s have seen a wide diversity of colours and schemes. Stratford depot outshopped their No. 47577 *Benjamin Gimbert GC* in a revised blue livery with silver roof, together with large numbers and logo. The locomotive is seen from its No. 1 end inside Stratford depot on 27th February 1987.

Colin J. Marsden

A high proportion of locomotives have now been given the "more yellow" livery. This is usually complemented with large numerals, logo and sometimes a grey painted roof. No. 47457 *Ben Line* is pictured inside the servicing shed at Bounds Green depot. The brightness of the high intensity headlight of the locomotive on the left should be noted.

Colin J. Marsden

With the introduction of sector ownership a number of Class 47s have been repainted in InterCity livery, to match the sector's rolling stock. Two InterCity examples, Nos 47501 and 47612 are posed inside Old Oak Common depot on 9th April 1987, the depot that has predominated in the application of InterCity livery.

Colin J. Marsden

One of the latest liveries to be applied to the Class 47 fleet is that of Freightliner, whose distinctive mid green and yellow colours, offset by the Freightliner name on a body side reflective panel, suits the body style well. No. 47258, an example fitted with green spot multiple control jumpers, is seen at Tilbury Freightliner terminal in company with a Class 57 rebuild.

Colin J. Marsden

In resplendent condition ETH fitted Class 47/4 No. 47585 *County of Cambridgeshire* passes Branston near Burton on Trent on 18th July 1986 with the Royal train conveying HM The Queen from Newcastle upon Tyne. It is usual practice for BR either to provide an immaculate or an ex works locomotive for Royal train duties.

John Tuffs

The Network SouthEast livery, introduced in Summer 1986 to provide an 'image' for the 'new' South East trading area has been applied to a small batch of Class 47/4 locomotives, orginally all being allocated to the ER, but some now being housed on the Western Region. No. 47581 *Great Eastern* is shown from its No. 2 end in this illustration. Note the Stratford cockney sparrow on the side.

Colin J. Marsden

The Class 47 livery changes continued in late 1987, when the first of many, No. 47079 was outshopped in the new Railfreight double grey colours. Sporting a revised front end No. 47079 shows off the new livery at the press launch at Ripple Lane on 15th October 1987. The shed plate of the Cheshire cat indicates that the locomotive is shedded at Crewe.

Colin J. Marsden

No. 2 End

No. 2 End

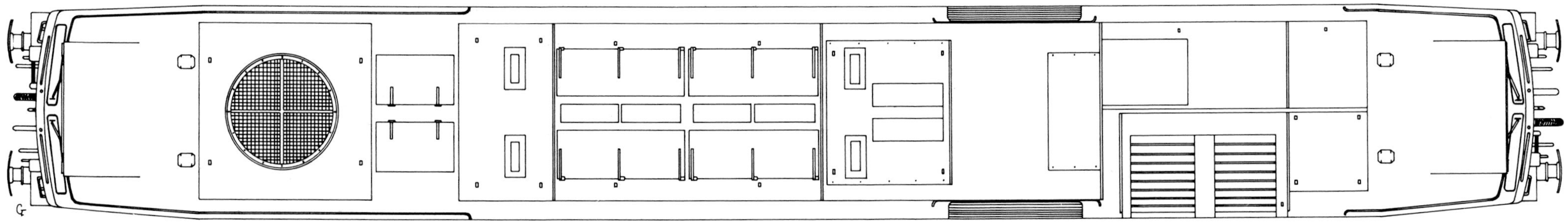

No. 2 End

No. 1 End

No. 1 End

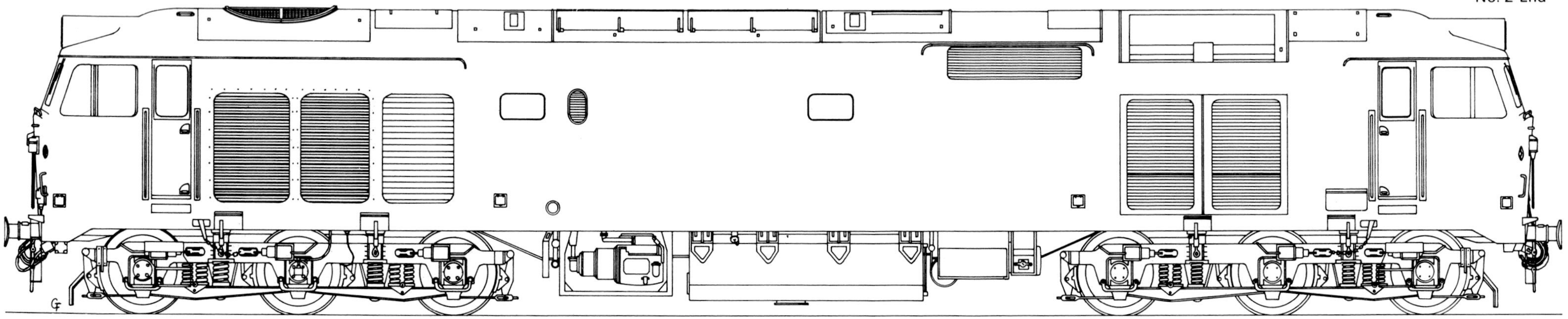

No. 1 End

DWG 206

DWG 207

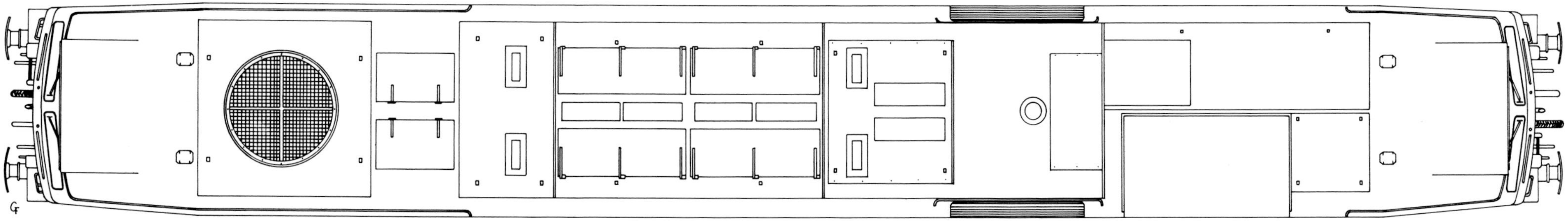

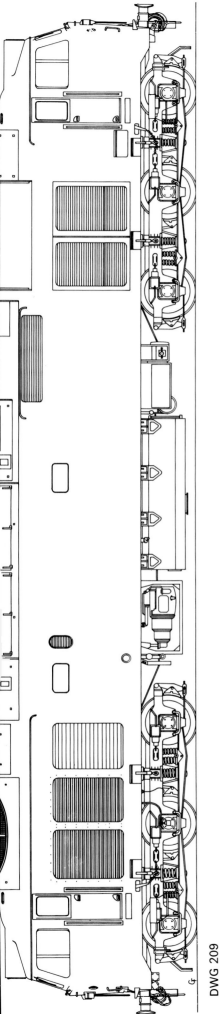

DWG 209

No. 2 End

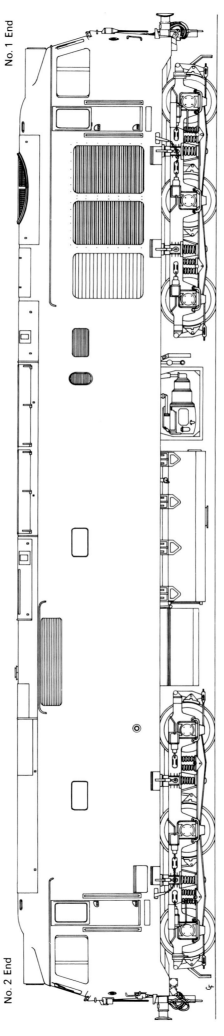

DWG 210

No. 1 End

Class 50 (D400–D449) 50001–50050, 50149

DWG 206
Class 50 roof detail, unrefurbished.

DWG 207
Class 50 side elevation, unrefurbished, No. 1 end to the left.

DWG 208
Class 50 roof detail, refurbished.

DWG 209
Class 50 side elevation, refurbished, No. 1 end to the left.

DWG 210
Class 50 side elevation, refurbished, No. 1 end to the right.

DWG 211
Class 50 front end detail, showing unrefurbished layout.

DWG 212
Class 50 front end detail, showing refurbished layout.

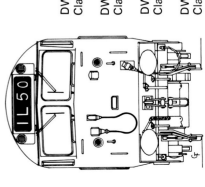

DWG 211

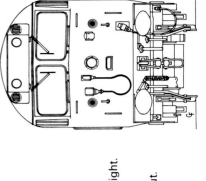

DWG 212

Class 50 (D400-D449)
50001-50050, 50149

Class	50	Route Availability	6
Former Class Codes	27/3	Multiple Coupling Restriction	Orange Square
Number Range TOPS (50/0)	50001-50050	Brake Force	59 tonnes
(50/1)	50149	Engine Type	English Electric
Former Number Range	D400-D449		16CSVT
Built by	EE	Engine Horsepower	2,700hp
Introduced (50/0)	1967-68	Power at Rail	2,070hp
(50/1)	1987	Tractive Effort	48,500lb
Wheel Arrangement	Co-Co	Cylinder Bore	10in
Weight (operational)	117 tonnes	Cylinder Stroke	12in
Height	12ft 10¾in	Main Generator Type	EE840-4B
Width	9ft 1¼in	Aux Generator Type	EE911-5C
Length	68ft 6in	ETS Generator Type	EE915-1B
Min Curve negotiable	4 chains	Number of Traction Motors	6
Maximum Speed (50/0)	100mph	Traction Motor Type	EE538-5A
(50/1)	80mph	Gear Ratio	53:18
Wheelbase	56ft 2in	Fuel Tank Capacity	1,055gal
Bogie Wheelbase	13ft 6in	Cooling Water Capacity	280gal
Bogie Pivot Centres	42ft 8in	Lub Oil Capacity	130gal
Wheel Diameter	3ft 7in		
Brake Type	Dual		
Sanding Equipment	Not fitted (Note: 1)		
Heating Type	Electric – Index 61		

1. Fitted with sanding equipment when built.

This fleet of 50 locomotives constructed by English Electric at Vulcan Foundry were a direct result of information obtained from the prototype locomotive No. DP2. The locomotives were constructed from early 1966 and when completed were initially leased to BR via an English Electric subsidiary company. Under the BR numerical classification system the locomotives became Class 50, and were originally numbered in the D400 series.

The original idea for the construction of these locomotives was to supply BR with a medium output diesel-electric suitable for modern day operating requirements, and benefiting from the many advances in rail traction since previous orders. Unlike many of the earlier designs this fleet came under the watchful eye of the BR design panel who stipulated a number of requirements in terms of shape, output and internal layout.

Construction of the first locomotive began at Vulcan Foundry in February 1966, but it was not completed until September 1967 when it was handed over to BR and commenced a series of test operations. During the course of construction it was announced that the locomotives would remain the property of English Electric, and be leased to BR through a separate company known as English Electric Leasings. This arrangement operated satisfactorily for many years but eventually, after their transfer to the Western Region, BR purchased the locomotives. Delivery of the 50 locomotives took just 14 months to complete and once in traffic were allocated to Crewe depot, from where they were

used on Anglo-Scottish passenger and freight services, often in pairs. When built only locomotives Nos D400 and D401 were fitted with multiple control equipment (orange square), this being subsequently fitted to all locomotives.

From 1972, during the run down of the diesel-hydraulic fleets, the WR started to become the home for the locomotives as the class was gradually displaced from the WCML by the introduction of Electric-Scot services. By the summer of 1976 all 50 locomotives had been transferred to the WR where they had taken over the majority of Paddington–Bristol and West of England services. Unfortunately their performance on the WR was poor and in 1978-79 availability was as low as 50% on most days. The problem was not easy to solve and the only solution was a complete re-build to eliminate some of the sophisticated electronics that were originally installed. A general refurbishment programme for this work was agreed and locomotives passed through BREL Doncaster Works between 1980 and 1983 for this major operation. After return their performance was considerably improved. Today the fleet is allocated to Laira and Old Oak Common, being used on WR internal services, some North East – South-West inter-regional duties and the Waterloo–Exeter route.

After taking up service on the WR, the BR naming scheme was introduced, which led to the names of naval shore establishments and ships being applied to the entire fleet. The liveries of this class have changed quite considerably over the years. When built, all were painted in BR corporate blue with full yellow ends. This remained standard until the summer of 1980 when, following refurbishment, No. 50023 was outshopped in 'revised' livery of blue with wrap-round yellow ends, black window surrounds and grey roof, together with large BR logo and numbers. In February 1984 No. 50007 was selected for renaming as *Sir Edward Elgar,* and was repainted in 'mock' GWR style green livery, complete with cast brass numbers and nameplates. The most significant alteration to Class 50 liveries came in May 1986, when Network SouthEast was launched and locomotives began to appear in that sector's colours.

In July-September 1987 locomotive No. 50049 was converted by Laira depot for use by the Railfreight sector. Its traction motors and bogies were replaced with refurbished Class 37 units, and many other technical alterations made.

Externally the locomotive was repainted into the then new Railfreight 'Speedlink' two-tone grey livery and renumbered 50149, being reclassified as Class 50/1. After the machine's release to traffic a number of problems were encountered and it was eventually returned to standard form.

To provide much-needed spare parts for the fleet, two members (Nos 50006 and 50011) were withdrawn in mid-1987, and several further withdrawals took place during 1987 and 1988. The last examples were finally withdrawn from BR stock in May 1994, but many were saved by enthusiast groups and by the end of 1999 a number had been returned to fully operational condition.

Today, some members of the class have been accepted by Railtrack for main-line running and this number is likely to increase over the next few years.

The first of the English Electric owned Type 4s, later to become Class 50, was completed at Vulcan Foundry in September 1967. In this view the locomotive is seen in the Vulcan yard where finishing touches were being carried out prior to a main line test.

GEC Traction

When constructed only the first two locomotives were fitted with multiple control jumpers, the remaining 48 being wired for the system to which the external jumper heads were later added. Looking strange without its front connections No. D437 is seen at Carlisle on 21st June 1969.

Colin J. Marsden

Once in service on BR the EE Type 4s were deployed on WCML services, in particular between Crewe and Glasgow where their performance was totally satisfactory. Coasting down Shap incline at Greenholme No. D433 heads a Rootes Car Company freightliner on 3rd June 1970.

John Cooper-Smith

When in use on WCML passenger duties the locomotives were often used in pairs, and it was for this that the multiple control jumpers were fitted during 1969-70. Still devoid of its nose end clutter No. D438 passes Wigan North Western with the 09.30 Linwood–Gosford Green car train during April 1969.

L. Riley

After their transfer to the WR the Class 50 fleet became the sole property of BR and were used on a multitude of WR internal services and inter-regional diagrams as well as the Waterloo–Exeter route. No. 50024 passes Talaton on 29th June 1981 with the 09.10 Waterloo–Exeter service.

Colin J. Marsden

Once on the WR the entire Class 50 fleet were given names associated with the Royal Navy. After a short period of WR operation performance was such that refurbishing was undertaken which resulted in a number of external alterations. When No. 50006 *Neptune* was released from Doncaster its new headlight was not installed and a blanking plate covered the front orifice. No. 50006 is seen passing Southcote Junction on 4th March 1980 with the 12.30 Paddington–Paignton service.

Colin J. Marsden

During the course of the Doncaster refurbishment a livery change was adopted, whereby locomotives were finished in 'modified' blue with wrap round yellow ends, black window surrounds, grey roof together with large numbers and logo. No. 50041 *Bulwark* is seen outside Old Oak Common depot on 15th February 1987.

Colin J. Marsden

To many people the revised livery was not aesthetically pleasing on the Class 50s, but it is certainly very striking. Storming towards the Capital near Slough on 22nd April 1987 No. 50008 *Thunderer* heads the 10.00 Penzance–Paddington.

Colin J. Marsden

In February 1984 No. 50007 was repainted by Laira depot into Brunswick green livery and renamed *Sir Edward Elgar*. Whilst the locomotive did and still does look smart in this scheme it is not authentic, as Class 50s were never painted green, while the renaming was very controversial amongst staff and enthusiasts. On 10th March 1984 No. 50007 passes New Malden with the 09.10 Waterloo–Exeter service.

Colin J. Marsden

Following the 1986 launch of Mr Chris Green's 'Network SouthEast' the Class 50s started to emerge in NSE colours. This re-livery of motive power might have been successful if the locomotives had been kept to NSE territory, but with the majority allocated to Laira, their operating area has ranged from Penzance to Birmingham, making something of a farce of 'dedicated' motive power fleets. On 18th April 1987 No. 50037 climbs away from Exeter Central with a Waterloo service.

Colin J. Marsden

Although the Class 50 fleet have always been fitted with snowplough brackets none were carried until 1986. Pulling off the Plymouth line at Aller Junction No. 50018 *Resolution,* complete with 3-piece miniature ploughs heads for Exeter with empty stock from Plymouth on 21st April 1987.

Colin J. Marsden

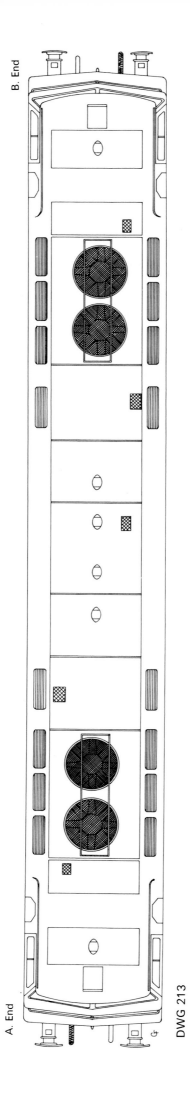

A. End

B. End

DWG 213

A. End

B. End

DWG 214

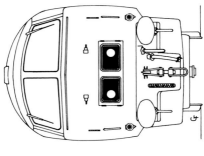

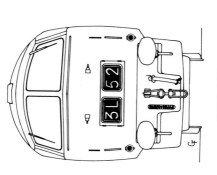

DWG 213
Class 52 roof detail.

DWG 214
Class 52 side elevation.

DWG 215
Class 52 front end in original condition with only vacuum braking.

DWG 216
Class 52 front end showing the dual brake fitment and dots in the route indicator box, as applied solely to locomotive No. D1023.

Class 52 (D1000–D1073)

Class	52	Multiple Coupling Restriction	Not Multiple Fitted
Former Class Codes	D27/1, later 27/1	Brake Force	82 tonnes
Number Range	D1000-D1073	Engine Type	2 x Maybach
Built by	BR Swindon &		MD655
	Crewe	Engine Horsepower (each)	1,350hp
Introduced	1961-64	Total Available Horsepower	2,700hp
Wheel Arrangement	C-C	Power at Rail	2,350hp
Weight (operational)	108 tonnes	Tractive Effort	72,600lb (Note: 2)
Height	12ft 11⁷/₈in	Cylinder Bore	7¹/₄in
Width	9ft	Cylinder Stroke	8¹/₄in
Length	68ft	Transmission Type	Voith L630rU
Min Curve negotiable	4¹/₂ chains	Fuel Tank Capacity	850gal
Maximum Speed	90mph	Cooling Water Capacity	gal
Wheelbase	54ft 8in	Lub Oil Capacity	gal
Bogie Wheelbase	12ft 2in	Boiler Water Capacity	800gal
Bogie Pivot Centres	42ft 6in	Boiler Fuel Supply	From main tank
Wheel Diameter	3ft 7in		
Brake Type	Vacuum (Note: 1)		
Sanding Equipment	Pneumatic		
Route Availability	6		
Heating Type	Steam – Spanner		
	Mk 111		

1. When constructed all locomotives had vacuum brakes. During the late 1960s/early 1970s a number were fitted with dual brake equipment.

2. Tractive effort later reduced to 70,000lb.

To provide additional main-line traction for the Western Region the BTC ordered a total of 74 diesel-hydraulic C-C locomotives during 1959-60. Construction contracts went to BR works at Swindon and Crewe with the number series allocated being D1000–D1073. All locomotives were given names prefixed *Western* and thus this fleet were always known as the 'Westerns'.

After the contracts had been awarded Swindon was first to make a start, and during early 1961 the locomotive could be seen taking shape. Completion of the first example, No. D1000 being during November, the locomotive was then the subject of extensive on works and active testing, entering general service from 20th December. The second of the build, No. D1001 emerged the following February and deliveries were then effected at the rate of about one per month until all Swindon locomotives (Nos D1000–D1029) were in service by mid 1964. Crewe Works construction commenced in early 1962 with their first locomotive, No. D1035 completed the following July. The Crewe machines (Nos D1035–D1073) were delivered at about two locomotives per month until December 1963. Towards the end of the booked Crewe build, Swindon works were still hard at work producing their quota and as the BTC was keen to get the locomotives into service as quickly as possible, the construction of locomotives Nos D1030–D1034 was transferred to Crewe. The entire 74 locomotives were in traffic by July 1964.

The power units used in the 'Westerns' were two Maybach MD650 units, each developing 1,350hp, while the transmissions were Voith L630rU sets. Once in full service the fleet was deployed on Paddington–Swansea, and West of England line duties where their performance was excellent, often availability figures of around 85% being recorded.

When built all locomotives had only vacuum train brake equipment, but as air brakes were being widely introduced, from the mid 1960s dual brake conversions were made to all but a handful of the locomotives. Train heating was provided by a centrally mounted Spanner Mk III boiler.

During the traction rationalisation policy of the late 1960s, when it was announced that diesel-hydraulic traction would be phased out, at the latest by the end of 1973, the 'Westerns' days were numbered. However the Westerns, or Class 52s as they became under the numeric classification system, survived until 27th February 1977 when the final locomotives were withdrawn.

At the time of the introduction of the 'Westerns' the WR were trying out various different livery schemes. The first locomotive, No. D1000 emerged painted in desert sand livery, while No. D1001 emerged in maroon, numbers D1002–04/35 being painted in green. No. D1015 when released in January 1963 was painted in golden ochre livery. After a few years in their various guises the entire fleet was re-painted into maroon with small yellow warning panels, this later giving way to standard blue with full yellow warning ends from late 1967.

The 'Westerns' were probably the most followed diesel class of all time, and after their withdrawal in 1977 no less than seven have been preserved in operational condition.

The 'Western' diesel-hydraulic class, later to become Class 52 under the numerical system were, without doubt the most followed modern traction class of all time. Taken only days after completion at Swindon Works No. D1009 *Western Invader* poses outside Swindon running depot in September 1962, painted in maroon livery with yellow buffer beam.

Colin Caddy

During the early 1960s the 'Western' fleet were adorned with small yellow warning panels, and it is perhaps in this scheme that the machines looked their best. In maroon with small panels No. D1039 *Western King* heads through Sonning Cutting with a Cardiff–Paddington express.

BR

In the final year of the Class 52s service a number of railtours were operated, taking the machines in many cases to pastures new. The final passenger train on BR to be Class 52 hauled was the BR operated "Western Tribute" special headed by Nos D1023 *Western Fusilier* and D1013, *Western Ranger* which is seen here south of Newport heading for Swansea on 26th February 1977.

Peter Gater

After withdrawal a total of seven locomotives were saved from the cutter's torch. No. D1035 illustrated, is the real No. D1010 *Western Campaigner,* which was purchased by Foster Yeoman and stored until 1986 at their Mendip quarry. The locomotive has now been restored to near original condition by the Diesel & Electric Group at Didcot. The machine is seen here looking rather forlorn at Merehead in August 1984.

Colin J. Marsden

No. 2 End

No. 1 End

DWG 217

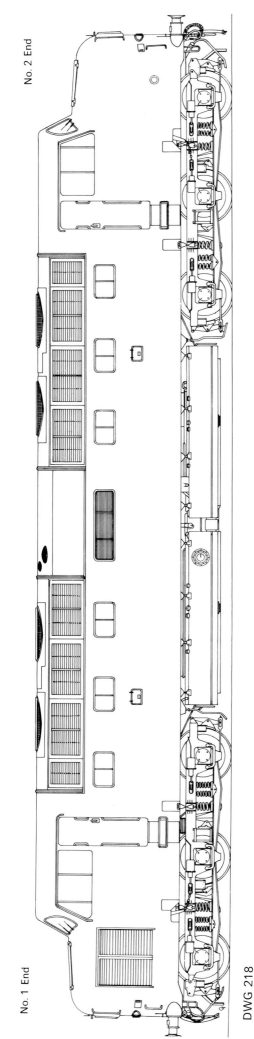

No. 2 End

No. 1 End

DWG 218

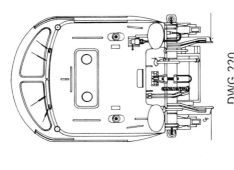

DWG 220

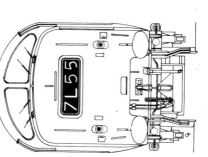

DWG 217
Class 55 roof detail.

DWG 218
Class 55 side elevation, showing original condition.

DWG 219
Class 55 front end layout showing the original configuration of steam heat and vacuum braking, together with an operational route indicator box.

DWG 220
Class 55 front end layout showing the revised fitments for dual heat, dual braking and marker lights in the redundant route indicator box.

Class 55 (D9000–D9021) 55001–55022

Class	55	Multiple Coupling Restriction	Not Fitted
Former Class Codes	D33/1, later 33/3	Brake Force	51 tonnes
Number Range TOPS	55001–55022	Engine Type	2 x Napier D18.25 'Deltic'
Former Number Range	D9000–D9022	Engine Horsepower (total)	3,300hp
Built by	EE Vulcan Foundry	Power at Rail	2,640hp
Introduced	1961-62	Tractive Effort	50,000lb
Wheel Arrangement	Co-Co	Cylinder Bore	7in
Weight (operational)	100 tonnes	Cylinder Stroke	3.45in
Height	12ft 11in	Main Generator Type	2 x EE 829-1A
Width	8ft 9¹/2in	Aux Generator Type	2 x EE 913-1A
Length	69ft 6in	Number of Traction Motors	6
Min Curve negotiable	4 chains	Traction Motor Type	EE 538A
Maximum Speed	100mph	Gear Ratio	59:21
Wheelbase	58ft 6in	Fuel Tank Capacity	826gal
Bogie Wheelbase	13ft 6in	Cooling Water Capacity	33gal
Bogie Pivot Centres	45ft	Lub Oil Capacity	50gal
Wheel Diameter	3ft 7in	Boiler Water Capacity	640gal
Brake Type	Dual (Note: 1)		
Sanding Equipment	Pneumatic		
Route Availability	5		
Heating Type	Dual (Note: 2)		
ETS Index	66		
Boiler Type	Spanner Mk 2		

1. When introduced the locomotives were fitted with vacuum brake equipment, dual brakes being fitted during the 1970s.

2. When built steam heat equipment was fitted, electric train heat equipment being added in the 1970s.

Following the success of the twin-engined 'Deltic' prototype, tried on the ER during the 1950s, the British Transport Commission (BTC) ordered a fleet of 22 production models of a similar design. These were to replace steam traction from the East Coast Main Line (ECML). The number series allocated to this fleet was originally D1000-D1021, but was subsequently amended to D9000-D9021, and under numerical classification the fleet became Class 55.

The order for the 22 production 'Deltic' locomotives was placed with English Electric in March 1958, construction of the machines being then sub-contracted to the Vulcan Foundry in Newton-le-Willows where the first locomotive started to take shape in early 1960. By the spring of 1961 the erecting shop at Vulcan was almost full of 'Deltic' locomotives, with no fewer than twelve under construction at one time. The first two locomotives were completed in January 1961; No. D9001 was the first to be delivered to Doncaster Works for testing, the original locomotive, No. D9000, remaining at Vulcan for special testing. The 22 'Deltic' locomotives were delivered over a period of just 15 months, being allocated after acceptance tests to the Eastern, North Eastern and Scottish Regions. Their duties were mainly confined to King's Cross-North East and Anglo-Scottish passenger services. Once in service their performance was excellent, with speeds of 100mph being quite possible. One drawback with the fleet was that no locomotive-train corridor connection was provided, so the previously non-stop London-Scotland expresses had to be revised for a crew change en route.

After their introduction the BTC decided to name the entire fleet. Locomotives allocated to the Eastern Region were named after racehorses while the North Eastern and Scottish allocations were named after regiments.

Each locomotive was fitted with two Napier D18.25 'Deltic' units, giving a total output of 3,300hp; electrical equipment was provided by English Electric. When constructed the locomotives were fitted with vacuum brake and steam heating equipment, these fitments later being updated to provide dual (vacuum/air) braking and steam/electric heating.

For their entire lives, until ousted by the introduction of IC125s, the 'Deltics' operated crack ECML expresses, as well as some Trans-Pennine services in their later years. Their performance was always excellent, but maintenance costs were very high with frequent visits to Doncaster Works being neceesary for power unit attention.

Following introduction of High Speed Trains on the ECML it was decided to withdraw the entire 'Deltic' fleet; the first casualties were Nos 55001 and 55020 in January 1980; with the remainder following by January 1982. Several of the class have been preserved, No. 55002 (D9002) by the National Railway Museum and five others by private societies. By the end of 1999 four of the fleet had been returned to main-line condition, being authorised to operate on Railtrack metals.

When constructed, the entire fleet was outshopped in two-tone green, yellow panels being added in the early 1960s, and some locomotives operating with full yellow ends on green livery. BR corporate blue was applied from late 1967. In the locomotives' later years the 4-character route indicator boxes were plated over and sealed beam marker-lights installed. In 1999 No. D9016, owned by the Deltic 9000 Fund, was restored to main-line condition at Brush where modern head- and marker lights were fitted; at the same time the locomotive was repainted in the mauve and white livery of its financial sponsor Porterbrook Leasing.

For deployment on the East Coast Main Line, as a replacement for the East Coast steam 'racehorses', a fleet of 22 production 'Deltic' locomotives was built by English Electric in 1960-61. The second of the build, No. D9001 in immaculate ex works condition is illustrated.

GEC Traction

The 'Deltic' fleet which became synonymous with the King's Cross crack expresses, with their 3,300hp available, were able to travel in excess of 100mph if required. In green livery with yellow warning panel No. D9012 *Crepello* is seen at King's Cross with a BR blue/grey exhibition train on 4th April 1966.

GEC Traction

Following the introduction of the standard corporate identity blue the entire 'Deltic' fleet was outshopped in this scheme, without the 'D' prefix to its number, No. 9010 *The King's Own Scottish Borderer* poses outside Haymarket depot.

Colin J. Marsden

Following the introduction of IC125 sets on the East Coast, the 'Deltic' fleet was relegated to secondary duties, firstly within the ER and then on some Trans-Pennine duties, until their final retirement in January 1982. On the outskirts of York No. 55019 *Royal Highland Fusilier* heads for the Yorkshire capital with the 14.04 service from King's Cross on 9th September 1981.

Colin J. Marsden

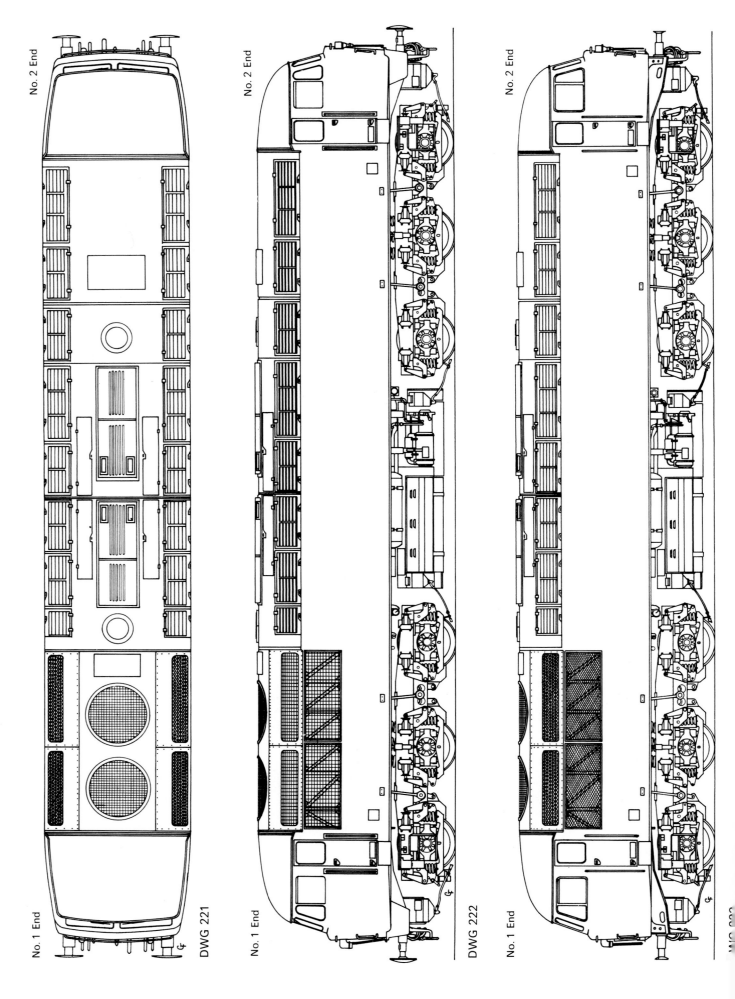

No. 2 End

No. 1 End

DWG 221

No. 2 End

No. 1 End

DWG 222

No. 2 End

No. 1 End

228

DWG 224

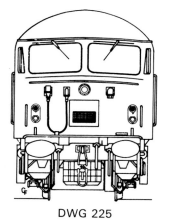

DWG 225

DWG 226

DWG 221
Class 56 roof detail.

DWG 222
Class 56 side elevation, showing the Romanian design (Nos 56001–30). No. 1 end being to the left.

DWG 223
Class 56 side elevation as applicable to BREL built Nos 56055–135, having the large horn box and oval buffers. The No. 1 end is on the left.

DWG 224
Class 56 front end layout showing the original Romanian style as applied to locomotives Nos 56001–30.

DWG 225
Class 56 front end layout as applicable to BREL built locomotives Nos 56031–055.

DWG 226
Class 56 front end layout as applicable to BREL built locomotives Nos 56056–135.

Class 56 56001–56135

Class	56	Engine Horsepower	3,250hp
Number Range TOPS	56001–56135	Power at Rail	2,400hp
Built by	Electroputere in Romania, BREL Doncaster & Crewe	Tractive Effort	61,800lb
		Cylinder Bore	10in
		Cylinder Stroke	12in
Introduced	1976-84	Main Alternator Type	Brush BA1101A
Wheel Arrangement	Co-Co	Aux Alternator Type	Brush BAA602A
Weight (operational)	126 tonnes	Number of Traction Motors	6
Height	13ft	Traction Motor Type	Brush TM73-62
Width	9ft 2in	Gear ratio	63:16
Length	63ft 6in	Fuel Tank Capacity	1,150gal
Min Curve negotiable	4 chains	Cooling Water Capacity	308gal
Maximum Speed	80mph	Lub Oil Capacity	120gal
Wheelbase	47ft 10in		
Bogie Wheelbase	13ft 5^7/8in		
Bogie Pivot Centres	37ft 8in		
Wheel Diameter	3ft 9in		
Brake Type	Air		
Sanding Equipment	Pneumatic		
Heating Type	Not fitted		
Route Availability	7		
Multiple Coupling Restriction	Red Diamond		
Brake Force	60 tonnes		
Engine Type	Ruston-Paxman 16RK3CT		

Major detail differences

No. 56042 is mounted on CP1 bogies.

Nos 56073/74 are fitted with remote control equipment and have roof mounted warning beacons.

Nos 56001–055 were built with small type horn grilles on the front, a lipped buffer beam, and inset marker lights.

Nos 56056–135 were built with a larger horn grille, protruding marker lights, and a body mounted step in place of the lipped buffer beam.

During 1973 when it became apparent that BR would be required to move a considerable amount of coal traffic in the near future, mainly due to the increased cost and general scarcity of oil, BR had something of a dilemma as what to do for traction. Most of their present fleets of locomotives were of the mixed traffic type, and indeed would soon be coming up for either retirement or refurbishing. The answer, not surprisingly, was found in the construction of new locomotives which became Class 56, and following several orders the production run extended to 135 locomotives.

Towards the end of 1974 BR invited tenders for the build from various British and continental traction builders, for the production of 60 Type 5 locomotives. Against much fierce competition from the USA, the Brush Group of Companies succeeded in winning the detail design and build contract, the actual construction contract (for 30 locomotives) was then sub contracted to a Brush subsidiary, Electroputere of Craiova in Romania. The remaining 30 locomotives of the order being constructed by BREL Doncaster. The Romanian built examples were assembled from mainly British components shipped to the Eastern Bloc country. After receipt of the order Electroputere commenced construction of their first locomotive (No. 56001) which was completed and shipped to England via the Zeebrugge–Harwich train ferry in August 1976.

Over the following twelve months all 30 of the overseas build were delivered but were not immediately placed in service as serious problems were identified. This caused many hundreds of hours' work for British depots and works, and the first Romanian locomotives finally entered service around the same time as the earliest British built examples. The first Doncaster built locomotives were constructed during late 1976/early 1977, with No. 56031 being handed over to operators in May 1977. Before it had completed its original order for 30 locomotives BREL was awarded follow-on contracts, and the group eventually produced a total of 105 similar locomotives. Construction at Doncaster continued uninterrupted until January 1983 when No. 56115 was completed, the final 20 locomotives being built at BREL Crewe. Such a change of works during a build was costly, but necessary because Doncaster was commencing the Class 58 contract and required the workshop space and resources. The Crewe built locomotives were all delivered by November 1984.

During the course of the build a number of minor detail differences were incorporated, these are detailed in either the drawings or illustrations.

Once in traffic the original locomotives were allocated to the Eastern and London Midland Regions, where they were deployed on merry-go-round (MGR) and block coal workings. As further machines entered service, the Western Region was allocated a small fleet for use on aggregate duties, as well as the port Talbot Llanwern iron ore diagrams. Performance of the Class 56s has generally been good, with few major problems occurring; WR allocated examples have always had the worst

availability, with those allocated to Toton and other depots seeming to operate continuously without problem!

When constructed, locomotives Nos 56001-083 were outshopped in standard BR blue with full yellow ends, while Nos 56084-135 were finished in 'revised' livery of blue body, wrap-round yellow ends, black window surrounds and grey roof, together with large numbers and logo. After the introduction of a new Railfreight livery of all over grey, several members of the fleet emerged in this scheme. In October 1987, when the new Railfreight sector liveries were launched, No. 56001 was repainted in double grey livery with its sub-sector logo on the side. Upon formation of the 'shadow privatisation' freight companies, two of the three — Transrail and Loadhaul — were allocated Class 56s. Loadhaul applied its distinctive black, orange and yellow livery to a handful of locomotives while Transrail applied its name and 'T' emblem to the triple grey colours. After the sale of the freight businesses to EWS, the now standard maroon and gold livery has been applied to many members of the class.

Withdrawal of the fleet commenced in the early 1990s, with less than half the original build total remaining in traffic by January 2000. The delivery of new Class 66s has taken its toll on the Class 56s. At the time of writing none had entered preservation, but it is expected that several will be saved by the enthusiast movement or purchased by another mainstream operator.

The first diesel locomotives to be delivered new to BR carrying the 5-figure TOPS number series were the purpose built Railfreight Class 56s, introduced from 1977. The first 83 locomotives of the build emerged in standard blue livery as displayed here on No. 56075 at Beighton.

Colin J. Marsden

The initial allocation of the Class 56s was to the Eastern and London Midland Regions for air brake block train operation. However after sufficient locomotives were in service the WR received an allocation. Sporting the revised "more yellow" livery, No. 56048 passes West Ealing on 17th February 1987 with a westbound empty ARC stone train.

Colin J. Marsden

The prototype Class 56, No. 56001 was the first such locomotive to appear in the new Railfreight sector triple grey livery, when it took part in the official press launch at Ripple Lane in October 1987. The logo of blue and yellow cubes on the side was the emblem of the Trainload Construction arm.

Colin J. Marsden

Painted in the distinctive black, orange and yellow Loadhaul livery, No. 56074 passes through Derby Midland station on 22nd May 1997 with a Wolverhampton steel terminal-Lackenby steel service formed of covered telescopic hood wagons.

Colin J. Marsden

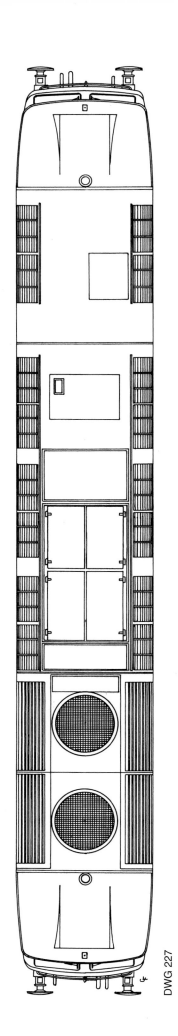

DWG 227

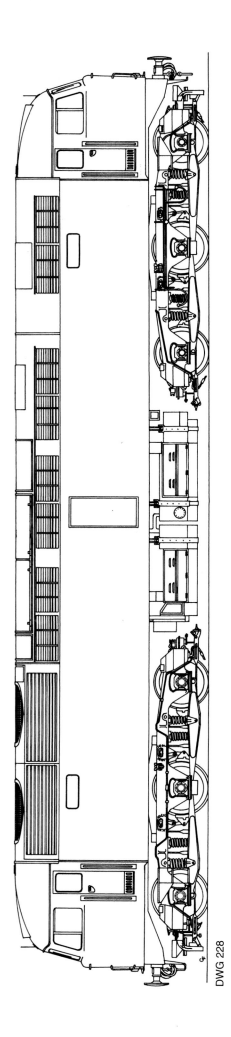

DWG 228

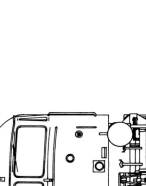

DWG 229

DWG 227
Class 57 roof detail, with No. 1 end on the left.

DWG 228
Class 57 side elevation, with No. 1 end on the left. Note the main difference from a Class 47 is the provision of bogie-mounted sandboxes.

DWG 229
Class 57 front end layout, showing the revised Class 47 buffer beam with only air brake equipment.

Class 57 57001-57012

Class	57	Route Availability	6
Number Range TOPS	57001-57012	Multiple Coupling	Not fitted
Rebuilt by	Brush Traction, Loughborough	Brake Force	68 tonnes
		Engine Type	GM 12-645E3
Introduced	1998-2000	Engine Horsepower	2,500hp
Wheel Arrangement	Co-Co	Power at Rail	1,900hp
Weight (operational)	120 tonnes	Tractive Effort	55,000lb
Height	12ft 10⅜in	Cylinder Bore	9¹⁄₁₆in
Width	9ft 2in	Cylinder Stroke	10in
Length	63ft 6in	Traction Alternator Type	Brush BA1101A
Min Curve negotiable	80m	Aux Alternator Type	Brush BAA602A
Maximum Speed	75mph	Number of Traction Motors	6
Wheelbase	51ft 6in	Traction Motor Type	Brush TM64-68
Bogie Wheelbase	14ft 6in	Gear Ratio	66:17
Bogie Pivot Centres	37ft 0in	Fuel Tank Capacity	1,470gal
Wheel Diameter	3ft 9in	Lub Oil Capacity	190gal
Brake Type	Air	Owner and Operator	Freightliner
Sanding Equipment	Pneumatic		(57007-012 funded by
Heating Type	Not fitted		Porterbrook)

One of the most surprising 'new' class introductions in recent years has been the 12-strong Class 57 fleet. These locomotivess are totally-rebuilt Class 47s, now installed with reconditioned General Motors 645 power units, coupled to reworked ex-Class 56 alternator groups.

The rebuilding work, undertaken by Brush of Loughborough, was a direct contract by Freightliner Ltd, as part of that company's post-privatisation drive radically to improve its traction fleet. As part of the rebuilding work, new cab interiors have been included, based on the principal of removing all redundant equipment, including the now-obsolete vacuum brake system. The positions of cab equipment were also revised to be more user-friendly, while at the same time new panelling and a behind-seat bulkhead were installed to minimise cab draughts.

The rebuild contract, placed for six locomotives in 1997 and a further six in 1999, saw Freightliner and Brush engineers work in partnership on the re-engining project. At an early stage it was decided, on grounds of economy, not to buy new engines but follow the American principle of engine remanufacture to obtain the required power unit. The chosen engines were sourced from VMV in Paducah, Kentucky, one of the longest-established engine rebuild companies in the world. The engines, fully bench-tested, were crated and shipped to Loughborough for the Brush-rebuilt alternator group to be fitted. The contract also called for the full rebuild of the original Brush bogies, which have now been fitted with sanding equipment.

Although the 2,500hp GM645 engine is technically a Type 4, the operating characteristics give it an output of Type 5, and thus the locomotives' deployment has replaced pairs of multiple-fitted Class 47s on some of the heaviest duties.

The first Class 57 to be completed was rolled out of the Brush works on 21st July 1998 and launched the new Freightliner livery of two-tone green, with large Freightliner name on the bodyside, mounted on a reflective ground. Yellow ends have been retained. All six of the first batch, the last of which entered traffic in spring 1999, have been named in a *Freightliner*-prefixed series, with the names selected by company staff. The first of the second batch of six emerged from Brush in October 1999.

The locomotives are allocated to Crewe Basford Hall, and are usually deployed on the Leeds, Southampton and Tilbury routes. The rebuilding work should give a further 15-20 years' operational life.

In autumn 1999 talks were progressing between Freightliner and Brush over the conversion of 12 locomotives fitted with Electric Train Supply for passenger work.

The first of the Class 57 conversions, No. 57001, rebuilt by Brush of Loughborough from Class 47 No. 47356, stands in the works yard at Brush on 21st July 1998, during the official handover of the first class member to its owner, Freightliner. This was also the first locomotive to sport the new Freightliner green and yellow livery.

Colin J. Marsden

With the first Freightliner-liveried Class 47, No. 47193, on the left, the first of the Class 57s, No. 57001, shunts off-shed at Ipswich in spring 1999. Ipswich depot, serving the major Freightliner terminal at Felixstowe, is a stronghold for the class.

Colin J. Marsden

The second of the conversions, No. 57002, modified from No. 47322, is seen passing Oxford on 10th June 1999 with the 03.51 Leeds-Southampton liner train service.

Darren Ford

The eighth of the Class 57 conversions made an historic visit to Earls Court Exhibition Centre on 8th-10th December 1999 to take part in the annual Intermodal exhibition, where it was a major part of the Freightliner stand. It is seen in the main hall mounted on its own section of track

Colin J. Marsden

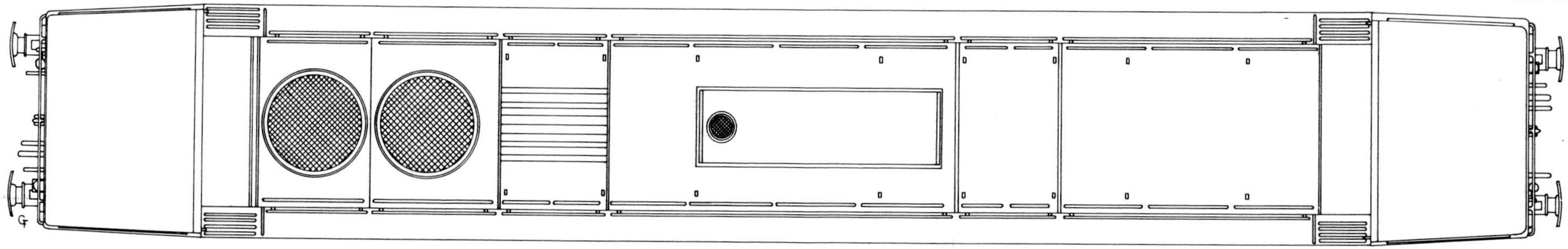

No. 2 End

No. 1 End

DWG 227

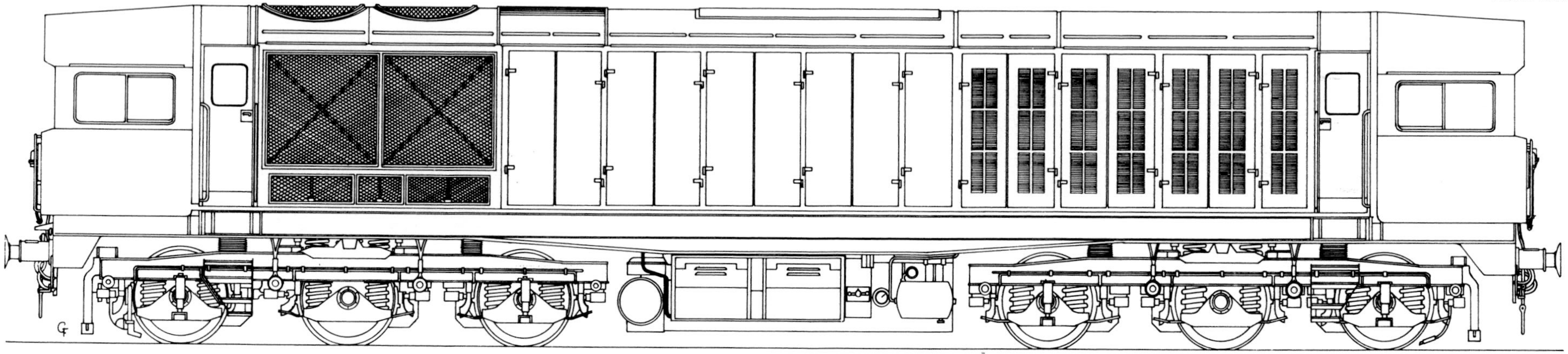

No. 2 End

No. 1 End

DWG 228

No. 2 End

No. 1 End

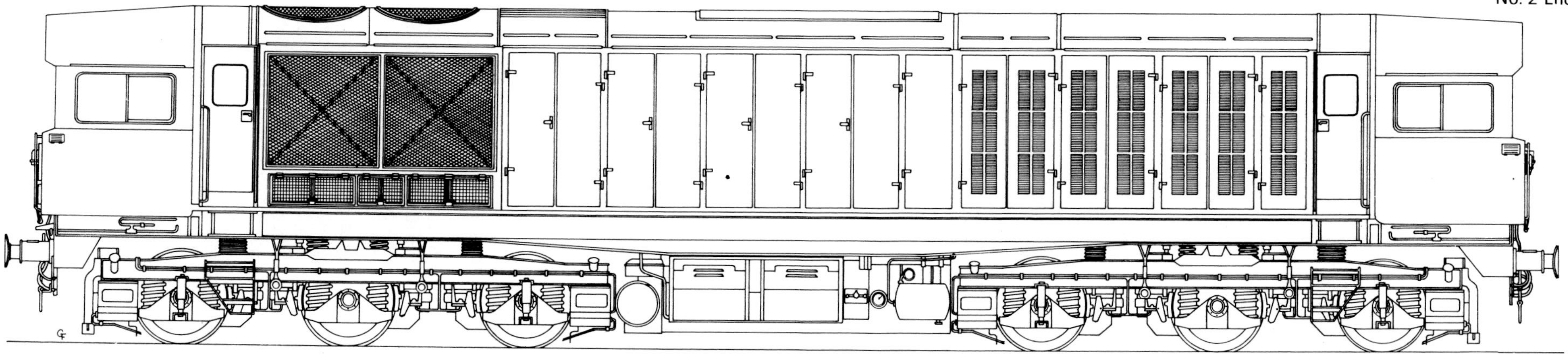

DWG 229

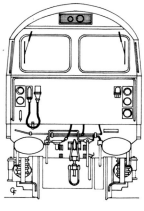

DWG 230

DWG 227
Class 58 roof details.

DWG 228
Class 58 side elevation, as applicable to Nos 58001–013.

DWG 229
Class 58 side elevation, as applicable to locomotives Nos 58036–050, fitted with compartment door handles, cab vent panel, and modified sandboxes.

DWG 230
Class 58 front end detail.

Class 58 58001–58050

Class	58	Multiple Coupling Restriction	Red Diamond
Number Range TOPS	58001–58050	Brake Force	62 tonnes
Built by	BREL Doncaster	Engine Type	Ruston-Paxman
Introduced	1983-87		12RK3ACT
Wheel Arrangement	Co-Co	Engine Horsepower	3,300hp
Weight (operational)	130 tonnes	Power at Rail	2,387hp
Height	12ft 10in	Tractive Effort	61,800lb
Width	8ft 10^1/$_2$in	Cylinder Bore	10in
Length	62ft 9^1/$_2$in	Cylinder Stroke	12in
Min Curve negotiable	4 chains	Main Alternator Type	Brush BA1101B
Maximum Speed	80mph	Aux Alternator Type	Brush BAA602B
Wheelbase	48ft 9in	Number of Traction Motors	6
Bogie Wheelbase	13ft 8^1/$_2$in	Traction Motor Type	Brush TM73-62
Bogie Pivot Centres	35ft 5^1/$_2$in	Gear Ratio	63:16
Wheel Diameter	3ft 8in	Fuel Tank Capacity	985gal
Brake Type	Air	Cooling Water Capacity	264gal
Sanding Equipment	Pneumatic	Lub Oil Capacity	110gal
Heating Type	Not fitted		
Route Availability	7		

No. 58050 is fitted with 'Sepex' traction equipment.

During the course of the Class 56 build, BR was keen to develop a new low-cost, purpose-built modular freight locomotive, which whilst fulfilling a BR requirement would hopefully take BR into the export locomotive market. During 1977 the BR design office at Derby prepared a report on the feasibility of a new generation freight locomotive, three main objectives being set: 1. Economy in design; 2. Ease, economy and minimum maintenance; 3. Export potential. In September 1979 it was decided to go ahead with the construction of a fleet of three locomotives, classified by BR as Class 58.

After the build contract for the three locomotives had been placed with BREL in September 1979, Doncaster Works was chosen for the construction work. From late 1979 through to early 1981 Doncaster Works was tooled for its new operation. The first stages of producing the modular locomotive came in the spring of 1981 when the underframe joists were cut for the first locomotive. During construction of the first three machines a subsequent contract was placed which took the production run to 35, and whilst this was being fulfilled a further order took the fleet to 50. Delivery of the first Class 58 was made to the Railfreight sector on 9th December 1982, but due to prolonged testing the locomotive did not 'take to the road' until the following year. Delivery of the fleet was a protracted affair, mainly due to late deliveries of components from outside manufacturers, with the last locomotive not being fully assembled until early 1987.

From new, the Class 58 fleet has always been allocated to Toton depot from where these locomtives have operated a variety of freight services; originally they were restricted to MGR coal traffic but in more recent years general freight flows have been the norm. Performance on the whole has been good, but the fleet has always had a tendency to suffer adhesion problems.

When locomotive No. 58050 was completed in early 1987 it was fitted with a 'Sepex' control system, installed by Brush, in an attempt to improve wheel-rail adhesion. However, many problems were encountered with this equipment and it was some nine months before the locomotive operated a revenue earning train.

Regrettably, BR's export plans for the class never came to fruition, with many foreign administrations making the trip to Doncaster to see the locomotives under construction and at work but no orders being forthcoming; following assembly of No. 58050, the works jigs were broken up.

When built, all locomotives were finished in Railfreight grey livery, with wrap-round yellow ends and a red frame. With the introduction of Railfreight sector liveries from October 1987 No. 58050 was outshopped by Stratford in the new triple grey scheme and bearing the Railfreight coal sub-sector embellishment on the side. Eventually the majority of the fleet were repainted in triple grey livery. Upon shadow privatisation of the freight business, Mainline Freight became the owner of the 50 strong fleet; a small number of locomotives were subsequently painted in the operator's blue livery, while others had a Mainline Freight decal applied to the triple grey bodywork. With full privatisation and the takeover of the freight business by EWS, maroon and gold has been the standard livery for repainted locomotives since mid-1997.

Until recently it was assumed that the Class 58 fleet would be 'safe' well into the third millennium; however, in 1999 a number of locos were placed in long-term store, thus providing spare parts for the remainder of the fleet. Full withdrawal of some class members is expected in 2000.

The modular constructed Class 58s designed and built by BR/BREL started to appear from BREL Doncaster in December 1982. The locomotives were a complete break from previous types in having the 'between cab' section narrower than full width. Many weeks prior to its official handing over No. 58001 poses in the Works yard, the No. 1 end being on the right.

Colin J. Marsden

The Class 58 assembly programme took over four years to complete. Whilst all locomotives were of basically the same physical appearance a number of technical modifications were incorporated in later examples. On 4th February 1986 No. 58036 poses outside the Doncaster Works weigh shop prior to entering service.

Colin J. Marsden

The entire Class 58 fleet are allocated to Toton depot in Nottinghamshire from where they are displayed mainly on the Railfreight coal sub-sectors traffic. Approaching Toton from the north No. 58015 heads a Bentinck–Ratcliffe 'trip' working on 5th November 1986.

Colin J. Marsden

Sepex fitted No. 58050 *Toton Traction Depot* was selected for repainting into sub-sector livery of double grey for the Ripple Lane press launch on 15th October 1987. The locomotive, with its non-standard 'Railfreight' legend on the front, together with the coal sub-sector and Toton depot crests is illustrated on the day of the livery launch.

Colin J. Marsden

Passing its place of birth, Mainline Freight blue liveried No. 58046 runs through Doncaster station on 25th June 1996 with a southbound loaded MGR train bound for Doncaster Decoy yard.

Colin J. Marsden

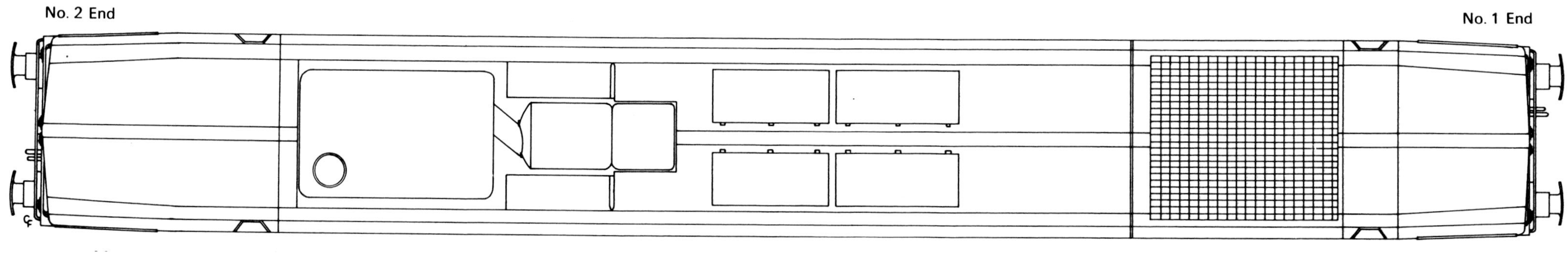

No. 2 End

DWG 234

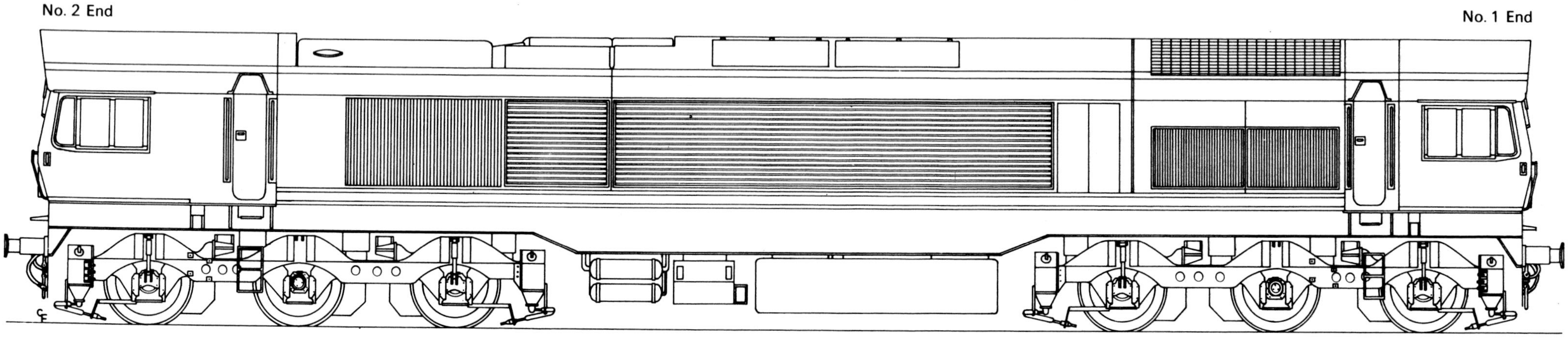

DWG235

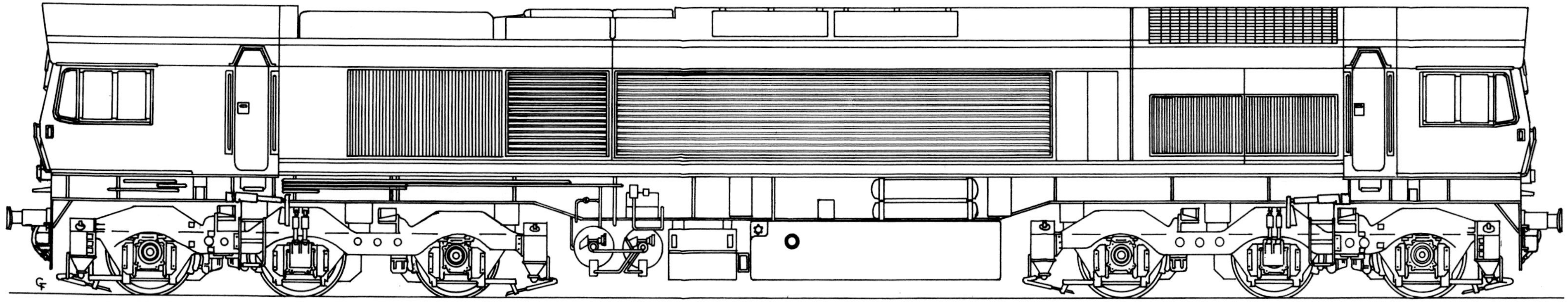

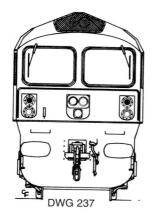
DWG 237

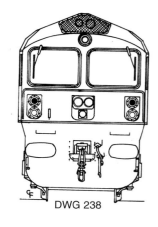
DWG 238

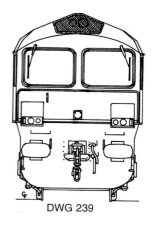
DWG 239

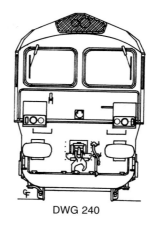
DWG 240

DWG 234
Class 59 roof detail.

DWG235
Class 59/0 side elevation; the No. 1 end is on the right.

DWG236
Side elevation of National Power/EWS Class 59/2, with No.1 end on the right.

DWG 237
Class 59/0 front end detail.

DWG 238
Class 59/0 front end variation, showing the additional marker light fitted above the cab windows of No. 59003 for operation in Germany.

DWG 239
Class 59/1 front end layout.

DWG 240
Class 59/2 front end layout, showing the buck-eye auto-coupler in the lowered position.

Class 59 59001-59206

Class		59
Model		JT26SS-55
Number Range TOPS	(59/0)	59001-59005
	(59/1)	59101-59104
	(59/2)	59201-59206
Built by	(59/0)	General Motors ElectroMotive Division LaGrange, Illinois, USA
	(59/1, 59/2)	General Motors Diesel Division London, Ontario, Canada
Introduced		1986-95
Wheel Arrangement		Co-Co
Weight (operational)		126 tonnes
Height		12ft 10in
Width		8ft 8¼in
Length		70ft 0½in
Min Curve negotiable		4 chains
Maximum Speed	(59/0, 59/1)	60mph
	(59/2)	75mph
Wheelbase		56ft 9in
Bogie Wheelbase		13ft 7in
Bogie Pivot Centres		43ft 6in
Wheel Diameter		3ft 6in

Brake Type		Air
Sanding Equipment		Pneumatic
Heating Type		Not fitted
Route Availability		7
Multiple Coupling		AAR type, Class 59, 66, 67
Brake Force		69 tonnes
Engine Type		EMD 16-645E3C
Engine Horsepower		3,300hp
Power at Rail		2,533hp
Tractive Effort		122,000lb
Cylinder Bore		9¹⁄₁₆in
Cylinder Stroke		10in
Traction Alternator Type		EMD AR11 MLD D14A
Bogie Type		HT-C
Number of Traction Motors		6
Traction Motor Type		EMD D77B
Gear Ratio		62:15
Fuel Tank Capacity		1,000gal
Cooling Water Capacity		212gal
Lub Oil Capacity		202gal
Owner and Operator	(59/0)	Foster Yeoman
	(59/1)	ARC/Hanson
	(59/2)	National Power, then EWS

The most radical change in British locomotive-operating policy came in the mid-1980s when, following considerable negotiation between the aggregate company Foster Yeoman and the BRB, agreement was reached for the company to operate a fleet of its own privately-owned locomotives on BR tracks. These were to head the firm's aggregate trains from its quarry complex at Merehead in the Mendip Hills, Somerset.

While BR was prepared to have locomotives idle for long periods around the network, a private company was not; an availability figure of 95% was required. As no British builder was able to guarantee this figure, Foster Yeoman looked to the USA, especially General Motors (GM), which had already built a yard switcher for the company. After much negotiation between Foster Yeoman, GM and the BRB, a deal was struck in November 1984, with GM being given the contract to design and build four locomotives. Construction was effected at the LaGrange Works in Illinois during 1985, with the

locomotives completed by mid-December. Shipment to England was made in January 1986 on board the 1,500-ton ship MV *Fairlift,* which docked at Southampton on 21st January. Three days later, after the locomotives had been offloaded, they were hauled as a 'train' from Southampton Docks to Merehead Quarry, where commissioning was carried out.

On 27th January the locomotives were hauled to the Railway Technical Centre, Derby, for weighing and final commissioning; they entered traffic in mid-February. Such was the success of the private-owner traction that a fifth locomotive was quickly ordered, and was delivered in June 1989.

Once the success of the Foster Yeoman operation was noted, other major private freight operators looked at owning their own traction, the next to make the change being ARC, also based in the Mendips and involved in aggregate. As the FY Class 59 design was now available from the General

241

Motors portfolio, ARC purchased four locomotives, classified Class 59/1 and numbered 59101-104. By the time these were ordered, General Motors had transferred all new locomotive construction to its massive Diesel Division plant at London, Ontario, Canada. The ARC locomotives, finished in mustard yellow and grey, were shipped to England in October 1990 and allocated to a new purpose-built facility at Whatley in Somerset.

The third and final private operator to buy the Class 59 design was National Power, which in 1991 ordered one locomotive of an identical design to the ARC Class 59/1s, this being delivered in 1993 for powering limestone traffic between Peak Forest and Drax Power Station. National Power soon found huge financial benefits from owning its own traction, and a further five locomotives were ordered in 1994 and delivered in 1995 for hauling high-capacity coal trains in the Yorkshire area.

The Somerset-based Foster Yeoman/ARC Class 59s have continued working their original traffic flows, but are today operated under the Mendip Rail banner, a company formed by the two businesses to transport aggregate. In early 1999, the ARC name gave way to Hanson, the firm's parent company. Some of the Foster Yeoman locomotives now sport a revised blue/silver livery, while the original ARC colours were slightly revised in 1998 to match the Yeoman paint style,

but retaining ARC yellow. Following the change of name, a new Hanson livery of blue, silver and brick red has been introduced.

The six locomotives owned by National Power were originally finished in the distinctive NP mid-blue with NP branding. They operated on their intended traffic flow for only a short time, as in April 1998 all six were sold to the English, Welsh & Scottish Railway (EWS), which repainted the fleet in its standard maroon and gold livery. The locomotives now perform a far wider range of duties, which takes them to many other parts of the country.

The performance of the Class 59s has been superb, with virtually no on-line failures being recorded. The power unit installed in all sub-types is a GM EMD 16-645E3C unit developing 3,300hp, electrical equipment also being provided by EMD.

In mid-1997 Foster Yeoman No. 59003 was sent to Germany to operate for a new company jointly owned by Foster Yeoman and DB Cargo, hauling high-capacity aggregate trains to various major construction sites. Before travelling to Germany via the Channel Tunnel, the locomotive was repainted at Eastleigh Works into a blue and red livery, receiving a number of technical modifications, including a high-level headlight above the cab windows to conform with European operating standards.

Shown from its No. 1 end, Foster Yeoman No. 59004, painted in the original silver and blue livery, stands outside Merehead depot on 25th June 1989. By the time this illustration was taken, a radio telephone (NRN) box had been fitted on the cab roof.

Colin J. Marsden

The all-over silver Foster Yeoman livery was changed, from 1998, to a basically Yeoman blue body offset by a silver base-band and roof. At the same time, a minimal-sized yellow end was applied, just between the buffer beam and base body line. No. 59005 is seen in the revised colours at Merehead in June 1998.

Colin J. Marsden

Prior to transfer to Germany to operate on the joint Yeoman/DB Cargo freight initiative, No. 59003 was outshopped in a new red and blue colour scheme by Wessex Traincare, Eastleigh. Sporting a roof headlight to meet European operating standards, no yellow end and a number of other technical modifications, No. 59003 *Yeoman Highlander* is seen at Merehead.

Colin J. Marsden

The second of the ARC locomptives, No. 59102, travels between Ealing Broadway and West Ealing on 24th June 1992 with empty low track force hoppers from Acton Yard to Southall Yard. The locomotive's silencer or No. 2 end is nearest the camera.

Colin J. Marsden

One of the classic locations to see a Class 59 powering a stone train is Fairwood Junction, where the Westbury station/yard and Westbury avoiding line join west of Westbury station. On 17th September 1991 No. 59101, then still unnamed, departs from Westbury Yard bound for Whatley Quarry with a rake of high-capacity ARC box wagons.

Colin J. Marsden

The six National Power Class 59/2s were very similar in body styling to the ARC Class 59/1s; the most noticeable difference was the provision of buck-eye couplings, now being removed. The doyen of the sub-class, No. 59201, is seen in National Power blue passing Wellingborough on 14th March 1994 on a commissioning special from Cricklewood to Derby RTC.

Colin J. Marsden

Following the transfer of the entire National Power rail operation to EWS in April 1998, all six Class 59/2 locomotives were repainted in the EWS house colours of maroon and gold by RFS, Doncaster. The first to be completed, No. 59201, is seen from its No. 1 end.

Colin J. Marsden

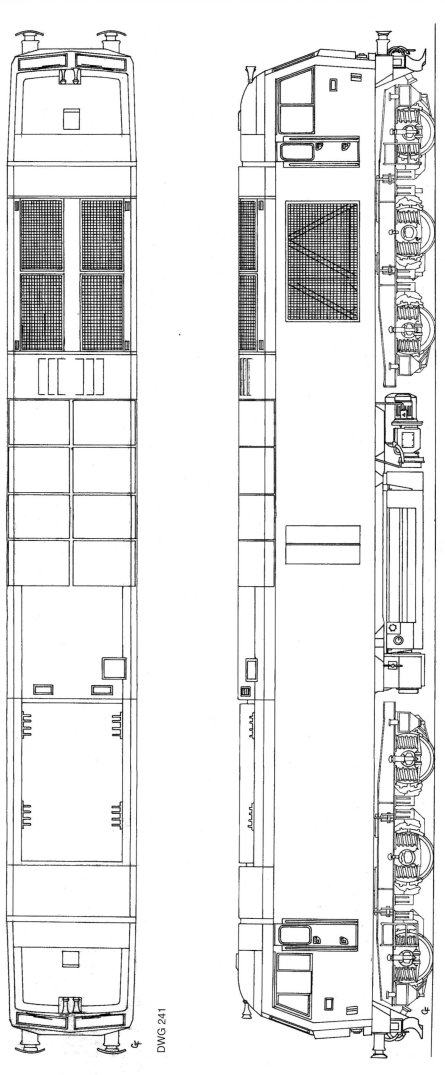

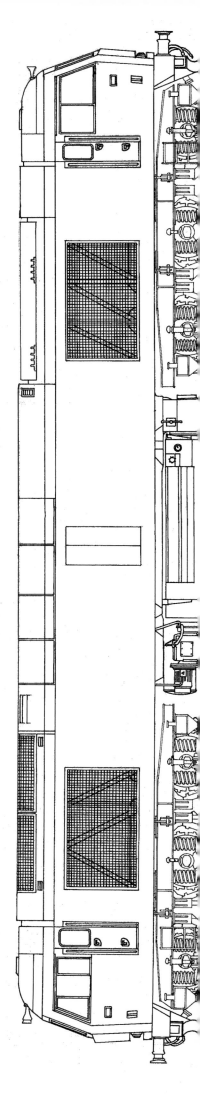

DWG 241

DWG 242

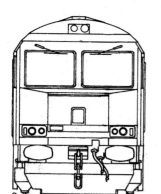

DWG 244

DWG 241
Class 60 roof detail; No. 1 end is on the right.

DWG 242
Class 60 side detail, with the No. 1 end on the right.

DWG 243
Class 60 side detail, with the No. 1 end on the right.

DWG 244
Class 60 front end detail.

Class 60 60001-60100

Class	60	Route Availability	7
Number Range TOPS	60001-60100	Multiple Coupling	Within class only
Built by	Brush Traction, Loughborough	Brake Force	74 tonnes
		Engine Type	Mirrlees 8MB275T
Introduced	1989-92	Engine Horsepower	3,100hp
Wheel Arrangement	Co-Co	Power at Rail	2,415hp
Weight (operational)	129 tonnes	Tractive Effort	106,500lb
Height	12ft 10¾in	Cylinder Bore	10¼in
Width	8ft 8in	Cylinder Stroke	12¼in
Length	70ft 0in	Traction Alternator Type	Brush BA1006A
Min Curve negotiable	80m	Aux Alternator Type	Brush BAA702A
Maximum Speed	62mph	Number of Traction Motors	6
Wheelbase	56ft 3⅛in	Traction Motor Type	Brush TM2161A
Bogie Wheelbase	13ft 6½in	Gear Ratio	97:17
Bogie Pivot Centres	42ft 9¾in	Fuel Tank Capacity	1,000gal
Wheel Diameter	3ft 7in	Cooling Water Capacity	125gal
Brake Type	Air PBL	Lub Oil Capacity	220gal
Sanding Equipment	Pneumatic	Owner and Operator	EWS
Heating Type	Not fitted		

Following the highly successful introduction of the General Motors Class 59s on to British tracks in 1986, the then British Rail Railfreight sector became painfully aware just how far behind its operation was in terms of heavy-haul diesel traction. Its fleet was predominantly old, inefficient and unreliable. Railfreight's Trainload divisions all wanted to invest in new traction and, with this in mind, funding was authorised to develop a new Type 5 diesel locomotive, designated Class 60.

The BRB went out to competitive tender on 10th August 1987 for the fleet of 100 locomotives, valued at around £125 million. Bids had to be received by 7th November of the same year, and of the six firms invited to tender for the contract, only three positive bids were received, these being from Metro-Cammell, Brush Traction and GEC Transportation. The Metro-Cammell bid was a non-starter; it offered a Metro-Cammell body with an option of traction packages, many untried, and could not offer performance guarantees as stipulated by the contract. GEC, which was the front-runner for a long time, was to go into partnership with General Motors and offer a state-of-the-art Class 59. GM did not submit a direct tender, as the company thought that the political climate of the day would preclude such an order going to a US company. If the GM/GEC deal had won the order, the locomotives would probably have been constructed at the then BREL Crewe Works, which already had a partnership agreement with GEC for the construction of the Class 91 electric locomotives. However, the eventual winner of the Class 60 order was Brush. This option offered a locomotive powered by either a Mirrlees or Ruston power unit, and used separately-excited (Sepex) traction control, as previously tested on the final Class 58, No. 58050. The contract for the 100 Class 60s was formally placed on 17th May 1988.

Brush used its Loughborough plant for the assembly of the locomotives, with bodyshells fabricated by Procor of Horbury and delivered pre-painted to Brush. Assembly was carried out in revamped erecting shops at Loughborough, with the locomotives emerging finished in the then standard triple grey livery, offset by the Trainload business sector logo of the on-line operator. The first locomotive, No. 60001, carrying the name *Steadfast,* was handed over to Railfreight on time on 30th June 1989 and driven under its own power to Toton.

During early deliveries many serious problems were identified; many involved computer software, but others involved bogie and structural defects. At one time the build was almost cancelled, and for many months in 1990/1 a large number of locomotives remained at Loughborough part-finished. Eventually, after some 16 months, the problems were ironed out, and the fleet settled down to provide a stable operating platform. The original division between operating sub-sectors was: Trainload Coal — 35; Trainload Construction — 25; Trainload Metals — 22; and Trainload Petroleum — 18. However, by the time the fleet entered service, this was largely changed, and soon the Trainload businesses gave way to preparations for private ownership, with the formation of Loadhaul, Transrail and Mainline Freight. When finally placed in traffic, the Class 60s displaced many older locomotives, either to other duties or for scrap.

With the launch of the three 'shadow' private companies, five locomotives were repainted in the highly distinctive Loadhaul black and orange colours, while three were finished in the aircraft blue livery of Mainline Freight. Transrail did not adopt a new livery. Most of the Class 60s had lost their Trainload sub-sector decals by the mid-1990s, in favour of business branding.

As part of the privatisation of Britain's railways, all the Trainload Freight operations were purchased by American-controlled Wisconsin Central, which formed the English, Welsh & Scottish Railway (EWS), the entire fleet becoming EWS property. The company's distinctive maroon and gold livery was first applied to No. 60019 at Brush in May 1996, and by autumn 1999 over 30% of the fleet had been repainted. Many of the original historical names applied to the Class 60s have now been removed, and some machines now carry business-related names.

The entire 100-strong Class 60 fleet was assembled at the Loughborough factory of Brush Traction. On 14th June 1991 Nos. 60074 and 60077 share space in the main erecting shop. The bodies for this fleet were supplied pre-painted to Brush from Procor at Horbury.

Colin J. Marsden

Although the delivery and entry into normal service of the 100 Class 60s was delayed, the fleet has settled down well, and now returns a low casualty/fleet mileage figure. On 7th July 1992 No. 60089 traverses the northbound slow line at Shipton-on-Benningborough, north of York, with a Milford Junction-Mossend empty hooded MGR train.

Colin J. Marsden

Following the division of the national Railfreight operation into three accountable units, Transrail, Mainline and Loadhaul, new liveries were adopted by Loadhaul and Mainline while Transrail simply applied new decals. Painted in full Loadhaul black, orange and yellow livery, No. 60038 passes Clay Cross Junction on 26th October 1995 with a Wolverhampton-Lackenby empty steel service.

Colin J. Marsden

Following the adoption of the new EWS maroon, gold and yellow livery, the first Class 60 to be outshopped in the new scheme was No. 60019, repainted by Brush at Loughborough to a very high 'showroom' standard. The locomotive is seen in immaculate EWS colours on 20th May 1996.

Colin J. Marsden

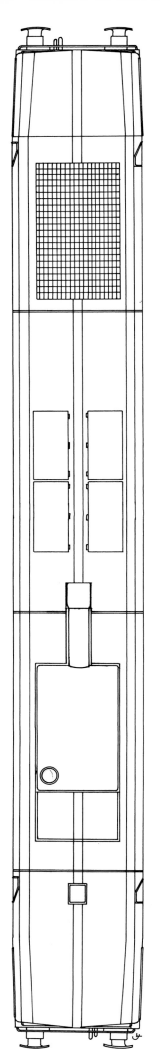

DWG 245

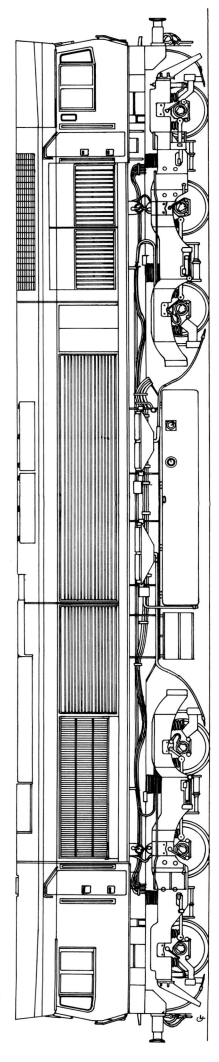

DWG 246

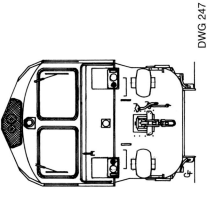

DWG 247

DWG 245
Class 66 roof detail, with No. 1 end on the left.

DWG 246
Class 66 side elevation, with No. 1 end on the left.

DWG 247
Class 66 front end layout

Class 66 66001-66250 66501-66520

Class	66	Multiple Coupling	AAR, Class 59, 66
Type	JT42CWR		and 67
Number Range TOPS (66/0)	66001-66250	Brake Force	68 tonnes
(66/5)	66501-66520	Engine Type	GM 12N-710G3B-EC
Built by	General Motors	Engine Horsepower	3,000hp
	Diesel Division,	Power at Rail	2,295hp
	London, Ontario,	Tractive Effort	92,000lb
	Canada	Cylinder Bore	9¹⁄₁₆in
Introduced	1998-2000	Cylinder Stroke	10½in
Wheel Arrangement	Co-Co	Traction Alternator Type	GM EMD AR8
Weight (operational)	126 tonnes	Companion Alternator Type	GM EMD CA6
Height	12ft 9½in	Number of Traction Motors	6
Width	8ft 8¼in	Traction Motor Type	GM EMD D43
Length	70ft 0½in	Gear Ratio	62:15
Min Curve negotiable	80m	Fuel Tank Capacity	1,730gal
Maximum Speed	75mph	Lub Oil Capacity	165gal
Wheelbase	56ft 9in	Sand Capacity	8 x 1.5cu ft
Bogie Wheelbase	13ft 7in	Owner and Operator (66/0)	EWS
Bogie Pivot Centres	43ft 6in	(66/5)	Freightliner
Wheel Diameter	3ft 6in		(66501-505:
Brake Type	Air, Westinghouse		Porterbrook;
	PBL3		66506-520:
Sanding Equipment	Pneumatic		Forward Trust)
Heating Type	Not fitted		
Bogie Type	HTCR		
Route Availability	7		

Following sale of the three ex-BR freight businesses — Loadhaul, Transrail and Mainline Freight — to the American Wisconsin Central company, the latter formed a British operation: the English, Welsh & Scottish Railway (EWS). Having also purchased BR's mail and parcels operation, Rail Express Systems, and intending to acquire Railfreight Distribution, EWS needed new locomotives to meet the projected upturn in British freight traffic. With its US parentage, EWS was not totally sold on the idea of buying British traction, and indeed few companies could offer anything which could meet its aspirations.

In 1996 it became apparent that around 250 new Type 5 locomotives were to be ordered, the order eventually going, not surprisingly, to General Motors. This company, which had previously built the Class 59s, could offer an up-to-date package in the Class 59 bodyshell, which was already accepted on Railtrack lines and could thus be introduced without problem or delay.

An order for 250 locomotives, designated Class 66 and using the GM EMD 710 series power unit, microprocessor control and radial steering bogies, was formally placed in 1997. Construction of the fleet was sub-contracted to GM's loco production plant in London, Ontario, Canada, with the first locomotive being shipped to England via Immingham Docks in April 1998.

Construction of the locomotives in Canada has been swift, with over 150 in Great Britain by October 1999. Their speedy introduction, with many being placed into service on freight duties straight from the dockside, saw the rapid withdrawal of older classes in late 1998 and throughout 1999. Their performance has, so far, been quite superb, with very few on-line failures recorded, and an availability figure surpassing that originally envisaged.

The EWS Class 66s, painted in the standard EWS maroon and gold livery, are all allocated to Toton but operate throughout the country. At the time of writing no major modifications have been carried out. Locomotive No. 66002 is of interest, for, after completion in Canada, it was transferred to a private test track in Pueblo, Colorado; following tests it was sent to the VMV reworking site in Paducah, Kentucky, and then back to London, Ontario, for final completion prior to shipping to England, a year after its construction.

Freightliner Ltd, which had been keen to develop a more robust and modern traction fleet in recent years, in addition to its Class 57 rebuilds, turned to General Motors for a new build order in spring 1999. Five standard Class 66s were ordered, numbered 66501-505, and were constructed alongside the EWS build. The five locomotives, painted in full Freightliner livery, were shipped to the UK via Newport Docks in July/August 1999, and are now allocated to Crewe Basford Hall depot. In August 1999 Freightliner signed a contract with Railtrack to provide traction for the latter's West Coast main line infrastructure trains. To power these, Freigtliner signed a further deal with General Motors for an additional 15 locomotives (66506-520), to be delivered in 2000.

All Class 66 locomotives are shipped to Great Britain from either the Canadian port of Halifax, Nova Scotia, or through Norfolk, Virginia, USA, transport being arranged by JumboLine Shipping.

At the time of writing EWS's order for 250 Class 66s was still being fulfilled by the General Motors Diesel Division plant in London, Ontario, Canada. This view of the main erecting shop taken on 2nd December 1998 shows locomotives Nos. 66071/073/069 under construction.

Colin J. Marsden

During 1998/9 the London erecting shop usually held between 15 and 20 locomotives under assembly at any one time, with over 90% of works space given over to the project. This December 1998 view shows Nos. 66065/066 nearing completion and ready for the paint shop.

Colin J. Marsden

Adjacent to the London construction plant is a GM-operated test track, which for about a mile runs parallel to the Canadian Pacific main line. Here No. 66052 is put through its paces on the test track on 1st December 1998. Prior to shipping to the United Kingdom, each locomotive is tested on its own and in multiple with others of the class.

Colin J. Marsden

By spring 1999 virtually the entire EWS network had seen Class 66 activity. On 16th February 1999 No. 66005 approaches Northam Junction, Southampton, with the Fawley-Eastleigh-Plymouth fuel service.

Colin J. Marsden

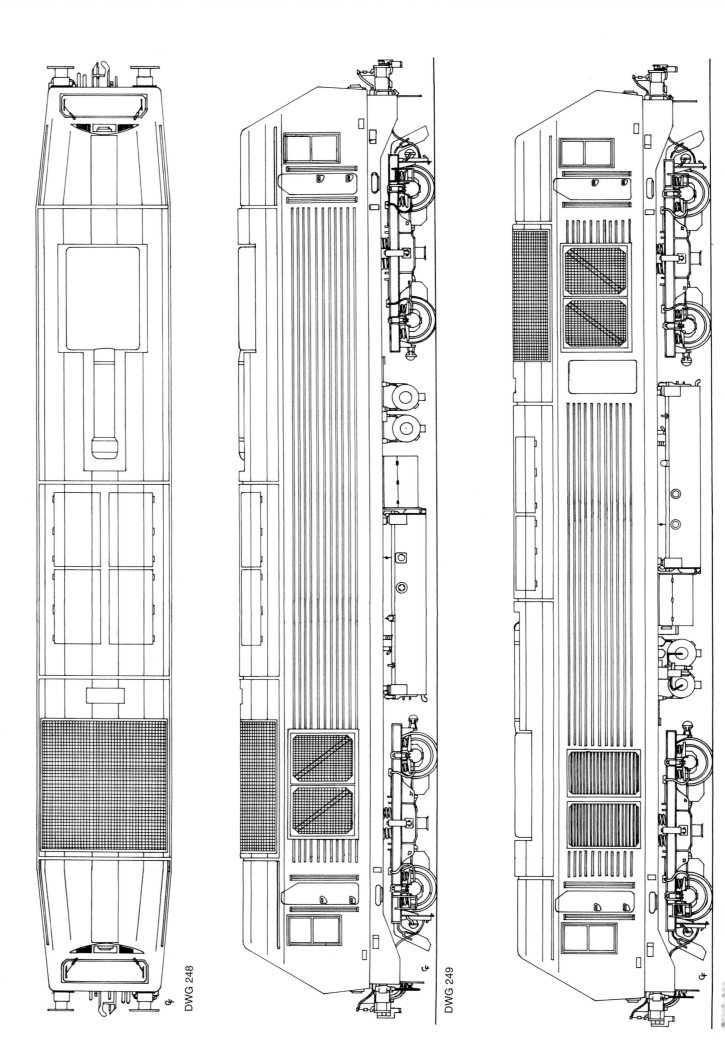

DWG 248

DWG 249

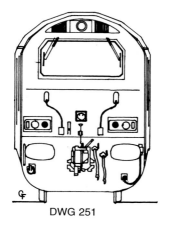

DWG 251

DWG 248
Class 67 roof detail, No. 1 end on right.

DWG 249
Class 67 side 'A' detail, No. 1 end on right.

DWG 250
Class 67 side 'A' detail, No. 1 end on left.

DWG 251
Class 67 front end detail.

Class 67 67001-67030

Class	67	Heating Type	Electric — index 66
Type	JT42 HW HS	Bogie Type	Alstom high-speed
Number Range TOPS	67001-67030	Route Availability	8
Built by	General Motors,	Multiple Coupling	AAR, Class 59, 66
sub-contracted to	Alstom, Valencia,		and 67
	Spain	Engine Type	GM 12N-710 G3B-EC
Introduced	1999-2000	Engine Horsepower	3,200hp
Wheel Arrangement	Bo-Bo	Power at Rail	3000hp
Weight (operational)	90 tonnes	Tractive Effort	31,750lb
Height	12ft 11½in	Cylinder Bore	9¼₆in
Width	8ft 10⅝in	Cylinder Stroke	10½in
Length	64ft 7¾in	Traction Alternator Type	GM AR9
Min Curve negotiable	75m	Companion Alternator Type	GM C6HEX
Maximum Speed	125mph	Number of Traction Motors	4
Bogie Pivot Centres	39ft 1¾in	Traction Motor Type	GM D43FM
Wheel Diameter	3ft 2in	Gear Ratio	59:28
Brake Type	Air, Westinghouse	Fuel Tank Capacity	1,135gal
	PBL3	Owner and Operator	EWS
Sanding Equipment	Pneumatic		

Following the purchase of freight operations in the UK by Wisconsin Central, trading as EWS, the quest began for a high-speed diesel locomotive as a direct replacement for the Class 47/7. Having ordered 250 Class 66s from General Motors, EWS planned to adapt this design, with a high-speed bogie suitable for 125 mph operation, and the provision of electric train supply. However, during the design stage, it was soon discovered that no suitable off-the-shelf high-speed Co-Co bogie was available, and EWS was thus forced to change its aspirations and go for a high-speed Bo-Bo locomotive. General Motors was awarded the contract for 30 locomotives, designated Class 67. GM's lack of experience in dealing with high-speed diesel traction in North America, together with tight production schedules at its Canadian plant, led to construction being sub-contracted to Alstom in Valencia, Spain. The two companies have a long-standing partnership in locomotive construction.

The Class 67 design shares the same powerplant as the Class 66, as well as much internal equipment, but a change was made in structural design; whereas the Class 66 employed a common underframe on to which component modules were attached, the Class 67 followed more traditional designs, being a full load-bearing structure. For the first time on a production fleet of diesel locomotives, a new design of coupling was used; known as a combination auto-coupler, the device combines a standard draw-hook with a US-style knuckle coupler, which can be swung into position for use when needed.

The entire Class 67 is assembled at the Valencia factory, close to the Mediterranean Sea. Prior to delivery to the UK, locomotive No. 67002 underwent a period of high-speed

running in Spain, to conform with General Motors' requirements; as much of the Spanish rail network is broad-gauge, the locomotive was transported to Alstom's depot at La Sagra, near Toledo, where the company maintains the AVE high-speed electric sets based on the French TGV. The Class 67 was authorised to operate in company with a RENFE Class 252 electric over the high-speed line from La Sagra towards Madrid to demonstrate its 125mph maximum speed and prove its design performance to be in keeping with the specification set out by EWS. The factory began construction of the first locomotive in summer 1999, with 22 under assembly by September. The first to be delivered to the UK, No. 67003, arrived at Newport Docks in early October. It had been projected that Railtrack would authorise the fleet for use within days of arrival but gauge and weight problems saw the first locomotive not starting trials until very late in December 1999. A number of finished locomotives were held in Spain awaiting sorting out of the problems in case major structural changes were required.

The deployment of the locomotives will be on fast Royal Mail services, mainly on the Penzance/Plymouth/Swansea-London-Newcastle routes. They will also be used to replace Class 47/7s used on charter work. Talks were in hand in late 1999 between EWS and Royal Mail over the Royal Mail 2000 project, which, if agreed, would revolutionise the mail by rail system. The project calls for the design and construction of a fleet of six-vehicle 125mph van sets with a DVT, enabling much easier access throughout the network and providing a far quicker and more reliable mail service. If the Royal Mail 2000 project goes ahead it is possible that a follow-on order for Class 67s could be placed.

No. 67003 stands on the test plant at Alstom's Valencia plant on 23rd September 1999. Each new Class 67 undergoes several days of static and dynamic testing on the Alstom 2.5km test track, which is built to metre, standard and broad gauge.

Colin J. Marsden

After completion at Valencia, the second locomotive of the build, No. 67002, was taken to Alstom's La Sagra depot, near Toledo, for testing at speeds of up to 125mph plus 10%, giving a maximum trial speed of 137.5mph. No. 67002 is seen next to the La Sagra single-track depot.

Colin J. Marsden

Locomotive No. 67019 takes shape in the Valencia fabrication shop in late September 1999. Unlike the Class 66, the Class 67 is a full load-bearing structure, and is assembled from medium-gauge steel at the Alstom factory. Many internal components are manufactured in the United States and the UK before being shipped to Spain for fitting.

Colin J. Marsden

The
Scottish Railway
Preservation Society

37413

CERBERUS

The "Irish Post Mail" Gwyddelig